• Your thirteen-year-old walks in, mor
uncommunicative. You try to cheer hi
thing you know, you're shouting. What happens? He
yells back at you as if you're the one with the problem.

• You set up a curfew for your fifteen-year-old. What
happens? The two of you get in a huge fight over the
curfew, and then he comes home late anyway.

• You think your daughter is hanging out with kids who
are doing drugs. You tell her she can't see those kids
anymore. What happens? You don't know. She just won't
tell you.

**It doesn't have to be this way. In this extraordinary
book, you'll discover a program that helps parents change
from feeling helpless and defeated to feeling successful.
It's called the "relationship approach," and it works
better than any other method to build a healthy, effective
relationship between you and the teenager you love.**

"This book could make a real difference in your family
living."

—Louise Bates Ames, Director, Gesell Institute

"Absolutely first-rate...I wish I'd had it twenty-five years
ago."
—Eda LeShan, author of *When Your Child Drives You Crazy*

"A wonderful, simple, and effective book."
—Dorothy Firman, author of *Daughters and Mothers*

"The best book I know on how parents can build a
working relationship with their teenagers."
—Roger Fisher, co-author of *Getting to Yes*

MIRA KIRSCHENBAUM and CHARLES FOSTER, Ph. D., are a husband
and wife team of family therapists. They have taught and supervised
other therapists and conducted research. They are founding directors
of the Brighton Family Therapy Associates, and together they have
raised two children. They live in Brighton, Massachusetts.

PARENT/ TEEN BREAK- THROUGH:
The Relationship Approach

Mira Kirshenbaum
and
Charles Foster, Ph.D.

A PLUME BOOK

PLUME
Published by the Penguin Group
Penguin Books USA Inc., 375 Hudson Street,
New York, New York 10014, U.S.A.
Penguin Books Ltd, 27 Wrights Lane,
London W8 5TZ, England
Penguin Books Australia Ltd, Ringwood,
Victoria, Australia
Penguin Books Canada Ltd, 10 Alcorn Avenue,
Toronto, Ontario, Canada M4V 3B2
Penguin Books (N.Z.) Ltd, 182–190 Wairau Road,
Auckland 10, New Zealand

Penguin Books Ltd, Registered Offices:
Harmondsworth, Middlesex, England

First published by Plume, an imprint of Dutton Signet, a division of Penguin Books USA
Inc.

First Printing, May, 1991
20   19   18   17   16

Copyright © Mira Kirshenbaum and Charles Foster, Ph.D., 1991
All rights reserved.

Ⓟ   REGISTERED TRADEMARK—MARCA REGISTRADA

LIBRARY OF CONGRESS CATALOGING IN PUBLICATION DATA:

Kirshenbaum, Mira.
    Parent/teen breakthrough : the relationship approach / Mira
Kirshenbaum and Charles Foster.
        p.   cm.
    Includes bibliographical references and index.
    ISBN 0-452-26616-5
    1. Parents and teenager—United States.   I. Foster, Charles,
    1946-.   II. Title.
HQ799.15.K57   1991   91-13580
306.874—dc20   CIP

PRINTED IN THE UNITED STATES OF AMERICA
Set in Caledonia
Designed by Leonard Telesca

Without limiting the rights under copyright reserved above, no part of this publication
may be reproduced, stored in or introduced into a retrieval system, or transmitted, in any
form, or by any means (electronic, mechanical, photocopying, recording, or otherwise),
without the prior written permission of both the copyright owner and the above publisher
of this book.

BOOKS ARE AVAILABLE AT QUANTITY DISCOUNTS WHEN USED TO PROMOTE PRODUCTS
OR SERVICES. FOR INFORMATION PLEASE WRITE TO PREMIUM MARKETING DIVISION,
PENGUIN BOOKS USA INC., 375 HUDSON STREET, NEW YORK, NEW YORK 10014.

To all the families and individuals who have let us help them—for showing us what works in parenting and what doesn't.

To our own parents—for putting up with us as teenagers and helping us learn how to be parents ourselves.

To our children—for teaching us the secret that having teenagers can be the best time for parents.

Contents

Acknowledgments

We feel very grateful to a lot of people. Without them, this book and whatever virtues it might possess would not have been possible. Some of these people have exerted a long and continuing influence on us; others have touched our lives for one crucial moment. But to all we say thank you: Shaye Areheart, Ruth Bork, Martin Buber, James Callahan, Lynette Cunningham, Thomas Dunn, Barry Dym, Joyce Engelson, Nancy Fain, Theresa Flor-Henry, Daniel Gasman, Paul Goodman, Sarah Greenberg, Richard Grossman, Jay Haley, Julie Hobbes, Kathleen Huntington, Kenneth Jones, Alfred Kazin, Larry Kessenich, Michael Kirshenbaum, Deirdre Levinson, Amy Mintzer, Salvador Minuchin, Gerrie Nussdorf, Rev. Howard C. Olsen, June Palmer, Barbara Phillips, Cynthia Roe, Gitta Sereny, Myron Sharaf, Isaac Bashevis Singer, David Slavin, Warren Sonbert, George Steiner, Walter Watson, Rosa Wexler, Carl Whitaker, and Harold Zyskind.

A special thanks must go to Peter Murkett for being there from before the beginning and for always providing encouragement when it was necessary.

We wish Geraldine Conner, Dody Giletti, and Pearl Karch were alive so we could express our gratitude toward them.

Our editor, Alexia Dorszynski, has worked hard to make this the best book it can be and to ensure that it will reach as many people as possible. We appreciate her contribution.

We feel very fortunate to have Ivy Fischer Stone of Fifi Oscard Associates as our agent. She believed in us, supported us, and helped make this book happen. We're profoundly grateful to her.

A very special thanks to Rachel Kirshenbaum for her enthusiam about this book and her thoughtful and helpful suggestions; to Hannah Kirshenbaum for honoring us by walking in one day and saying, "Hey, why don't you guys write a book about parenting teenagers?"—and to both of them for their love and support.

Our love and gratitude goes to Mira's mother, Sonia Freund, who went through danger and deprivation to bring Mira through war-torn Europe to America, and for continuing to be a model of a strong woman.

A Note to Parents of Teenagers

Well, this is it—your last chance to be a really good parent. As a matter of fact, your kid's adolescence is your *best* chance to be a really good parent. It used to be thought (Freud and all that) that early childhood was the critical period for your making a difference in how your kid turned out. But there is more and more evidence that nothing has more impact on what your kid does with his life and how he feels about himself than what you do during his adolescence.

This is also your last chance to do something for yourself. The way you parent now will determine how much you will enjoy your life with your teenager for the next several years. Perhaps more important, it will determine whether you can be friends with your kid for the thirty or forty years you are both adults.

Your kid's adolescence is the time for you to give yourself and your teenager a future that feels good and works well for both of you. We wrote *Parent/Teen Breakthrough* to help you make this happen.

THE PROBLEM —AND THE SOLUTION

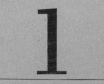

PART 1

Why Good Parents Go Wrong 1

If you're like most parents of teenagers, you wish you could break through the barriers that have prevented your good intentions from getting good results. Until now, your life has probably been filled with far too many moments like these:

- Your thirteen-year-old walks around the house morose and uncommunicative. You want him to cheer up or at least say *something* like a normal human being. You try to talk to him, and the next thing you know you're shouting. And what happens? He yells back at you as if you're the one with the problem.
- You see that your fourteen-year-old is not studying, and you try to persuade her to hit the books. You want her to start getting good grades so she'll have a chance to get into a good college. And what happens? She goes up to her room all right, but you're sure she's not studying, and when you ask her what she's doing she says she's already finished her homework.
- You set up a curfew so your fifteen-year-old won't be out too late and get into trouble. And what happens? The two of you get into a huge fight over the curfew, and then he comes home late anyway.
- You think that your sixteen-year-old is hanging out with

kids who are doing drugs. You tell her she can't see those kids anymore. And what happens? You don't know. She just won't tell you.

- You've dropped your eighteen-year-old off at college, and you wonder whether the emotional distance there's been between you was inevitable. Now you look forward to some healing. And what happens? Well, when he phones or writes he's polite—but warmth seems lost forever.

No wonder parents dread their kids' teen years as a kind of terrible Dark Ages that only time and sheer endurance will get them through.

Good News

Well, *it doesn't have to be this way.*

As family therapists we've worked with hundreds of parents and teenagers and have read all the research. We've also brought up two typical teenagers ourselves. And we looked for a way to help parents break through from feeling defeated to feeling successful. We knew that this solution would have to answer the question, "What's the critical difference between successful and unsuccessful parents of teenagers?" We also knew that the solution would have to be based on

- What *really works*—not theories or anyone's opinion about what should work
- What parents can *easily use*—something simple that any parent can put into effect in the middle of the distractions and confusions of everyday life.

What we discovered was a new way of thinking about parenting teenagers that will transform this hellish time into a time when you feel good about being a parent *and* fulfill all your responsibilities to your teenager *and* begin to know and appreciate the budding adult you've worked so hard to produce.

Using this new way of thinking—what we call *the relationship approach*—you'll be able to

- Deal with the things about your teenager that give you trouble minute by minute and day by day
- Help your teenager get ready for the time when she'll be on her own
- Form a close and loving relationship with your teenager that will endure for the thirty or forty years you are both adults

And you'll find that it's far easier to do this than what you've been doing so far.

What's Been the Problem Until Now?

Has bringing up your teenager been so tough up until now because there's something wrong with him? Probably not. There may be times when he scares, worries, and infuriates you, but that doesn't mean he's not normal. The fact is that normal teen behavior covers a much wider range than most parents think. So even if your own teenager is far from perfect, you can still bet he's OK, enjoy being his parent, and feel you're doing a good job.

Well, then, is the problem that there's something wrong with *you?* Again, probably not. We've found that most adults have what it takes to end the daily battles and to be the best possible parent for their teenager. The very talents and skills you already use in other areas of your life will make you a terrific parent for your teenager.

Is the problem that you just don't have the right tools and techniques at your fingertips, that everything would be great if you knew how to say this or do that at just the right time and in just the right way? Definitely not. Successful parenting isn't a science. When your kid does something that gets you upset, it happens fast and your emotions churn, and you don't have the time or composure to apply a complicated technology.

Or is the problem just that parents and teens are somehow ordained by nature to go through hell together? Not at all. Many parents—neither saints nor geniuses—both enjoy their teenagers and do a good job at being their parents.

So what really is the problem? What keeps smart, well-intentioned parents stuck in painful, frustrating battles with their teenagers?

What the Problem Really Is

Ruth is typical of most parents of teenagers. Listen to the words she uses when she talks about parenting her son. She talks about him being "out of control," about keeping him "on the right path," about "guiding" him, about "setting patterns," about "riding herd" on him. "It's just what I did when he was little," she told us. "It worked then, so why should I change my methods now?"

What makes Ruth typical is that she subscribes to the belief that the key to producing a good teenager and a successful, well-adjusted adult is "to straighten him out" now before he's fully formed. When you listen to Ruth's words, they all have to do with "straightening out." But is straightening out really the solution?

The fact is that in spite of Ruth's confidence that she is doing the right thing with her son, she knows that when her own parents do the same kinds of things to her, she hates it. Here she is, a full-fledged adult, and yet how many times has she been annoyed by her parents' "helpful" attempts to "improve" her, to straighten *her* out?

Their tactics are sometimes indirect: "Don't you think you've been using too much makeup, dear?" or "It seems to me parents today spend too much time working and not enough time with their kids." And sometimes their tactics are confrontational: "You spend way too much money," or "If you don't divorce that bum, you can forget about asking me for any more help."

Ruth finds this infuriating. She knows that her parents have good intentions, but she doesn't like being treated this way.

And yet Ruth does with her own kids what her parents do to her; the minute she puts on her "parent" hat she's convinced that "straightening her kid out" is the right thing to do. If you ask Ruth about this contradiction, she says, "Yeah, but I know that I'm OK. I don't know that my kid's going to be OK."

Perhaps the "straightening-out" philosophy that Ruth and most people subscribe to can be summed up this way:

- Typical teen behaviors often turn into real problems.
- These behaviors are a kind of deviance or going off the track.
- The solution to this deviance is parental control.

The anticipated payoff from struggling for control is supposed to be like the moment when, after years of putting orthodontic control on crooked teeth, you proudly point to your grown-up child's dazzling, straight-toothed smile and say, "That cost us thousands of dollars and it was worth every penny." In the same way, you look forward to pointing to your grown-up child's perfect life and proudly saying, "That cost us a lot of heartache—all those times I had to make him do things he didn't want to do when other parents would have just let him do what he wanted—but look at him now."

But with teenagers, as opposed to crooked teeth, the payoff doesn't come. *It can't.* And here's why.

You know that mere hopes and wishes won't turn snaggled into straight teeth. Whether the problem is crooked teeth or unruly teens, *"straightening out" requires force.* So in an effort to be a "good" parent, you make rules and demands. You criticize and lecture and urge and suggest and push. You do some threatening and punishing. You may try to get tough or to use psychology. Whatever the means, you try to get some *control* over your teenager.

And so, trying to gain control in one way or another becomes the approach most parents use to bring up their teenagers. It seems to make sense. Just ask yourself, what feels like the biggest problem you have with your teenager? It's that you can't control him, isn't it? That you can't make him do what you want and be who you want him to be. If you could control him, there would be no problems, no worries, no fights.

Now ask yourself how you deal with not being in control. You try to gain control, don't you? This is true today more than ever. Whether it's fear of drugs or fear of their kid not getting into a good college, parents are determined to get tough to prevent their kid from wandering off the right path.

But is the control approach really the solution? No. As much as they *look* as if they need straightening out (and God knows it's hard to look at most teenagers without feeling that they're desperately in need of some straightening out somewhere), teenagers are not like crooked teeth. Instead of gradually but smoothly straightening out in response to your attempts to gain control over them, teenagers are programmed by nature to fight back. *With teenagers, instead of producing "straightening out," trying to gain control only produces resistance, which only produces more problems. So control is not the solution. Control is the problem.*

The control approach may sound good, but unfortunately the cycle of controlling and resisting feeds on itself. The more you try to gain control, the more your teenager resists. Anger leads to opposition, which leads to more anger and more opposition. Punishment leads to evasion, which leads to more punishment and more evasion. Criticism leads to secrecy, which leads to more criticism and more secrecy. No wonder the control approach feels like trying to spread cold butter on soft bread: it just tears the bread apart, and the solution isn't to spread harder.

And that's why parents like Ruth complain that it feels so painful to bring up a teenager. It's no wonder she sees her teenagers becoming more and more distant from her. No wonder she's afraid they'll resent her as she does her own parents. No wonder she feels so helpless. The control approach is the real problem.

Many parents deal with all this by becoming permissive or just giving up. But ignoring things like your kid coming home at all hours, treating you with disrespect, or getting awful grades doesn't feel good either. And being permissive does not solve any problems. Giving up doesn't bring you and your teenager any closer.

So there you are, wanting to do a good job, a parent in the midst of your day-to-day battles with your teenager, in the midst of worrying about his future. It doesn't seem you have any other alternative: if you don't like what you see and you're not getting what you want, what else can you do besides fight for control or give up?

No wonder parents of teenagers feel so trapped.

Well, take heart. There is a way out. And the first step out of the trap is understanding just what the control approach really is and why it can never work.

The Control Approach: What It Is and Why It Can't Work

2

We know that most parents don't use the control approach because they are mean; they use it because they're doing their best to be helpful and to cope with a rebellious teenager. It's instinctive to try to control something that's out of control. It's what your parents did. It's what your friends do (or say they do). It's what a lot of the media and many experts tell you to do. Most of all, control worked for you when your kid was little; it made you feel competent and successful as a parent. And many parents think there is no real alternative.

So we hope you understand that when we say good parents go wrong because they end up using the control approach, we don't intend any blame. The most skillful and sensitive, the friendliest and most caring people may feel there's no alternative to battling for control with their teenagers.

The issue isn't blame; the issue is gaining understanding that will help you stop using an approach that can't work so you can start using an approach that will work. And understanding begins as you see just how deeply the control approach has infiltrated your parenting.

How to Know When You're Using the Control Approach

Sometimes the control approach is very easy to recognize. Regardless of your intentions—and most parents intend only to do a good job—when you impose limits, rules, and punishments on your teenager, you're using the control approach. Why else would you use limits, rules, and punishments? Since teenagers don't instinctively and automatically act the way you'd like them to, parents try to make their teenagers do things the kids wouldn't otherwise do—they try to control them.

But the control approach is far broader than just making a lot of rules and then making a big deal when your rules are violated. If it's hard for you to see yourself as someone who tries to gain control, maybe this will help. Ask yourself how often you've said things like

- "I try not to let her get away with . . ."
- "I fight with her whenever she wants to . . ."
- "It's a lot of hard work, some of the things I do, but it's for his own good . . ."
- "I'm not going to let myself be a patsy when he . . ."
- "Look, it's just reasonable that she should let herself be guided by me. If she won't . . . I have to try to get her to do it."
- "He just doesn't know what he's capable of, so I have to push him if he's ever going to . . ."
- "I know he can do a lot better, and he'll thank me later on for getting after him now . . ."
- "I'm just trying to be helpful when I make her . . ."
- "I feel I have to teach her to . . ."
- "He won't learn good patterns if I don't . . ."

Can there be many parents of teenagers who *haven't* said things like these? Well, if you've been doing so, it means you've been trying to control your teenager.

If you're still not sure if you've been using the control approach, ask yourself whether your teenager has been acting secretive, or sullen, or rebellious, or angry. Many parents think this kind of behavior either is a sign that something is wrong with their kid or is an inevitable part of adolescence. Well, it isn't. Most of the time it's a sign of a normal teenager's reaction to a controlling parent.

One reason some parents don't recognize they are trying to gain control is that so much controlling goes on *indirectly*. Control isn't only saying, "Come straight home from school or else," or "Take off that ridiculous shirt immediately." Perhaps more frequently, it's surrounding your teenager with a shower of comments, suggestions, opinions, warnings, and lectures that have the effect of trying to gain control.

For example, do you ever find yourself trying to get your teenager to do something indirectly by

- "Just asking" if he's done his homework?
- Making "helpful hints" to your daughter about how she can improve her appearance?
- Casually pointing out the "right way" to do things?
- Offering opinions about your teenager's friends?
- Explaining over and over again, in dozens of different ways, how drugs ruin people's lives?
- Telling your eleven-year-old she doesn't need a bra?
- Lecturing about the value of hard work?
- Complaining about the mess your kid leaves in the kitchen?
- Bombarding your kid with messages that there's no limit to what he can accomplish if he only puts his mind to it?

Marie, for example, prided herself on not being controlling, but when we met with the family it turned out that her son, Stu, constantly felt controlled by her. What was going on? Here's the kind of thing Marie kept doing. She didn't directly tell Stu how to do his chores. But she always managed to be around when he was doing them, and the minute he didn't do things the way she wanted she would make seemingly innocuous statements like, "The dish towel is in the drawer"—giving information to control how he did the job.

Marie didn't try to control directly, but her *desire* was for control and her actions showed it. And her son felt it. Stu's constant resistance to his mother, which Marie experienced all too often, was caused by her constant striving for indirect control, which she couldn't see at all until it was finally pointed out to her.

If you want to know how you look, what's important isn't your mental picture of yourself but what you see in the mirror. In the same way, *it's not what you think you're doing that determines whether you're being controlling; it's how the other person reacts to what you're doing.*

Here's another example. Tom was concerned about what he saw as his thirteen-year-old son Rob's irresponsibility. Rob kept forgetting to do his homework, losing money, and leaving valuables at friends' houses. Tom was afraid that this behavior would stick and that Rob would grow up unable to survive in the real world. But Tom also had a real horror of being one of "those parents who tell their kids what to do all the time."

What Tom did instead was to tell Rob stories. Mostly they were about work. And all these work stories were about someone who was careless or heedless or thoughtless or anything less than totally vigilant and diligent, and in these stories the person's irresponsibility always led to something bad happening. Tom also told a lot of stories about how someone acted very responsibly and accomplished a great deal and was rewarded for it.

When we asked him, Tom wasn't even aware of what he was doing. He thought he was being a good father because he was talking to his teenager. But the talking was all about the same thing. And Tom was aware that many times Rob didn't want to listen to him because he was "boring." So they fought over whether Tom was boring and over Rob's seemingly perverse reluctance to "listen to his dad."

Tom was only able to realize how controlling he was when he was shown what his stories were *not*. They were never about anyone who was irresponsible and yet who somehow came through OK. They were never about anyone who was responsible and yet still got in trouble. They were never about anything but work and responsibility.

Here are some other examples that might help clarify what we mean by direct versus indirect control:

- *Directly*, a parent might threaten not to pay for a kid's college education unless the kid goes to the parent's alma mater. *Indirectly*, the parent might constantly talk about how great his alma mater is. But they're both control.
- *Directly*, a parent might demand that his kid come into the family business. *Indirectly*, a parent might constantly make guilt-inducing comments about having to sell the family business if the kid doesn't come into it. Again, both statements are controlling.
- *Directly*, a parent might make rules about when her daughter has to be home from a date. *Indirectly*, a parent might cross-examine her daughter about every detail of what goes on during a date. But both are control.
- *Directly*, a parent might try to tell her teenager what to wear. *Indirectly*, a parent might constantly talk about how nice certain other kids look. But directly or indirectly, it's all control.

You may have the best of motives. You may think you're being terrifically subtle. Or you may not even be aware of what you're doing. But even when you wage war indirectly, you're still a foot soldier in the Great Parental Battle for Control.

Why the Control Approach Can't Work

You'd be surprised at how many parents don't care about how painful and frustrating it is to use the control approach. "So what," they say, "if trying to control a teenager is no fun. Sure it's a dirty job, but someone's got to do it."

But we're saying not only that the control approach is painful and frustrating for everyone concerned, but that *it just can't work.* The control approach isn't like simonizing your car, where you do a lot of rubbing but you get a nice shine. Instead, the control approach is like trying to polish your car with steel wool. Work hard at *that* and you'll ruin your car.

Parents desperately want to understand what's going on in the confusing business of trying to bring up a teenager. And we believe that once you understand just why the control approach can't work, it'll be very hard to continue to use it.

Reason 1: The control approach can't work because adolescence programs teenagers to resist control, and their ability to resist is stronger than parents' ability to win.

Remember when your kid was little and you used to tell her to go to bed? "Do I have to?" she'd say. Or maybe, "I don't want to." Well, maybe she'd fuss, but eventually she did go to bed. And you'd tuck her in and give her a kiss, the fussing forgotten.

But dealing with a teenager is not something harder, like dealing with a big, more-difficult-to-manage child. It's something completely different. At some point, if you tell your teenager it's time to go to bed, she's not merely going to put up a fuss; instead, she's going to challenge you and say, "You can't tell me when to go to bed anymore."

When your kid enters adolescence the whole game changes. Her underlying motivation is no longer to be nurtured and protected, even though you've just gotten good at doing these very things. In the teen years, your kid's life is dominated by a new and specific job: *getting ready to leave home.*

This job starts right at the beginning of adolescence, certainly by age thirteen and often as early as age nine. One day your kid is sweet, cute, and cooperative. The next day it seems she's changed entirely—and she has. It's hard to tell which is worse, her rebellious attitude or the fact that she's getting swept up in a cheap, seemingly destructive teen culture. This job of getting ready to leave home continues throughout the seemingly endless middle-teen years, when her emotional focus shifts from her wise parents to her wild friends. She drives you crazy as she demands both freedom and the right to act irresponsibly. And the job of leaving home is so important and so difficult that most people are in their late twenties before it's completed. Kids may look grown-up toward the end of adolescence, but even at this late stage they're still doing things like asking for money, experimenting with who they are, and floundering around in relationships.

Adolescence takes roughly five thousand days from beginning to end; at the beginning a ten- or eleven-year-old adolescent is almost indistinguishable from a child, while at the end a twenty-four- or five-year-old is almost indistinguishable from an adult. But whatever the age or stage, what sets adolescence apart is the fact that

> *getting ready to leave home is the central reality around which your teenager organizes his existence.*

A child can't really imagine leaving home. But when that child becomes a teenager—even though he still may look a lot like a child—getting ready to leave home becomes his main job, his reason for being.

We're not saying this is conscious. For example, your teenager doesn't spend hours hanging out with friends for the express purpose of getting ready to leave home. But hanging out with friends, like most of the other things a teenager does, *functions* to make leaving home possible. To a parent it can look as though teenagers hang out with friends so they can act like jerks. But, functionally, learning to hang out with friends is part of the process by which a teenager moves himself from the world of his parents to the world of his peers. And, after all, it's with their peers that adults spend their lives.

In other words, the point of adolescence isn't the behaviors you see—rebellion, or being immature, or doing dangerous things. And the point isn't learning to play by the rules— even though you'd like that. Sure, some or all of these things take place, but the point of adolescence is something that's invisible. The point is that your teenager is making the profound transformation of himself from being a parent-dependent child to being a self-dependent adult.

Now, finally, you can make sense of every single thing your teenager does, whatever her age. All you have to know is that during the five thousand days of adolescence everything your teenager does is based on getting ready to leave home. And to leave home she has to accomplish two main tasks.

- She has to go from being a person who's taken care of to being a person who takes care of herself. This means she has the job of *becoming self-reliant.*
- She has to go from being identified as your child to being her own person. This means she has the job of *developing her own identity.*

We said that this will enable you to make sense of everything your teenager does. Here are two examples.

- Goofing off in school? It doesn't prove much to walk a tightrope that's lying on the ground. But if you can put that tightrope up in the air and take the net away, it's risky as hell but it sure demonstrates self-reliance. Goofing off in school can be a teenager's way of knocking away the safety props society provides and proving that he can be OK without school.
- Watching MTV? This doesn't make for much of an identity, except in one crucial respect—you the parent probably don't like it. And while being different from you isn't much, it's a crucial step on the road to developing a separate identity.

Of course, most parents wish their kids could accomplish these tasks by doing things "the right way" and by following tried-and-true paths. "Why won't he listen to me?" every parent of a teenager wonders. It seems to make sense: you made enough mistakes of your own and you know about lots of other mistakes people can make. So you naturally want to save your teenager from making those mistakes.

But what's hard for parents to realize is that adolescence is *not* about *not* making mistakes. It's only about getting ready to leave home. And teenagers know instinctively that if they are going to become self-reliant and develop their own identity, they have to experiment, take risks, and maybe make a lot of mistakes. In the process, teenagers will do things that look stupid or scary to you, just when you're desperately wishing they'd get their act together. But from your teenager's point of view, she risks becoming an automaton if she just follows orders and does things "the right way." And automatons are not self-reliant; nor do they have their own identity. Automatons can't leave home.

So the noisiness and obnoxiousness, the strange clothes, the crazy experiments, and, most of all, the resistance to your attempts to gain control (as helpful and commonsensical as those attempts might be) are all part of the normal process by which a kid transforms herself from child to adult. Adolescence is not a sickness or a mistake or a defect. It's not a miscalculation of nature. Instead, adolescence—with all of its frustrating resistance to parental control—is necessary for a person's survival as an adult.

How One Teenager Can Outnumber Two Parents

What makes adolescence even harder for parents to manage is that as an adult you're many things, and being a parent of a teenager is just one of them. As a teenager, you're only one thing, and that is someone who is getting ready to leave home. When you try to control your teenager, you're fighting the central reality of her existence with only a part of yours. She will fight you as if her life depends on it because, in a way, it does. And she'll win.

So there you are with your curfews and groundings and lectures, continuing to put out the message "I'm doing this to straighten you out" or "This is for your own good," just the way you did when she was little and was more or less willing to accept it. But way before *you* may be ready for *her* to leave home, she stops hearing these messages the way you'd like her to, as ways of expressing "protection" or "help." Instead, what she hears is "threat to independence!" or "danger to self!"

The harder she tries to do her job of becoming her own person, the more your attempts at taking control backfire. You push, and she just has to push back. It's called polarization, and this polarization is the graveyard of parents' good intentions.

And your teenager's drive to become her own person is not something you can reason away, overcome, or work around. This drive is too important to your teenager emotionally; it becomes more and more of a practical reality for her every day. Both emotionally and practically, your teenager is just not interested in being straightened out. You once had a handle on her because you were the center of her world, but that handle is fast disappearing. Other things besides you become important in her life—friends, clothes, sports. There are just too many variables and too much slippage in the system for you to be able to get control.

Some people believe that it's normal for teenagers to fight with their parents, or that fighting with them helps kids grow up. But this isn't true either. It *is* true that leaving home has to happen, but it doesn't have to happen by fighting. A parent is not a kind of barbell that a teenager has to keep pushing away in order to gain strength. Ninety percent of parent-teen fights come from the teenager's reaction to the parent's attempt to gain control. The only thing these fights over control create is a noxious atmosphere of anger and distance.

But, some people ask, what about all the adults in their twenties and thirties who come back to live with their parents? Well, it's true there are a lot of these people, particularly in these times of high divorce rates and housing costs. But in percentage terms these "boomerang babies" are a tiny minority. And most of them desperately want to get back out on their own.

So, your kid's becoming a teenager means that both of you are in a completely different game. The control that may have been nurturing and protecting when she was a child becomes a threat now that she's a teenager. The control you used before is now an obstacle to her doing the job of getting ready to leave home, the job nature has programmed her for.

Reason 2: Parents can't win the battle for control because the day-to-day reality of teen life makes attaining parental control impossible.

Look at it like this. Is your teenager with you most of the day? No. It's much truer to say that your teenager is away from you most of the day.

According to a study in which researchers followed teens through their daily lives, parents spend less than fifty minutes a day alone with their teenagers, and most of these minutes are spent doing chores, eating, and watching television. It's the rare parent who spends more than *five* minutes out of her busy day in direct, one-to-one contact with her teenager. Even mothers who work as homemakers spend barely more time with their teenagers than mothers who work outside the home.

On the other hand, *teenagers spend 85 percent of their waking hours either alone or away from their family.* And in those long hours when your teenager is away from you, do you have any power to make him do what you want? Of course not. Even some of the most "carefully supervised" girls get pregnant. Even the teenagers whose parents try to discipline them most tightly may still take drugs. Even some teenagers whose parents lead them by the hand through every homework assignment find ways to screw up on tests.

And so the best-laid plans of a parent who battles for control come to nothing.

Of course you know this. That's why when parents think about what their kids do before they come home from school and while they're alone in their room, they dream of achieving a kind of *remote control.* They try to find a way to have control even when their teenager is not around, the way they hope they've trained the dog not to sleep on the sofa even when they are not in the house. Unfortunately, the techniques parents use to gain remote control are as inefficient and ineffective as wearing oven mitts to thread a needle.

See how many of the following techniques you use; they're the ones most parents use to try to maintain some control over their teenagers when the parents are not around.

The Guilt Technique

You might say, "When you bring home a terrible report card like that, it upsets your father."

- The response you want: "I'll study very hard every single day."
- The response you usually get (but don't know it because your kid keeps it to herself): "You can make me stare at the book, but you can't make me learn."

The Threat Technique

You might say, "If I catch you coming home drunk, you can forget about ever having the car again."

- The response you want: "Oh, then, I'll never drink again."
- The response you usually get (but don't know it because your kid keeps it to herself): "Then I'll make sure you don't catch me."

The Comparison Technique

You might say, "I wish you were more like your cousin. She always seems to find something to say to her parents. Why can't *you* talk to us?"

- The response you want: "I'll go to her right now and ask for pointers on how to talk to you."
- The response you usually get (but don't know it because your kid keeps it to himself): "I didn't like her before,

but now I really hate her guts, and I'd do anything not to be the way she is."

The Bribery Technique

You might say, "We'll buy you a car if you manage to get into a good college."

- The response you want: "Well, I'll study every minute so I can get that car."
- The response you usually get (but don't know it because your kid keeps it to herself): "OK, let's see, if I cheat and take easier courses, maybe I'll have a chance."

The Lecture/Lesson/Teaching Technique

You might say, "If you work hard you can be anything you want to be. Here's what you must do. First, . . ."

- The response you want: "Thanks for pointing that out; I hadn't realized."
- The response you usually get (but don't know it because your kid keeps it to himself): "Ronald Reagan didn't work hard. My boss, the assistant manager at Burger King, does work hard. You figure it out."

There you have it: what really happens when parents try to achieve remote control. No wonder well-intentioned parents are so frustrated.

Reason 3: Battling for control can't work because temporary victories lead to permanent defeats.

OK, let's say you put your foot down this time, and, miracle of miracles, your teenager did what you told her to. Sure, there was fighting, anger, slammed doors—but, hell, she's just a kid. Anyway, you won.

Did you? Don't count on it.

Here's why. If you really listen to teenagers, what you hear over and over is, "I wish I could talk to my parents. But they have their stupid rules, and that seems to be all they care about. I can't talk to them about anything because they just get mad and fight about it. So when I have a problem, all I can do is talk to my friends."

For example, fourteen-year-old Cynthia was offered a chance to participate in an advanced study program at her junior high school. But she didn't want to participate because none of her friends were. Her parents yelled, bribed, and threatened, and she finally agreed to join the program.

Was this a victory? A successful use of the control approach? Let's look more carefully at the invisible price Cynthia's parents paid. Let's look at how Cynthia—like any other normal teenager—reacted to her parents' victory in the battle for control.

What happened was that Cynthia decided she couldn't talk to her parents. Why should she talk to them? She didn't feel they listened. Why would any teenager want to talk if the only result was getting yelled at or lectured to? When your parents gave you a tough time, did that make it easier for you to talk to them? Even the best of teenagers with the best of parents clams up all too often. Why make it even harder?

Some parents say, "Who cares if my kid talks to me? Talking's not important. What's important is getting her to do the right thing." But your teenager's ability to talk to you, fully and freely, isn't a luxury option; *your teenager's ability to talk to you is the main vehicle by which you can get the changes you've been trying to get by battling for control, including getting her to "do the right thing."*

Look at what happened to Cynthia. Sure, she did enroll in the program her parents pushed her into. But her grades slowly deteriorated and, even worse, she kept her problems from her parents because she felt she couldn't talk to them about how she hated math or about how she felt her English teacher was mean to her. Things slowly and (from her parents' point of view) mysteriously got out of hand.

And why wouldn't they? Imagine how many planes would fall from the skies if pilots couldn't talk to air traffic controllers. In the same way, because Cynthia didn't talk to them, her parents lost the opportunity to provide her with any real guidance. By the end of the year Cynthia was out of the program.

Every time you battle for control, your kid feels that you don't see her or care about her as a person. She feels she's not important to you—only your rules are. Convinced that you don't understand her, she gives up trying to talk to you. Why bother? Being in control is obviously more important to you than her needs and her life.

Yes, your teenager can prevent herself from getting yelled at by "behaving," but the less you're able to watch over her every minute, the easier it is for her to hide her "misbehaving." After all, which is easier—spending hours studying or just not telling your parents you're having trouble in school? Which is easier—having a fight with your parents in which you try to get them to understand your needs or just coming home on time and then sneaking out later? The answer is obvious.

So your teenager gives an internal sigh of relief as she stops telling you about her life. Sure, you may have gained a little control in the short run, but the long-run cost is losing access to your teenager.

What makes all this even worse is that the less your teenager talks to you, the more out of touch you feel. And the more out of touch you feel, the more powerless you feel. And the more powerless you feel, the more you try to gain control—with the result that your teenager will talk to you still less.

You simply can't purchase access and influence with the coin of control. Your parents couldn't with you, could they? Many adults still feel they can't confide in their parents. And yet their silence only seems to goad those aging parents into being all the more intrusive and controlling, and all the more someone to avoid. Well, this vicious cycle started in adolescence.

Reason 4: The battle for control can't work because too often a parental victory is just an illusion.

OK. You laid down the law. "You *will* be home by eleven." "You *will* be grounded for the next month." "You *will* refrain from taking drugs." "You *will* do your homework." "You *will* get engaged to the right kind of person."

Then what?

She does what she wants anyway.

In one very typical situation, Bill started making a big fuss about the time his daughter Susan had to be home. Susan didn't even bother arguing. She just made a game of her curfew and a monkey of her father. There were all the times when she was just a little late, late enough for her to feel triumphant and yet close enough to her curfew so her father felt stupid making a big deal of it. And then there were all the times when she pretended to be sleeping over a friend's house but was actually out carousing. And there were all the times when she snuck out of the house after she came home and after her father had gone to bed confident that he was able to control her.

Teenagers believe that what *you* don't know won't hurt *them*. If you catch your teenager at something, she only becomes more resolved not to get caught again. If you tell her not to do something, she tries to find a way for you not to find out she's doing it. As a result, your battle for control only builds walls that keep you in the dark about what's going on with your teenager.

What makes battling for control even more absurd is that before long your kid goes off to college or joins the army or gets his own place, and then, even if the lid was on before, all bets are off and he does lots of the things you weren't letting him do anyway. And he does them with a vengeance—just ask the residents of towns where college kids go on spring break.

For the great majority of kids—the ones whose parents had fought so hard to rein them in—leaving home is a moment to experience not their maturity but their liberation. The goofing off, drinking, sexual experimentation, and general irresponsibility that take place on college campuses—some students engage in a sometimes lethal game called "elevator surfing"—make it clear what an illusion any temporary parental victory in the battle for control was.

So not only is the control approach a losing game, one that strips you of your assets, but even when you think you've won, the payoff is in counterfeit currency. When you try to cash in on your victory, there's nothing there.

Reason 5: Parents can't win the battle for control because fighting for control is too exhausting for parents.

Think about all the times when you drew that line in the sand and dared your kid to step over it. What happened? By the time you came to the end of the fights, and the end of the exceptions you were forced to make, and the end of the times you forgot to make the rules stick, and the end of the punishments that were too much trouble to enforce, and the end of your suspicion that your kid was stepping over the line behind your back—by the time you came to the end of all this, it was hard to get yourself to draw another line in the sand.

It even sounds exhausting. As a result of this, your teenager is left not only with a feeling that she can do what she wants but also with a nagging sense of anxiety or a loss of respect for you.

Because it's so likely that you will eventually surrender in the battle for control, your teenager will too often find herself having to deal with a parent who feels frustrated and defeated. No wonder many parents of teenagers are bitter. Fighting for control has turned them into losers. And it's painful for a teenager to see her parent as a defeated loser. What makes this even more tragic is that parents who fight for control think they are making their kid respect them, when in fact they're only destroying respect.

A classic example of this was when Janet was trying to get her daughter Mollie to do her homework. There were so many battles about what Mollie's assignments really were and whether she'd really done them, so many times Mollie procrastinated just a little and Janet felt like a fool making a big deal about it, so many exceptions for things like clubs, sports, and work, that eventually Janet just gave up, not with a whimper but a bang. "From now on," Janet yelled at Mollie, "you can do as little homework as you damn well please. I don't care anymore. Just don't come to me when you get into trouble."

Of course Janet didn't mean this, but she didn't know what to do with her frustration. And so now Mollie doesn't know what to do either. She tries not doing her homework and nothing terrible happens. It starts to occur to Mollie that maybe she can do anything she wants. But instead of feeling liberated and confident, Mollie feels troubled. Teenagers need their parents. They don't need them to battle for control, but they do need them to be there.

So surrendering is not a solution. It's just an inevitable toxic by-product of the battle for control. Actually, maybe it's not so toxic. After all, parental surrender prevents even more damage from happening. Perhaps the main reason parent-teen relationships and parent–adult child relationships aren't as bad as they might be is that parents so often give up the struggle.

Reason 6: The control approach can't work because parents' efforts to make teenagers "set good patterns" fail in the face of teenagers' resistance.

Most parents believe that, somehow, sheer repetition will create internal controls, the way kids believe that making an ugly face often enough will somehow make your face freeze. If you can make your kid do the right thing often enough it will somehow "take" and become a part of her. The idea is that control is the mold, repetition is the hardening of the plaster, and good behavior is the sculpture that's produced.

"So maybe," parents say, "if I get her in the habit of cleaning up her room (albeit by guilt or threats) she'll grow up a tidy person." Or, "If I make her do her homework every night (albeit by bribes or comparisons) it will become such a habit that when she gets to college she'll do it by herself without my needing to be there to supervise her."

But in most cases, *successful "pattern-setting" is an illusion.* Sure, pattern-setting is great when you're dealing with someone who is cooperative and who wants to be poured into a mold, like, say, the kid who does what the coach wants because she wants to make the basketball team. In cases like these, the behavior flows naturally from the kid's desires. But when people talk about setting patterns they're usually talking about patterns that go against the grain of their teenager's desires.

And the problems with "setting patterns" occur precisely when you most want them to work: when you run into resistance. If you have to fight to make your teenager follow a pattern, then that pattern will usually not take.

The reason for this is that *when you try to establish a pattern in the face of resistance, what gets most deeply established is the pattern of resisting.* The more you push, the more you strengthen and stimulate your teenager's desire to push back. The more you have already pushed, the more your kid holds on to her memories of resistance.

Remember that a teenager's only job is getting ready to leave home. Since this means becoming self-reliant and becoming her own person, every time you say, "Do it my way," your teenager feels a threat to her ability to rely on herself and to achieve a unique identity, no matter how wise and helpful "your way" may be. A teenager is as protective of her fragile, still-forming independence as a bird hatching an egg. If you attempt to establish a pattern that challenges her independence, you are just asking for a fight.

Of course you'll always find the adult who will stand up and say, "But I'm glad my parents made me practice the piano when I was a teenager." Yes, but for every one of these adults, there are a hundred others who went on to hate music, and perhaps even their parents, and who never wanted to touch the piano again. The same thing is true for keeping one's room neat, doing one's homework, saving money, standing up straight, working hard, and all the other things for which parents try to set a pattern.*

For example, Linda spent every sad Saturday of her teen years fighting with her mother about cleaning her room before she went out. Linda's mother used every weapon in the parental arsenal: lectures, bribes, threats, guilt, yelling and screaming, and all the rest. But the legacy of all that isn't clean rooms—Linda is now probably no neater or messier than anybody else. Instead the legacy is Linda's ineffaceable memories of fighting and anger. The things her mother did to "set a pattern" only made Linda hate her mother and gave Linda fewer rather than more reasons to do what her mother wanted. And this is not an unusual story. This is the norm.

Reason 7: Battling for control can't work because parents generally don't have much impact on how their kids turn out.

This may sound like a shocker, but it really is true. Scientists have looked high and low, but if you put them all in a room they won't be able to agree on the magic bullet guaranteeing successful kids or the poison pill guaranteeing failures. All parents—strict or lenient, permissive or protective, ambitious or indifferent—produce their share of successful and unsuccessful kids.

Why some kids turn out to be successes and others don't is not the only mystery. Even if two kids in the same family are successes, why does one choose one route to success and the other choose another route? Why does one choose one occupation and another choose differently? Why does one kid in a family want to go into the family business and the other refuse to have anything to do with it?

Yes, parents don't have much impact on how their kids turn out. But the little impact parents have comes from what *they* do, not what they make their kids do. For instance, since

*This doesn't mean you can't influence your teenager. Soon we'll show you how to use the relationship approach to have real leverage in getting your teenager to do some of the things you're sure he should do.

medical schools are filled with the children of doctors, the very best way for you to get your kid to become a doctor is for you to be a doctor. In other words, the major way you can have impact on your teenager is for you to be the way you want your kid to be. Controlling yourself is a hundred times more effective than trying to control your kid—and it has none of the costs.

Don't get us wrong. We know that really bad parents can have really bad effects on the way their kids turn out. Abusive parents and profoundly neglectful parents are responsible for lots of really messed-up kids. And a handful of parents probably have a talent for turning messed-up kids into healthy ones.

But these extremes are rare. Much more common are the 95 percent or even 99 percent of parents in the vast middle range, whose parenting techniques have surprisingly little impact on how happy or successful their kids turn out to be. And the ironic thing is that almost all of these parents believe control works. They ask, "Should I try to get more control?" "Is it terrible if I don't have control?" "How can I get more control?"

And it's to these parents that we say, "The kinds of things you're worrying about—doing more of this or less of that— are really not likely to have that much of an effect on the success or failure of your kid."

What does have a bad effect is the battle for control itself. It makes life hard for you and your teenager—when all the evidence is that it's not worth it. In other words, the control approach is the equivalent of performing a violent and exhausting rain dance to make it rain. There won't be any rain, but you will get worn out.

Reason 8: Parents can't win the battle for control because it results in their ending up physically or emotionally estranged from their kids.

Battling for control can not only poison your present; it can destroy your chance of having a future with your teenager. Just ask Heather. Here's what she told us:

My mother and father never really understood me or cared about who I was as a person. All they wanted was for me to be the way *they* wanted me to be, a good student, ambitious, that kind of thing. Whenever I was the way *I* wanted to be, they really didn't like me. I could tell. I could only take their not liking me for so long before I started not liking them back. I'm a really good person, but they couldn't see it, and I hate them for that. It's really kind of sad, but we don't have much to do with each other anymore.

Heather's future with her parents was destroyed by the poison of disappointment, and that disappointment came directly out of her parents' efforts to make Heather be a certain way.

This theme emerges every time you talk to a teenager: *teenagers want to be seen and treated as separate individuals.* "I'm not you," they'll say. "I'm not who you want me to be. I am just me. I want you to see me as I am and treat me as a separate individual." When you attempt to gain control over your teenager, you threaten her sense of herself as her own person. Nothing is more likely to provoke an extreme reaction from her.

Of course, the things you want her to do and the ways you want her to behave make perfect sense from your point of view. They're totally obvious and logical to you. Aren't kids supposed to work hard, be polite, and stay out of trouble?

But the fact that this makes complete sense isn't the point— at least not to your teenager. The way she sees it (and you'll only accomplish something as a parent if you take the way your kid sees things as your starting point), you have this cookie-cutter idea of how kids are supposed to be, and the cookie cutter has a rigid shape. And she's the one who gets cut by the edges of your cookie cutter. You see "common sense" and "doing things the right way," but all your kid sees is that damned cookie cutter and all she wants to do is get out of the way.

This is one of the reasons many adults complain about their relationships with their own parents. Whether for the best or worst of motives, when your parent tries to gain control he sets himself up in opposition to the adult you've become. In the fight between self and parent, you're always going to side with your self unless your self has been destroyed.

It's the same with your teenager. If the only way she can become self-reliant and develop her own sense of who she is is to get away from you, she will. And you'll both lose.

Reason 9: Parents shouldn't battle for control because their seeming victories too often hurt their teenagers.

There's something worse than your losing the battle for control. You could win.

Take Fran. When they talk about how they brought her up, Fran's parents tell stories about how they used to get her to do what they knew was right, even when she fought them. They managed to make Fran study and work hard in school, even though studying really didn't feel good to her and she preferred spending time with her friends.

And for a while it looked as though Fran turned out great. She always got the best grades, she went to one of the best graduate schools, and she became a successful chemist. Everyone they knew pointed to Fran's parents as proof of the kind of wonderful results you should be able to get by being tough and demanding, by being unafraid to use discipline, by being masters of control.

A fairy tale? A success story?

No, it turned out to be a horror story. Or maybe a ghost story would be more accurate. Because when the horrors started happening, Fran had in some sense become a ghost.

A couple of years after she started publishing the results of her research, Fran went through a period when she would look in the mirror and literally not recognize herself. Instead of becoming her own person, she'd become a stranger to herself. She felt her achievement had been built on the foundation of her parents' desires, rather than her own, and on the seeming success of their battle for control.

The point is that the teenager *always* wins the battle for control, even if the teenager in this case is trapped inside a thirty-three-year-old woman who is finally rebelling in a very sad way. In Fran's case, this rebellion took the form of headaches, depression, and mistakes at work. In other words, Fran was reduced to rebelling in the same ways as the most desperate of teenagers, ways that resulted in her hurting herself. She said to us at one point, "I don't know who I am or what I want, but it seems to me as if I'm going through a lot of pain to find out."

The damage done by the control approach is often invisible in the moment, not showing up in some cases until years later. But there's no way out. Your kid pays now or she pays later. When parents go so far in imposing their sense of the "proper" way to do things that they ignore who their teenager is as a separate individual, their teenagers can grow up agreeing to hate the things about themselves their parents hated. What happens when a person is stuck with certain characteristics (like not wanting to study) and is made to hate those characteristics? The result is that the person swallows an encyclopedia of depression-making statements about how he is no good for feeling or wanting or being who he is instead of who his parents want him to be.

As evidence of this, pay attention to what goes on in your own head the next time you're down in the dumps. It's usually more than just, "I'm blue, I'm blue, I'm blue." For most people feeling depressed means having a head filled with statements like, "I'm stupid. I'm never going to get anywhere. I'm just not good enough." These statements don't come from nowhere. They are often echoes of your parents' well-intentioned efforts to change you.

When a parent imposes control and manages to override his teenager's resistance, the parent has substituted his self for his teenager's self. He's performed a kind of soul transplant. And as the years go by the kid doesn't say, "Thanks for substituting your good self for my no-good, immature self." Instead, the teenager and then the adult, like Fran, spends those years in a difficult and often painful struggle to reclaim a lost self that she could have had all along. Can any victory in the battle for control be worth that?

* * *

There they are then, nine big pieces of evidence that the control approach can't work. Yes, control *seems* commonsensical—but only because it worked when your kid was little. Adolescence is a new ball game. Teenagers are not big children, nor are they immature adults. They are a third kind of person, one whose very being is organized around getting ready to leave home. Teenagers may act so irresponsibly that they seem to be crying out for control, but because of who a teenager is and what the job of adolescence is, battling for control does not and cannot work.

Fortunately, there is a solution to the problem of how you can be the best possible parent and at the same time enjoy living with your teenager: the relationship approach.

The Relationship Approach: What It Is and What It Will Give You

3

Many parents feel a sense of loss when they realize battling for control no longer makes sense. It's almost like losing an old friend. Sure, it was an old friend that kept getting you into trouble and made you feel bad, but it was familiar. "Maybe I *should* stop battling for control," parents say, "but what am I going to do instead? Give up and just be permissive?"

Hildy was one of these parents. Listen to what she told us it was like for her to struggle with her fifteen-year-old son Danny:

Danny had been getting pretty obnoxious. It was impossible to tell him anything. He would never listen to me, though God knows I tried to get him to, and when he opened his mouth, all he did was grunt. He was so infuriating. What had happened to my baby? It's funny—the worse things got, the more I kept saying he was just being a typical teenager. I wanted to shake him. I kept getting into this scold/yell/nag thing about his not talking, his not listening.

I wanted to make him do the things I wanted him to do. They were for his own good! Getting after him like that had worked when he was little, so I was sort of trained to do that. You know . . . "If you're going to get tough, mister, I'll get tough."

But things just got worse. I knew that what I was doing wasn't working, but I didn't know what else to do.

How do you solve this dilemma? What's the alternative to battling for control?

Well, your parenting can only be successful if it's based on understanding what adolescence is all about. Since he's getting ready to leave home, being a child is the very last thing your teenager wants to be. If you continue to act like a parent trying to be in control, your teenager will fight you, because when you come on as the parent, he feels like a child. This is so threatening that he'll do whatever he has to to shut you out. And if you keep insisting on being the controlling parent, he'll shut you out forever. The sad stories of the strained and painful relationships between adults and their parents are usually caused by mom and dad's continuing efforts to stay in control.

The solution is to begin the process of having an adult relationship with your teenager now. That way you acknowledge the adult part of him he most wants to develop. And so you become a welcome person in his life, not someone to resist. *And only by being a welcome person in your teenager's life can you—with all that you have to offer—find a place in his life and gain access to him so you can communicate with him, do your job as his parent, and enjoy your teenager as a person.*

Just as adolescence is the special stage where your teenager gets ready to leave home, it's also the special stage where you get ready to have the relationship with your teenager that you're going to have with him for the rest of your life. This means that being successful as the parent of a teenager becomes astonishingly simple: the way to break through the barriers that have prevented you from getting good results is to use what we call *the relationship approach.* Instead of trying to control your teenager,

Work only at improving your relationship with your teenager. If you think something will improve your relationship, do it; if not, don't.

And that's all you have to do.

This really amounts to a revolutionary new way of thinking about how to parent a teenager. By focusing on only one area—your relationship with your teenager—you'll find you're doing everything necessary to be the best possible parent. With the relationship approach you can cope with your teenager today *and* help him get ready for the future—and still come out of it with you both liking each other and wanting to spend time together.

The relationship approach means not putting your energy into the struggle to improve your teenager, as you did in your previous role as "the parent." You must stop worrying if *he's* OK and instead put your energy into making sure that the *two of you together* are OK. Amazingly, when you switch from trying to improve your teenager to trying to improve your relationship with your teenager, you end up having the maximum possible influence with him.

It's really very easy. You don't need to master a complicated list of things to say and do in any situation. To use the relationship approach you need to do only the things you already do every day to improve *any* relationship:

- Make sure the two of you are talking to each other and, just as important, listening. Lecturing, scolding, judging, and nagging hurt relationships. But talking and listening help.
- Make sure you do things together that feel good. If all you are to your teenager is someone who criticizes and complains, he won't want to spend time with you. But if you do things together, you'll provide opportunities for you and your teenager to communicate.
- Make sure you pay attention to how well the two of you are getting along, and try to iron out problems between the two of you. If you allow bad feelings to develop in the hope of gaining control, you'll end up with neither

a relationship nor control. But if you work at clearing away bad feelings, you'll gain both access to your teenager and your only chance of having influence with him.

- Make sure you're both getting your needs met, and be sensitive to your teenager's needs. Getting into battles over things you think *he* should do by imposing rules will hurt your relationship. But having a discussion about what both of you need will enable you and your teenager to agree on solutions.

This last point needs emphasizing. The fact that you're trying to strengthen your relationship with your teenager does *not* mean that you have to abdicate your responsibilities as a parent. What distinguishes successful parents isn't that they avoid fights by letting their kids get away with murder. It's that they fulfill their responsibilities by building on the cornerstone of a good relationship.

Hildy told us what happened when she switched her priorities from trying to improve Danny to improving their relationship. Here's what she said:

It was easier than I'd thought. For me the relationship approach had to do with what was inside my head. I had to let go of the idea that I could keep on doing the same old job I had when Danny was little—except that now, since he was a teenager, I'd have to get tougher.

At first, I was afraid that having a good relationship meant giving in and being a patsy. But that wasn't it. Once I stopped trying to make Danny do what I wanted him to do and just tried to get along with him the way I do with my friends, things changed. Now we do things for each other because we care about each other. It was just sort of natural for me because, you know, I know how to be a really good friend.

I guess I shouldn't say "I just tried to get along with him"—that makes it sound like I gave up trying to be a mother. I didn't. In the past I'd given up when I got tired of all the fighting, and that hadn't felt very good. No, it was more like I said, "OK, what do I need and what does Danny need and what does our relationship need?" And we'd talk about it.

It didn't always work like magic, but sometimes it sort of felt that way. When I stopped fighting, I stopped being the enemy, and when I stopped worrying, I stopped being . . . I don't know, I stopped being a jerk, I guess, to him. I could really be a good parent for Danny without making a martyr of myself and without making both of us crazy.

Hildy had thought that to do her job as a parent she had to fight for control even though that meant having an angry and uncommunicative teenager. The control approach is really the it's-a-dirty-job-but-someone's-got-to-do-it approach. But with the relationship approach she found—as you will—that she could finally do her job as a parent successfully and enjoy her teenager at the same time.

Payoffs from Using the Relationship Approach

When you try to strengthen your relationship with your teenager, you'll get a lot more than a good relationship. Here are some of the other payoffs you'll get from using the relationship approach.

Payoff 1: A good relationship with your teenager will give you the kind of influence you want.

Sure, having a good relationship with your teenager will make living with her a lot easier. But the first question many parents ask us about the relationship approach is, "Yeah, but how will just getting along with my kid give me influence? I'm the parent. I don't want to tie my hands."

You don't have to worry. To see how the relationship approach will give you influence, think about the people who have influence over you. Your best friend, for instance. Does she have influence over you because she demands it? Or because she's the smartest person in the world? No. Your friend has influence because the two of you talk to each other. Because you let her get close to you. Because you care about her.

So it's the communication and the closeness and the caring you have with your friend that gives her influence. And this can happen for you and your teenager. You don't have to wait until long years have cooled the anger that battling for control creates. You have it in your power to act now so that your teenager will talk to you and will let you get close to her and so that you strengthen the real caring that's possible between you. Only that communication, closeness, and caring will give you real influence with your teenager.

Payoff 2: The better your relationship with your teenager, the better you'll feel as a parent.

You can learn a lot by asking parents whose kids have grown up and left home what they wish they had done differently when their kids were teenagers. Almost never do they wish they'd been tougher and fought harder to gain control. Instead, overwhelmingly they say things like:

"I wish we'd been closer."
"I wish we hadn't fought so much."
"I wish we'd communicated more."
"I wish I'd gotten to know my kids better."
"I wish I'd shown more caring instead of always criticizing."
"I wish I hadn't worried so much, and acted so much out of worry."
"I wish we'd known more about each other's lives."

In other words, when it was too late, when patterns of anger and distance had already set in, these parents learned this simple truth: that only by having a good relationship with your teenager can you feel good about the job you have done as a parent.

Parents who battle for control have problems with self-esteem. There they are, trying to straighten their teenager out, to make her do the right thing now so she'll be OK later on. Their teenager fights them, and they have no idea how she'll turn out. Instead of rewards, all they get are battles and hopes. So how can they feel good about themselves?

On the other hand, using the relationship approach has a magical effect on how good you feel about yourself as a parent. Instead of your self-esteem being buffeted by frustration in the present and being a hostage to an unknown future, you'll get daily evidence of the state of your parenting by looking at the current state of your relationship with your teenager. This will make your life easier. If the two of you have difficulties, you can do something quickly to solve the problems that have come up between you and get immediate, visible results. If you find out why your kid's not talking to you now, and solve the problem now, and start communicating again now, you can feel better today rather than having to imagine yourself feeling better twenty years in the future.

Payoff 3: With the relationship approach, you get a solid and enduring future with your son or daughter.

If you spend his teen years struggling with your teenager, then as you see him leaving your life and starting his own life all the distance you've created somehow becomes greater, and the loss feels more bitter. In the end you're relieved to be rid of each other. And what do you have to show for all your time, money, energy, and struggle? At best, empty bragging about a kid who is basically a stranger.

And it's a fallacy that after years of painful and bitter struggles, kids always "come around" when they become adults and finally understand what their parents were trying to do. The anger and distance don't end. When a teenager has to spend his entire adolescence building up patterns of resisting his parents' control, these patterns and the anger that fueled them live on like toxic waste, poisoning that relationship forever.

But when you use the relationship approach you can spend

the thirty or forty years that you're both adults in a relationship filled with love and respect. This happens very easily because during the most stressful and difficult years—the teen years—you've focused on the most important thing: your relationship. You've laid a foundation of love and respect.

And really successful parents understand this. If Sally and Johnny do well in their lives it will be because of what Sally and Johnny do. The credit or blame will be theirs alone. And so you can relax. You don't have to worry about making a gigantic future for an entire human being. You just have to pay attention to the part of his future that is your relationship with him.

By focusing on the relationship, a parent bestows a great gift: the adult child is freed up to say, "My life is mine. I'm responsible for it." And a parent gives herself a great gift because her adult child can go on to say to her, "I'm happy to include you in my life."

Payoff 4: When you use the relationship approach you save time.

Part of the seductive power of battling for control is that you think it won't take much time. With one lightning raid (you feel) you can swoop down, impose rules and punishments, and turn the whole situation around on a dime. Your teenager comes home with a bad report card? Why not just yell, punish, and be done with it? Bang. You just set a limit. Pow. You threaten. Wham. You punish. What could be faster than that?

But it doesn't work. In the real world, battling for control just sets you up for more battles, and, of course, for defeat. You still have a kid who resists you, and he's that much more sullen and resentful. In the time you think you've saved, you have the leisure to contemplate what a really miserable attitude your kid has. And because the problem doesn't go away, there are more time-consuming battles over it in the future.

The relationship approach takes far *less* time than battling for control. In relationship-approach families, parents' investment in improving the relationship with their teenagers pays off because they can simply say, "Please do this because it's important to me"—and the kids do it because their parent's feelings are important to them.

So the real answer to parents who are concerned about their limited time is this: yes, you don't have any time to waste. Therefore, you ought to use every minute of your time in the most productive way. And therefore, even if you have only five minutes, spend it trying to have a better relationship with your teenager. Everything else you want will come from that.

Payoff 5: By using the relationship approach, you get a teenager who's a pleasure to live with.

Remember how pressured you felt as a teenager? There was pressure from thinking about a looming, wide-ranging future that extended from tomorrow's math test and the dance on Saturday night, through getting into college, up to choosing a profession and finding a mate. There was the complex and sometimes conflicting network of peer pressure. There was pressure from teachers. And finally there was the internal pressure that came from your hormones and hopes, your fears and fantasies.

If you as the parent apply another set of pressures—even though you do it because you're concerned—then you become just another thing to get away from. You become something to be avoided, rather than a resource.

You know that you're pressuring your teenager and that he's resisting if he keeps telling you things like, "This is none of your business," "Why don't you leave me alone?" or "You don't really know me." He acts just like a pressured adult. He blows up easily. He avoids you. He's attracted to escapism. He may be depressed. And if he uses a strategy of not talking to you, you may fail to recognize the full extent of your pressure and his resistance.

But parents who use the relationship approach find they can actually enjoy their kids. When they're not busy resisting their parents' pressure, teenagers can be charming, fun, creative, thought-provoking, and affectionate—just the way you and your friends were when you were teenagers. And ultimately, when you can enjoy your teenager, the two of you have an opportunity to experience the love that exists between you.

In a sample of teenagers we interviewed, the overwhelming majority wanted the same things from their parents: trust, respect, attention, independence, communication, and being treated like an individual—all qualities that have to do with having a good parent-teen relationship. Surprisingly, the teenagers we interviewed rarely mentioned that they wanted additional privileges or hoped that their parents made fewer demands on them. But they wanted their parents' demands to come in the context of a good relationship, because that way the demands could be discussed and could seem fair.

Payoff 6: The relationship approach allows you to stop feeling confused, stressed, and overwhelmed in dealing with your teenager. You always know clearly and simply what to do.

On Monday your kid is sullen and hostile. On Tuesday he tells you he wants to go to a rock concert that coming weekend. On Wednesday you finally reach the boiling point over all the stuff he's left around the house. Thursday he brings home a bad report card. And on Friday he tells you you're a lousy parent because you never listen to him, you never care about him, you never take his side.

This is typical. All teenagers assault their parents with behaviors, attitudes, beliefs, and styles that do everything from making your flesh crawl to sending you into shock. So you constantly have to decide what behavior to focus on. And if you're like most parents, you deal with things as they come up, and most of the time you're overwhelmed.

Most parents are also confused by all the different directives they carry around: Be firm. Be fair. Be loving. Be tough to get him ready for the real world. Save him from himself.

Leave him alone to make his own mistakes. Be someone he can talk to. Don't let him think he can get away with things. . . . And the list goes on. The effect of all these conflicting and confusing directives is to heighten your feeling of being overwhelmed, particularly during those times when you most want to be clear and effective.

The relationship approach helps with both of the causes of your feeling overwhelmed—your teenager's behaviors and your inner directives. Now you only have to focus on things that affect your relationship with your teenager. The number of problems you have to deal with and solutions you have to come up with shrinks as you move from trying to perfect an entire human being to getting along with one kid, your Joe or Jane. It's an infinitely more manageable universe. And that helps you be the relaxed, warm, effective, and confident parent you'd like to be.

Well, there it is, the solution to the problem of how you can be the best possible parent for your teenager. Remember, the relationship approach says that all you have to do to be a successful parent is:

Work only at improving your relationship with your teenager. If you think something will improve your relationship, do it; if not, don't.

When the going gets rough and you start feeling confused and overwhelmed, this is all you'll have to remember. It's as if instead of having to decipher a complicated map every time you wanted to take a step, you only have to glance at your compass and go in one straightforward direction: improving your relationship with your teenager. Nothing else is necessary.

And there are many payoffs from using the relationship approach:

- You will find that nothing will give you more influence with your teenager.

- You will feel successful as a parent.
- You will build a solid and enduring future with your teenager.
- You will save time.
- You will get a teenager who's a pleasure to live with.
- You will no longer have to feel confused, stressed, and overwhelmed in dealing with your teenager.
- You will always know clearly and simply what to do.

Getting Started with the Relationship Approach

4

You can begin to put the relationship approach into action immediately.

One of the many good things about the relationship approach is that it builds on *your* strengths. Like most adults, you already know how to have a good relationship with somebody. You do it all the time with friends, coworkers, and everyone else in your life. You also probably have a unique style of maintaining good relationships with people. Humor, intimacy, support, and shared activities are some of the different ways adults relate to their friends.

But the question for most parents isn't how to have a good relationship with just anyone, it's how to start having a good relationship with their teenager. Here's what to do.

First Steps in Getting Started

When your teenager acts in any of the ways that make you want to yell, or impose a rule, or bring down a punishment, or criticize, or lecture, or nag, or pick at her, or do any of the things parents typically do, *stop*.

That's really the first step in using the relationship approach: blocking off all your old, control-approach behavior.

Just accomplishing this step—not doing anything new, just stopping doing all the things that don't work—will go far in ending that terrible push-resist dynamic of parent-teen relationships.

But what do you do instead? Just think of something else to say, something that will strengthen your relationship with your teenager. Let questions like the following serve as a kind of filter to keep out the harmful words and let in the helpful words:

- Will saying this make us feel warmer and closer?
- Will this make us feel better about each other?
- Will this make it easier for us to talk to each other?
- Will this help both of us get our needs met?
- Is this the kind of thing I might say to a friend who was going through a rough time?
- Is this the kind of thing that will show my kid that I'm trying to take care of our relationship?

If you guess that what you're about to say will strengthen the relationship, say it. And if you don't think that what you're about to say will improve your relationship, if it's just more of the same old scold/yell/nag/lecture/punish stuff you've been doing, if it's the kind of thing *you'd* hate to hear if you were going through a rough time and your friend or your mother said it to you, then simply *don't say it*, even if you're itching to gain some control.

The relationship approach is as simple as that. You stop the old behavior, you try to think of something that will make you and your teen feel good about each other, and you trust yourself to come up with something helpful. What you say doesn't have to be wise or wonderful. It can be banal or awkward. But if it's in the direction of helping rather than hurting your relationship, you're on the right track.

If you try but time goes by and you still can't think of something healing or helpful to say, that's OK. Unless your kid is bleeding to death or has stopped breathing, you don't have to do—or say—*anything* right away. You can wait until you think of something that will make the two of you feel better about each other.

One mother waited two weeks after her daughter came home with a bad report card before she was able to think of anything other than put-downs and punishments. Her silence was eerie, but it wasn't harmful. Then, when she did finally come up with something that was helpful for her daughter *and* that strengthened the bond between them, there were no damage and debris to clear away.

Think of it this way. You can waste time if you respond too quickly, because the habits of speech parents get into are all too likely to cause trouble and take a long time to clear up. The more slowly you respond—particularly when you're just beginning to use the relationship approach—the more time you'll actually save, because you'll avoid making a mess of the situation. And even if you have to count to ten or wait ten days, you'll end up with a good solution.

If the first words that you think of saying aren't terrific, stop worrying. When they're upset, even the most successful parents in the world find themselves thinking of stupid, unproductive things to say. The difference is that successful parents keep these destructive comments to themselves until they can think of something better. And you can do that too.

Now suppose you let some time go by and you think of something to say that sounds better than the stuff you've been saying. How can you be confident it will make the two of you feel better about each other? Just ask yourself if it would make you feel better if a friend said it to you. Or ask yourself if this was the kind of thing you found helpful when you were a teenager.

You can trust yourself. You don't need a degree in adolescent psychology or interpersonal relations. Since all the relationship approach asks you to do is improve your relationship with your teenager, it calls for nothing more from you than the people skills you already use in other areas of your life. You'll find it's much easier than what you've been doing. And you'll be able to use it whatever your situation, whatever your kid is like, whatever his age, and even if you're afraid there's something seriously wrong with him.

What It Means to Be a Successful Parent

A week after he started using the relationship approach with his two teenagers, Frank, a divorced father, called us and said,

> It's hard for me to let go of wanting control because I want some evidence that will make me feel that my kids are good kids and I've been a success as a parent. And when I get evidence to the contrary I feel I'm a bad parent and they're bad kids, and that makes me feel terrible. I need to feel I'm accomplishing something with those kids.

For Frank and for most parents who want to use the relationship approach, dealing with these feelings is the most important thing they need to do to get started. Who wouldn't want to get that stamp of approval, to have your kid do and be those things that would make it absolutely clear you've done a great job? Who wouldn't feel like a successful parent if his kid graduated valedictorian of her high school class and, while pre-med in an Ivy League college, managed to be captain of her school's field hockey team?

But most parents have to live without those gold stars on the parental report card. If your kid's like most teenagers, he's done pretty well in some areas, struggled in others. Too often it just doesn't add up to anything you can point to as proof positive of your success. And this casts a pall of grim disapproval over the parent-teen relationship. As you search your teenager for signs that you've done a good job and that he's a good kid, he feels he has to get away from you to save himself from your disappointment. This means he feels he has to do his job of leaving home in private, because when you walk into the messy workshop of his adolescence, filled with unfinished tasks, all you see are mistakes and confusion. And that's all you comment on too, because you don't have a crystal ball that shows how this will all come together one day in the future in the form of an adult who may be less than a smash hit but is still successful in the sense that he's become self-reliant and achieved an identity.

For your kid's happiness and your own, you must redefine what it means to be successful as the parent of a teenager. It's destructive to define success in terms of how smart or ambitious your kid is or in terms of what she's accomplished. The truth is that if your kid's accomplishment is the kind of thing you could brag about, then it probably has nothing to do with your real success as a parent. Remember: the things parents do generally have little impact on how their kids turn out.

Instead, redefine success for yourself. Get started using the relationship approach by defining success as having a good relationship with your teenager. In other words, start thinking of yourself as a success if

- Your kid talks to you.
- Your kid listens to you.
- There's an easy atmosphere of give-and-take between you.
- You can have fights and can make up.
- You laugh together.
- You spend time together.
- Your kid comes to you for advice from time to time.
- You have fun together.
- There's a growing sense of your having an adult-to-adult relationship.
- Your kid tells you some of his problems.
- Your kid introduces you to the people in his life.
- You can get your needs met with him even if you sometimes have to struggle to do so.

Now there can be an end to your confusion and frustration. Rather than being abstract or remote, your relationship with your teenager is always right in front of you, ready for inspection, and *it's the only thing you have any control over.* And, as you'll see in the next chapter, a good relationship is the best way to have influence over your teenager.

This, then, is what it means to use the relationship approach. Whenever you're about to launch into your old controlling behavior, stop and try to think of something that will

- Make the two of you feel warmer and closer
- Make you feel better about each other
- Help both of you get your needs met
- Be the kind of thing you might say to a friend who was going through a rough time
- Be the kind of thing that will show your teenager that you're trying to take care of the relationship

Then, whenever you're feeling the desire to control because you see your kid is less than perfect or different from the way you'd like him to be, remember that you are now redefining what it means to be successful as a parent. Now, success *only* means having a good relationship with your teenager. Everything else—having the right kind of influence, taking care of yourself, protecting your kid, and solving problems—will follow from your using the relationship approach.

USING THE RELATIONSHIP APPROACH

PART

How to Influence Your Teenager   5

It just doesn't make sense to some parents at first. "A good relationship!?" they say. "My kid's threatened with drugs/AIDS/failing grades/bad attitudes, and all you want me to do is have a good relationship with her!? If I don't struggle with my teenager, how can I make her a better person?"

Of course you're not going to feel you're the best parent for your teenager if you think the relationship approach just means letting him get away with murder. Any parent also desperately wants to have influence over her teenager, so she can really feel she's doing her job as a parent. You can use the relationship approach to make sure you have that influence.

Suppose, to take a situation that bothers many parents, you want your teenager to speak like an articulate person instead of mumbling, grunting, and using repetitive, meaningless slang. If you struggle with her about this, more likely than not your kid will feel that all you want to do is control her. And so she'll avoid you, oppose you, or make fun of you.

Here's how the relationship approach will help get you influence. You've got a lot to offer as a role model. Anything you do that generates resistance and distance damages your effectiveness. Anything you do that generates warmth and closeness gives your teenager more contact with all that you have to offer. So, for example, if you want to influence how well your kid speaks, forge a good relationship with her. A good relationship will increase contact with you as a model and decrease resistance to what you have to offer. And since you do have a lot to offer, the more contact with you, the better.

This approach works with every other problem or issue, whether it's avoiding drugs, working hard, being a caring person, or any of the other values and behaviors you might want to pass on.

So one way the relationship approach gives parents influence is that it allows teenagers to emulate them. But most parents of teenagers also want a more direct, active kind of influence. And the relationship approach will give you that too. In fact, a good relationship works like a superhighway that lets you drive straight through to your teenager's heart and mind. It gives you the kind of direct access that parents who keep trying to control their teenagers can only dream about.

Of course, a good relationship doesn't translate into influence by magic. It works this way: when you have a good relationship with your teenager, you'll have influence because

- You'll get precious information from her.
- She'll listen to you.
- She'll *want* to do what's really important to you.

Let's look at how you can make these work for you.

Getting More Information from Your Teenager

This is the first, most important, and most overlooked step in the process of having influence. When you don't know what's going on with your teenager, you're like someone driving blindfolded on a moonless night with no lights. You can't see where you're going and you can't see how to get there. Your control of the steering wheel is only based on guesses. Isn't a crash inevitable?

That's why no issue in parenting teenagers is more crucial than *whether you'll get the truth* when you ask questions like

- "Did you do your homework?"
- "Where are you going?"
- "What's going on between you and that boy [or girl] you're seeing?"
- "Are you taking drugs?"

And we mean "the truth"—not the "right" answer and not just good news. In fact one of the best ways to know if you're successfully parenting your teenager is to ask yourself whether your kid tells you scary or disturbing things. You must hear from your kid when she's played hooky or been exposed to drugs. These things go on in every single teenager's life, and your job is to improve your relationship so your kid will tell you about them.

If you respond to the truth by getting upset, imposing punishments, yelling, criticizing, nagging, or lecturing, then any teenager in her right mind is going to figure out that lies and silence work better than the truth. You will hear only reassuring—but false—things like, "Of course I've done my homework," "I'm going to a friend's house to study for tomorrow's test," "We're just dating," "I'm not interested in drugs."

And if you don't know what's going on, your attempts at influence will be blind and misguided. Your doctor has to know everything that's going on with you before she can write a prescription. She can't help you if her diagnosis is based only on her assumptions and your lies. It's the same for you and your teenager.

Something of a miracle happens when you stop trying to control your teenager. Because she's not facing demands, criticisms, threats, and punishments, she'll know you won't use what she says against her. She'll feel safe confiding in you. Then you'll finally know what's really going on in your kid's life. The lights will come on; the blindfold will come off. *The number one complaint among teenagers is, "I can't talk to my parents."* So by focusing on the relationship and making it easier for your teenager to talk to you, you'll satisfy one of your teenager's deepest needs.

When your teenager talks to you, and especially when she tells you "bad news," you get real power, the kind of power you thought you'd get by battling for control. *It's only when she can talk to you that you can focus on what's most important in her life.*

For example, let's say your high-school-age daughter seems to be getting serious about some boy and you're afraid that she'll get used, pregnant, or hurt in some way. If you deal with this by trying to control the situation—say, by forbidding her to see the boy or making her curfew earlier—then your teenager (who's struggling to rely on herself and become her own person) can only take care of herself by not telling you what she's doing. You could end up thinking you're in the driver's seat when you've really been left by the side of the road, with all your influence in a ditch.

But if you're more interested in your relationship (making it one in which people listen to each other) than in control (when people try to tell each other what to do), your teenager won't feel threatened by telling you things. You'll find out how she feels and what's really going on. Maybe you'll find out that she feels more ambivalent about the boy than you thought. Maybe she has fears you haven't known about. Maybe she's having sex but not using birth control. Maybe you haven't realized some of the ways in which she's ignorant. Whatever the case, you'll know what's going on and what you have to deal with. You'll have traded the *illusion* of control for real information—and come away the winner.

Of course, when your teenager tells you things that are scary or disappointing ("Mom, I think I'm pregnant."), you may very well feel that you don't want to hear them. That's a very natural reaction to bad news. But it's much better— and gives you much more influence—to have an unpleasant moment in an open, trusting relationship than what feels like a pleasant moment but is really a lie in a relationship based on distance and distrust.

What you're really doing by making it easy for your teenager to talk to you is making a kind of deal with him. It's as if you were saying, "I'll give up yelling, punishing, and lecturing when you tell me something. Instead, I'll just listen and really try to hear what you're saying. In exchange you'll tell me what's going on in your life." Most teenagers will make this deal. And most parents are made winners by this deal.

Listening to your teenager comes in handy all the time. It's a skill you can use even if your teenager is defying you. There your daughter stands, saying she simply refuses to come home by twelve-thirty, her usual curfew—a situation in which you can lose power by fighting for control. You can say, "You'll be home by twelve-thirty or else," but in the long run, saying that kind of thing doesn't work. There are too many ways your teenager can sabotage you. On the other hand, you can gain power by listening. A question like, "Why is it so important to you that you stay out later than twelve-thirty?" will make your teenager feel her needs are being taken into account and that she has a chance to influence you.

Nothing else will give you as much power. For one thing, you get information about what's going on with your daughter, and information is always power. What's more, by making your daughter feel you've taken her needs into account, you make her feel good about you; therefore, she's more likely to want to please you and more likely to take *your* needs into account.

How to Speed Up the Process of Getting Your Teenager to Talk to You

First of all, your teenager *will* tell you all kinds of things if you just stop judging, worrying, punishing, and getting angry—in other words, stop trying to control her. It may not happen tomorrow or the day after tomorrow, but very soon she will get the idea that when she talks, you'll listen and nothing bad will happen to her.

How can you make this happen faster? Tell your teenager what you're trying to do. Tell her you're out of the control business. Tell her that from now on you want to have a good relationship with her, and that means the two of you have to be able to talk to each other, and *that* means you're going to listen to her.

Get ready for her to test you. Count on it: when you're proudest of your decision to stop controlling, your teenager will walk in and tell you some particularly upsetting bit of news, calculated to make you fall back into your old scold/yell/nag routine. Instead of falling into the trap, be grateful. This is your big moment. Sometimes nothing is harder than just listening without pushing the panic button. But if you pass this one simple test, then the way is open for all kinds of future communication.

And to pass the test all you have to do is say something like, "I'm glad you told me. It's important to me that you can tell me things like that." And then don't say anything else. There will be plenty of opportunities later to take care of your needs and concerns.

In fact, listening—not judging, not even commenting—can be very powerful in getting your teenager to talk to you. Think of it this way: there's a fixed number of words between you, and the more words *you* use the fewer there are for *her*. And the fewer words that are available to her the less you hear, and the less you hear the more you're in the dark. *And your effectiveness as a parent comes much, much more from what you hear than from what you say.* When your kid is talking, bite your tongue and just listen.

Another thing you can do to make it easier for your teenager to talk to you is to avoid making any assumptions about what your kid is saying. Parents spend too much time thinking they understand their kids. This makes teenagers angry and makes them decide not to talk to their parents. Why bother talking when your parent always misunderstands?

For example, one day Sally told her very successful father that she wasn't ambitious. Don started yelling: "What do you want to be, a bum?" But Sally, who was about to go off to college, only meant that she didn't have fixed career goals yet and that what she wanted was to do well in college without worrying about keeping to some preordained plan. Don would have understood this if he had only asked her what she meant. Instead, he yelled at her, making it harder for her to talk to him in the future.

To avoid making the wrong assumptions and to keep information flowing from your teenager, *ask questions.* If your daughter says she's in love, your fears *could* make you hit the roof or start lecturing. But your priority has to be making it easier for your teenager to talk to you. So ask her what being in love means to her. Let her talk all about her feelings and thoughts. Otherwise, you don't know what you should be responding to.

Remember, though, the point of asking questions is to generate information and help your teenager open up, not to give him the third degree. Pushing for answers in a way that hurts your relationship with your teenager just puts you right back in the futile battle for control. Trust takes time to build.

What about the times when you ask a question gently and sincerely and your kid still refuses to answer? (This happens to all parents.) What can you do about it? In spite of the fact that it feels as if she were provoking you to battle for control, your daughter's refusal to answer your question is only her way of saying, "I'm getting older; I don't belong to you the way I used to, and some things are just private now." In other words, she's setting up a boundary—and she'll be grateful if you respect it.

When your kid sets up a boundary, you might feel that you're losing control and maybe even losing her. But to a teenager, every boundary powerfully symbolizes both becoming self-reliant and achieving an identity. When you attack the boundary you attack her at the very core of her mission.

It may seem like a paradox, but it's absolutely true nonetheless: the more you respect your kid's boundaries, the more she'll talk to you. And *of course* she'll talk to you: your respecting her means she can feel safe. So if your teenager says, "That's none of your business," the response that works best is something like, "I'm not asking so I can trap you into some kind of admission but only so we can get closer. I hope you'll tell me when you're ready."

In fact, asking questions is one of the best ways to secure

real power and strengthen the relationship at the same time. Questions—sincere, interested, nonjudgmental questions—break through walls instead of building them. They are much better than the scolding, complaining, or commanding you usually do when you feel powerless.

But you have to ask the question as if you really wanted to break through those walls, as if you really wanted the brand-new information that will make you both feel close and powerful. Teenagers hate being given the third degree; they're suspicious of how powerful your information can make you. So make the question a treat and not a trick.

It's a treat if you ask questions because you really want to know and because the answers will help you get closer to your teenager. So don't ask her as if you're Perry Mason preparing a cross-examination and looking for that one damning piece of self-incriminating evidence that will enable you to spring the trap shut. For example, if you say to your thirteen-year-old, "Are there going to be boys at this party?" and she says yes, don't come back with, "Aha! *That's* why I don't want you coming home late! I *knew* there'd be a good reason." When you respond that way you destroy trust, and since mistrust destroys relationships, you lose your chance to have any influence.

Nor does it work to ask questions that are really disguised attempts to push and prod. Perhaps, for example, your teenager has agreed to clean out the garage, but time has gone by and nothing has happened. The very same question—"When are you going to do it?"—could result in a defensive "Stop bugging me, will you?" or in a simple "Later this afternoon after the football game." It all depends upon how you ask it. If you get the defensive answer, or want to prevent getting that answer, you can say, "I'm not asking this to bug you; I just want to know so I can make plans. When are you going to do the garage?"

Here are some more suggestions on how to ask questions in a way that builds bridges instead of walls:

- If you don't understand the way your teenager is acting, you could ask, "What does it mean to you that you're . . . ?"

- If your teenager insists on doing something you don't approve of, you could ask, "Why is this so important to you?"
- If you feel your teenager is giving you a hard time and that nothing seems to satisfy her, you could ask, "What do you *really* want?"
- If your teenager starts acting in ways that make no sense to you, you could ask, "How do you want me to think about what you're doing?"
- If your teenager seems sullen, obnoxious, and miserable, you could ask, "How can I be helpful to you?"

These questions put out the fires of resistance and at the same time nourish closeness. It may not all happen immediately, but it *starts* happening immediately. If you ask in a spirit of caring rather than as part of a scheme to blame or change your teenager, you will make progress. All you have to do is ask questions that help you to talk to each other.

Now you'll be one of the lucky parents. Your kid will be one of those teenagers who can say to her friends, "I can tell my parents anything."

Getting Your Teenager to Listen to You

Now, while getting your teenager to talk to you is the first and most important part of having influence, most parents won't really feel they have influence unless they can get their teenagers to listen to them. And one of the complaints we hear most frequently from parents is that their teenagers won't listen.

"So what do you do?" we ask.

"I yell [or lecture]," they admit.

"Does that work?"

"No."

"What do you do then?"

"I yell louder [or lecture more]."

But the solution isn't to shove what you have to say down your kid's throat. Getting him to listen to you isn't like getting your dog to swallow a pill. The reason teenagers don't listen isn't that they're defective or that they hate you or even that they're "just teenagers." It's that their supersensitive antennae pick up the smallest hint of an attempt at control. By refusing to listen, a teenager is saying, "Hey, you're not really trying to talk to me. You're just trying to control me. You're yelling at me, telling me I'm not OK the way I am. Why should I listen to that?"

Sadly, the less teenagers listen, the more many parents fight to make them listen—which only guarantees that they won't listen at all. But the less you try to control, the more she hears what you have to say as simple information rather than an attempt at control, as offering her choices rather than attempting to make her choices for her, as sharing your experience rather than attempting to limit hers. She can come close to you because she trusts that the information you're giving is not going to jump out and bite her. She can listen to you say you don't like something because she knows that your words are not accompanied by your saying she must do something.

You know this is true because you know it works with your friends. If your friend knows you care about her, you'll find that she will often listen even if you're upset, even if you yell. Why? Because she knows you can't control her. She doesn't have to defend herself, or worry about resisting your control.

So if your message is that good grades are important, your teenager will be able to listen to this only to the extent that you're not trying to make her study or be the kind of person who wants to study. If your message is that drugs are bad, she'll be able to listen only to the extent that you're not trying to control who she hangs out with, where she goes, and what she does when she gets there.

Of course there's always a part of you that wants control, and at first it might make you feel helpless if you're always saying things like, "I can't tell you what to do but . . ." Yet these are the very words that make teenagers pay attention! Saying, "You've got to . . . ," or "This is the way it is . . . ," just makes teenagers tune out.

Some parents confuse what we're saying here with "permissiveness" or "letting the kid get away with murder." In fact there's no connection. You're a real person with real needs, and if you let your teenager step all over you you'll damage the relationship between you from the other end: she may not resent you, but you'll resent her.

So having the best possible relationship with your teenager also means somehow reconciling her needs with your needs. Both are important. Whatever the issue, the problem, or the situation, you and your kid are sitting on a pile of things you want from each other. Even if the issue is something as simple as the acceptable volume for playing the stereo, you can neither ignore your preference for quiet nor her preference for her own music. But unless the two of you are talking and listening to each other, you won't know what the other prefers. And unless you've worked to eliminate control and have the best possible relationship with your kid, she won't want to meet your needs.

How to Get Your Teenager to Listen to You

Your teenager will listen to you when she doesn't feel you're trying to control her. Let's say she comes home and says, "Jennifer [her best friend] has been smoking," and you've listened to what she has to say about this, and you've asked her what this means to her and how she feels about it and what she's planning to do about it. The first rule in getting her to listen to you is to stop thinking about trying to make her do what you want. You can't make her obey you anyway, so you might as well make it possible for her to hear you. Attach a kind of anticontrol filter to your lips. Whatever you're thinking of saying, ask yourself if it's likely to make your teenager say, "You can't tell me what to do. I'll do what I want."

To see how this anticontrol filter works, listen to the difference between these two sentences:

- "You're going to be in big trouble if I catch you smoking."
- "I get scared when I think about you smoking."

The first sentence is likely to produce a you-can't-tell-me-what-to-do response from your teenager. The second sentence is likely to produce an I-don't-want-you-to-be-scared response from her. Your kid can listen to your words because you're just presenting her with a fact about how you feel.

And that's the key: talk about how you feel. Would you say to a friend, "If you don't stop smoking I'm going to punish you"? Or would you be more likely to say, and would your friend be more likely to hear you, if you said, "I can't make you stop smoking, but I'm afraid you're going to get lung cancer and I'm going to lose you."

The more you talk about how you feel, the more you become a real person to your kid. Show her that real people—even if they are parents—are often confused and conflicted about how they feel. You want your kid to do well in school, but, for example, you may also remember how much you hated school. You want her to stay away from drugs, but you remember how much you enjoyed smoking pot in college. The specific issue doesn't matter. The point is that the more real you are—the more you are a person and the less a controller—the more your kid's ears and heart will open to what you have to say. And the better your kid will feel about you, which leads us to the next point.

Getting Your Teenager to Do What's Really Important to You

Here's where the rubber hits the road. The essence of the relationship approach is that *when the two of you have a good relationship, your teenager will WANT to do many of the things you struggle unsuccessfully to make her do now. She'll want to do these things simply because they're important to you, and you're important to her.*

Is this pie in the sky? Is this just a feel-good fantasy?

No, it's the cold, hard truth. Being a teenager means your kid is more and more her own person every day. Anytime you try to control her by trying to make her do what you want, you threaten the most important thing in the world to her right now: her independence. She doesn't resist you because she's just being ornery. No, she resists because you tell her, "You have to do this," or "What's wrong with you for not doing that?" Don't set yourself up in opposition to one of the most powerful forces in the world: a teenager's drive to independence and selfhood. Trying to do so is a loser's game. No response is more likely than, "You can't make me," or "I like things the way they are."

But, believe it or not, your teenager loves you. That's a wonderful foundation to build on. If you have a good relationship with her, she even *likes* you, and the foundation is still stronger. And if you respect her, she'll respect you. Then the foundation is as solid as can be. It is only this love and liking and respect that give you any influence at all— *nothing else.*

How to Get Your Teenager to Do What's Really Important to You

The only powerful parents in the world are those who have a good relationship with their teenager. True, they don't have the power that controlling parents dream of, the power to make their kids turn on a dime. No parent has that kind of power. But they do have the only possible kind of power, the kind that comes when you say, "I can't make you do this, but it would mean a lot to me if you did"—and your kid then wants to cooperate.

Parents who keep trying, and failing, to make their teenagers do what they want often can't believe that a teenager would ever cooperate voluntarily. But in fact these parents are just like people who run after the family cat and can never catch it. The best way to get the cat is to open a can of cat food (because food is important to cats) and let him come to you. The right way to get a teenager to cooperate is to build a warm and strong relationship with her—because that's what's important to teenagers.*

---

*The tragedy is that many parents can't believe that their teenagers want a good

When you have this kind of relationship with your teenager, you can say, "Please do this for me," and a large part of her will want to. Your chances of getting what you want will be vastly increased. With a good relationship your words call forth results, not resistance. But if you demand something from your teenager, you will only make her want to defy you, vastly decreasing your chances of getting what you want.

Here's an example of what you can get from having a good relationship with your teenager. Lisa, fifteen, came to her parents about wanting to go to a rock concert on a school night. It was the usual story: all her friends were going, she'd be home early, she'd already done all her schoolwork, she promised she wouldn't be tired for school the following day, and so on. And, oh yes, it would just be this one time.

"We don't want you to go," the parents said.

"You know, you can't stop me," Lisa said, testing to see if they were trying to control her.

They refused to take the bait. They knew that short of physical restraint or dire threats they really *couldn't* stop her. Nor did they want to try. They knew that the control game doesn't produce winners, only resentment.

What they had going for them was a good relationship with her. "You're right, we can't stop you, but we don't want you to go. Your grades have not been very good and it just doesn't feel right to us that you'd go out on a school night. It's your life, but we really don't like your going out."

This stumped her. Lisa cared about how her parents felt. They hadn't eroded her respect for them by a long history of ridiculous attempts at impossible control. She knew there was a good chance they were right. Lisa was the one who'd been saying she wanted to start getting good grades. And their trusting what she did was important to her: she knew that their trust had resulted in her having a lot more freedom than many of her friends.

Lisa decided not to go—without any anger and resent-

---

relationship. They don't see any evidence for it. But the reason they feel only their kids' desire for distance is that that's what the control approach has created.

ment. It was her decision, and she couldn't blame her parents for it. (If she'd been seventeen instead of fifteen, it's possible Lisa would have gone anyway. The relationship approach is not a back-door way of reenlisting in the battle for control. But Lisa's parents still would have been winners, because the point isn't control.) Her parents' handling of the situation gave them influence. Lisa was able to hear their thinking. She was touched by their values in a way that didn't make her resist them. Her affection for her parents was strengthened, giving them the greatest power of all—the power of their daughter wanting to do things because she cared for them.

There's another reason why creating an atmosphere of mutual caring gives you influence. Normal teenagers can be very lonely. It may be hard for you to believe this if what you generally see is your teenager hanging out with friends or talking on the phone. And the last thing she wants to do is admit her loneliness to you, because it's critical that you of all people see her marching forward in the process of becoming self-reliant. But your caring can soothe her loneliness. She'll be willing to let you influence her to preserve your caring.

Still, as powerful as your caring is, sometimes it's just not powerful enough. You can have the best relationship in the world with your kid, and she can care for you a lot, *but she's getting ready to leave home* and so even her caring for you won't always get her to do what you want.

Then what? This is when parents can get frustrated and end up using the control approach again. But you know that doesn't work. There is something, however, that does work, almost like magic, to give you influence.

The Magic Question

OK. You've listened to your teenager. Your teenager has listened to you. You've said, "Please do this for me," but in spite of her real caring for you, your teenager just hasn't been able to give you what you want.

The solution to this comes right out of the recipe for how to have a good relationship. Relationships are strengthened by two people caring for each other, but they're also strengthened by two people doing things for each other. Since you know how to have good relationships with people, you already know how to do this. You just have to apply it to your relationship with your teenager.

To get that last measure of influence, when you've asked for something and your teenager has said no in spite of all kinds of communicating and caring going on between you, just ask the magic question:

"What do you need to give me what I need?"

For example, you could ask, "What do you need to clean up the kitchen after dinner without my nagging you or our having a fight?" Or, "What do you need to get home by midnight and to give me a call before you leave the party?"

When you've done everything else, this is what will give you the best chance of breaking through that last wall of your teenager's resistance. It works because it turns a command-and-control situation into "Let's Make A Deal." Instead of taking control, you're sharing power. It's like the difference between somebody stealing your car and somebody making you a cash offer for your car: you feel a lot better when someone offers you something in exchange for what you're giving up. And who can say no to a good deal?

So the better your relationship with your teenager, the more likely it is that you will get incredible bargains. In our experience, a teenager won't usually ask that much in return for giving you what you want. Often all it has to be is a token, just enough to satisfy his dignity. And the more you ask the magic question, the better your relationship with your teenager will be. Asking plugs you into a cycle where each fruitful deal you make leads to you and your teenager feeling better about each other and getting more of your needs met.

Unfortunately some parents don't like to do this, because they're worried about their own dignity. "What!? Make a deal with my own kid? You want to make me a beggar in my own house?"

Of course not. But while you should never be a beggar, you can no longer be the boss. That's what adolescence means. The magic question "What do you need to give me what I need?" takes into account the fact that in the world of parent-teen relationships, solutions must be negotiated. They cannot be imposed. The older your teenager gets, the more this is true. And the younger your teenager is when you start doing this, the more the two of you will be in the habit of negotiating solutions when he gets older and the going gets tougher.

And that's what the magic question is all about really: a negotiation in which something is talked about, worked out, and mutually agreed upon. It's no big deal to make a deal. It's just you and your teenager sitting down together and talking and realizing that both of you will probably have to pay a price if both of you are going to get what you want. And you aren't paying that price because your kid is holding you up at gunpoint or because you've lost your prestige. No, that price simply recognizes the reality that you can't get what you want unless you take what your kid wants into account.

We said at the very beginning of this book that we've based the relationship approach on what makes successful parents different from unsuccessful ones. And one of the biggest differences is that successful parents accept that both parents and teenagers have needs and that, even if there's a little struggling involved, good solutions take everyone's needs into account. Unsuccessful parents believe that parents are wise and teenagers are foolish and that only parents know what teenagers need. This is a recipe for disaster.

You're negotiating with your teenager not because you're a wimp, or because you're afraid of her, or because you don't care. No, you're negotiating with your teenager because imposing rules makes bad relationships worse, while negotiating solutions makes good relationships better.

What's more, by going through a negotiation you'll learn things about your teenager that you wouldn't learn otherwise, and you'll communicate things to your teenager that wouldn't get through otherwise. By making your relationship better in this way, you'll be in an even stronger position to have influence.

Using the Magic Question to Get Influence

How do you make this work for you? And what happens after you say, "What do you need to give me what I need?"

There are three possibilities. One is that your kid will mention something you can give her, and then there's no problem. For example, "OK, I won't go to that rock concert tonight—if you let me go to that rock concert a week from Saturday and stay over Betsy's house afterward." If that's OK with you, then you've got a deal.

Another possibility is that your kid will say he doesn't know what he needs, and then the two of you have to talk until you come up with something. For example, initially he can't think of a single thing you can do that would make him spend another minute studying, because he hates studying so much. You can't seem to suggest any offers he likes. Finally you say, "What's really the problem here?" As the two of you talk it turns out that your kid hates his school, the other kids, the teachers, everything. As you listen to his complaints, you find they have some validity. It turns out there really are problems with the school.

Now you have something to offer him that works. "Let's try to find you another school. It won't happen right away, and you'll probably need good grades to transfer, but if you study hard now I promise we'll solve the school problem." Your teenager will feel some hope, and you've got a deal.

Of course, it doesn't have to be this radical. Just don't let the negotiations get bogged down because your teenager can't think of what he needs to give you what you need. That doesn't mean you can't make a deal; that usually means only that you need to use a little creativity in digging to find out what the problem is.

The third possibility is that your kid will say he needs something that you don't feel you can give him. You'll be surprised at how rarely this happens, but what do you do if you come to an impasse? Then the two of you have to arrive at some kind of compromise between what he wants and what you can give. If both of you give up a little of what you want, you'll get a solution. *And less-than-perfect solutions that work are infinitely better than perfect solutions that never happen.*

Here's an example of how a mother and daughter dealt with an impasse like this. Again, what's important here isn't the particular solution they came up with, but the process they used to come up with it.

Helen wanted her daughter, Karen, to stay home the summer before her first year of college, instead of going to work as a lifeguard at a resort as Karen had been planning. Helen had been sick and so she felt she really needed help both with the house and with Karen's younger brothers and sisters.

"Mom, I'm sorry, but no," Karen said, after they'd talked for a while. "I've been looking forward my whole life to doing this."

After Helen asked Karen, "What do you need to give me what I need?" Karen finally said all she could think of was getting paid at least as much as she would have gotten paid as a lifeguard. She'd be giving up her summer but at least she'd get the money she needed for college.

But Helen couldn't afford this.

They had to find a way out of this impasse. Helen needed help. Karen needed money. And Karen felt she needed the experience of working at the resort she'd been looking forward to for so long.

What made the crucial difference in Helen and Karen arriving at some kind of solution was seeing each other as partners rather than antagonists. *Two people seeing each other as partners rather than antagonists is the key to successful negotiation.* Over the last couple of years Helen and Karen had managed to build a pretty good relationship, and they didn't want to destroy it over this impasse. So they talked together out of a sense of respect for both of their needs, as if they were business partners trying to come up with something to help their joint business.

Karen and Helen did arrive at a satisfactory solution, but

it's important to remember that another parent and teenager might have come up with a different solution. Once they were approaching each other as partners and were focused on what they really needed rather than on what they were demanding of each other, it was an easy step to generate new options and new ideas. Usually, goodwill, creativity, and a problem-solving approach will break through any impasse.*

As they talked, Helen realized that she didn't need help sixteen hours a day; she really needed help only a couple of hours a day. Karen realized that this was a very special situation and that her mother really needed help. It turned out that Karen had a friend who was looking for a job where she could work only a few hours a day. Karen offered to pay half her friend's wages if her mother paid the other half. Paying half of the friend's part-time wages would still leave Karen with a lot of earnings from the summer. And it wouldn't be placing too much of a financial burden on her mother, particularly since Helen didn't want to ruin Karen's summer.

To prevent hitting a stalemate when you negotiate with your teenager, remember to *expand your range of options and throw more possibilities into the negotiating pot.* If you and your teenager are getting along, then negotiations are only likely to break down when you have too narrow a range of options. With Helen and Karen the breakthrough came when they included money and Karen's friend in the solution.

So what you and your teenager need to do if you're stuck is generate more possibilities. It's very hard to get unstuck if all you can talk about is whether she can or can't have the car, or whether he can or can't have the money for the trip. But there are always other things you can throw in the pot—like money, chores, other people, other actions, and breaking things down into smaller pieces. All this can create more options. And the more options you have, the more likely it is that you and your teenager will be able to figure out what she needs in order to give you what you need.

* * *

*If you want to learn more about how to negotiate successfully, the best book is Roger Fisher and William Ury's *Getting to Yes* (New York: Penguin, 1983).

The relationship approach will enable you to get what you could never get from the control approach: real influence. It's very simple. You can have a good relationship and have influence if you

- Get more information from your teenager by listening and asking questions
- Get your teenager to listen to you by making sure you're conveying real information, either about the world or about how you feel
- Get your teenager to do what's important to you by preserving the real caring in your relationship and using your teenager's caring rather than your attempts at control as the mechanism
- Use the magic question, "What do you need to give me what I need?"

Notice something very important. We probably haven't told you things you didn't already know about relationships. All we did was show you how to apply what you already use in other contexts to your relationship with your teenager.

The Relationship Approach in Action

6

Let's look at how you can use the relationship approach right now to deal with some typical situations. It's not these specific situations that are the issue here, though. It's seeing the relationship approach in action. Later we'll go into more detail and provide more ideas about how to deal with situations like these. But now what's important is for you to see how much influence you can get just by focusing on improving your relationship with your teenager.

Your fifteen-year-old daughter has just announced that this coming Friday night she wants to stay out long past her curfew. What do you do?

If you're like most parents, your first thought is probably to say something like, "Hey, we've made the rule and that's that." Or, "You'll come home when I tell you to come home, do you understand?" Or, "As long as you're in my house, you'll do things my way." Or, "No daughter of mine is going to stay out late like some tramp." Or, "What are you trying to do, make me crazy with worry?" It's even possible that some parents would say, "Hey, I don't care when you come home," all the while feeling angry and helpless inside.

What should *you* do, if you want to use the relationship approach? First, while you're still in shock or confused, stop before you say anything. Rein in your first instinctive thoughts and feelings until you've asked yourself whether expressing them will make the relationship between you and your teenager better.

It doesn't matter how justified or righteous you feel at first. A little thought will convince you that however noble your motives, simply laying down the law is going to make your relationship worse. Two bad things can happen when you lay down the law: either your teenager will be goaded into disobeying you, or she'll comply but resolve to keep you in the dark in the future. Either way, she'll see you as someone to oppose or resist.

So what *do* you do? Any good solution will be based on the fact that a relationship is a two-way superhighway. So you think about information and access. You think about the fact that the only way you're going to be successful is if you and your daughter both get your needs met. Because that's the only way to make your relationship stronger.

OK. Your needs. Her needs. That's your clue. Whatever you say now has to have something to do with two people getting their needs met. Just as in any other relationship. Just the way you wish your parents had dealt with you.

Don't worry about being wise or brilliant or about saying exactly the right thing. The point is that saying *anything* that will help the relationship even a little is a lot better than what you were probably going to say when you were ready to lay down the law.

There are lots of good things you could say:

- You could try to get more information: "Why do you feel you can't get home by your curfew?" (When people know more about each other they feel closer.)
- You could say how you feel: "This makes me feel you're growing up too fast, and that's hard for me to accept." (When you share your feelings with your teenager, you seem more like a real human being than just a person playing the role of parent, and it's easier for your teenager to feel closer to you.)
- You could ask for what you want directly: "It would

really mean a lot to me if you came home by midnight. Would you do that for me?" (By asking, you show that you're not pulling your rank and are treating your kid with respect, and this makes it much easier for him to feel good about you.)

- You could try to work out some kind of solution: "Two-thirty seems awfully late to me. Let's see if we can agree on some time that will feel fair to both of us." (When people solve problems together, they feel better about each other.)

Whatever feels right *is* right, in the context of improving your relationship. The relationship approach liberates you from the need to find the perfect solution.

Let's say, to pick one solution at random, that you suggest working out a new time that feels fair to both of you. Now your teenager has the opportunity to explain the particular circumstances of her evening (this is a school dance that traditionally ends late; this is a special occasion she won't repeat; as long as she's up and around by noon she'll have plenty of time to do all her chores). This makes her feel good, appreciated, taken seriously, and cared for.

And now you have an opportunity to make *your* needs and concerns clear (you're worried about drunks on the road, or about her getting to sleep so late that she spends Saturday in bed and isn't available to help with the household chores). You're a real person, and real people have feelings. As long as you're not trying to control your kid, she'll not only listen to your feelings, but she'll hear them and respect them.

Now both sides have full information. But what's to prevent this discussion from turning into an angry fight? What's to prevent your teenager's selfishness and irresponsibility from sabotaging your efforts to arrive at a mutually agreeable solution?

No wonder we keep emphasizing that strengthening the relationship is so important! The stronger the relationship, the easier the process of negotiation, because there's more desire to cooperate on both sides. Now you can ask the magic question. "What do you need to agree to be home by midnight so I won't worry about your being out so late with those older kids?" Your teenager could, of course, come up with hundreds of good answers to this question. The point is that there's always at least one answer that will work for you. If you've maintained a good relationship, you'll get to that answer faster, because then both of you will care more about arriving at solutions than being victorious.

Let's say your relationship is lousy right now. All the more reason to focus on strengthening it. It's just going to take a little extra patience. But at least now you only have one thing to focus on. Strengthening your relationship will be the vehicle that brings you to a solution.

You only have to know how you feel. It's even OK if you feel bad because you don't have any control over your teenager! It's not battling for control if you say, "I feel sad now because I wish I had more control over you." All you're doing is acknowledging a reality (that you have no control) and how you feel about it (wishing you had some).

Suppose your daughter is making promises, and all you can remember are all the promises she's made and broken in the past. What your relationship needs here is to rebuild trust; for you to have a good relationship with your teenager, you need to trust her to take care of herself and to keep her word and to come home at an agreed time. And your teenager needs to trust you to be fair and understanding.

So talk about trust with your teenager, about how your trust has been damaged and needs to be rebuilt, about why it's so important to you, and about how much better things will be when the two of you trust each other again. Don't just say, "I can't trust you." That kind of blaming statement does nothing for relationships. Instead, say something like, "We've got a problem with trust here," and let her know that coming home at a time you consider more reasonable will build your trust in her—and the more you trust her, the more likely you are to let her stay out later in the future.

Bring whatever you're talking about back to your relationship. Your teenager will appreciate this. Your relationship is important to her, too. For one thing, she loves you. For another, she realizes that her life will be a lot easier and happier if the two of you have a good relationship.

Let's assume that in spite of a few angry outbursts the two of you agree on a curfew that's a little later than you would have liked and earlier than your teenager wanted. Good. So what if you weren't able to impose the curfew you first wanted to impose? Look at what you've gotten in return. Because the curfew was arrived at jointly, your teenager now has some compelling reasons for observing it:

- For one thing she feels some sense of ownership: it's *her* curfew because she had a part in setting it up.
- For another thing, she's feeling good about you, that you're a fair and understanding person. And that's why at least part of her now wants to observe the curfew.
- Finally, because she understands that the reason for setting up a curfew isn't to impose control but to build trust, and because she understands that the more you trust her the more freedom she'll ultimately have, she'll *want* to observe the curfew.

But what if, after all this, your teenager walks in an hour after your agreed-upon curfew? What *doesn't* work is the old rules-and-punishments approach. Remember, the reality of adolescence is that, whether you like it or not, you don't have the power to enforce either rules or punishments. Instead, the critical difference in using the relationship approach is that you deal with things that are real and that both of you have power over—and those things are trust and consequences.

Trust is the currency of relationships. If you spend too much of it, you have to build up the bank account again. The way to deal with your teenager's breaking the curfew is to deal with the fact that the major consequence of a breach of trust is that *people who are trusted get to do things people who are not trusted don't get to do.*

So your kid's coming home late doesn't just mean that she broke a rule but that she violated your trust. And as a consequence, the next time she wants something that requires your trust, such as borrowing the family car to visit a friend who lives an hour away, she's going to have to confront your diminished trust and therefore the greater likelihood that you won't let her use the car.

This works because it's based on reality, on how people feel, and not on the games parents and teenagers play with rules and punishments. Teenagers understand very well that their parents' trust is a resource that can give them tremendous freedom. They're highly motivated to preserve this trust. In addition, they understand perfectly well the idea of trust and consequences because they use it with their friends.

So when your teenager comes home an hour after the curfew you agreed upon, of course she'll experience your anger and disappointment, because those are real consequences of someone breaking an agreement. And of course you'll let her know that what she's done has made it harder for you to trust her. And the consequence of your diminished trust is that in the near future she won't be able to do some of the things she'd need your trust to be able to do. And of course the two of you will have to go through a period of rebuilding trust, of continuing to make agreements and observing these agreements, because each new agreement that's observed builds trust back up again.

Just one more thing. Since teenagers are the messy, careless people they so often are, even the best of them won't keep all agreements. But in our experience, when teenagers grow up in an atmosphere where freedom builds on trust and trust builds on keeping agreements, they are much less likely to break agreements in the first place. When they do, they'll still have to suffer the consequences, but it will happen much less often.

And what if your teenager comes home just ten minutes late? We said that the relationship approach isn't a technology and that successful parents handle things in different ways. So it's up to you. If to you ten minutes means the agreement is broken, then that's your reality. If ten minutes isn't a big deal to you, then you have a different reality. What's important is only that you take the way you actually feel and deal with it in the context of the relationship approach.

Your son's just come home with a poor report card. You gave him the usual lecture and he went to his room, supposedly to study. Now you hear the stereo blaring, just the way it has every evening. What do you do?

Again, the first thing to do is stop your instinctive responses. The blowing up you were about to do, the lecturing about how he's ruining his future, the grounding him for a week, the name-calling, the threatening to take away his stereo—stop before you do any of this. Such tactics can only damage your relationship.

Remember how little real power you have to turn him into this or that kind of person. Whatever he makes of himself in the future is in his own hands. All the limits, structures, and rules in the world, and all the wise words you're capable of delivering, won't make him become a motivated student. But just as overreacting is a bad idea, doing nothing isn't good either. Right now you're having strong feelings about that report card. Those feelings can hurt your relationship or they can help it. And maybe if your relationship is in good shape you'll find some way to be useful to him.

Give it a shot. Your feelings might as well bring you closer together. Maybe if the two of you can talk about how you feel . . . maybe you don't even have to agree . . . maybe if you can just understand what the other is feeling . . . maybe if your relationship were better . . . you'd have an easier time getting through to him.

Stop and think: What if your best friend had just screwed up on her job? How would you handle it?

Maybe you wouldn't even talk to her about it right away. So with your teenager maybe you should wait awhile and then go out and do something together and bring it up at that point. Remember: *your job as a parent is not to improve your teenager but to improve your relationship with your teenager.*

All right. Although it may feel a little weird, you do nothing immediately. You give your son time to lick his wounds.

But then a couple of days later you knock on your son's door and suggest the two of you go out and get a burger. He looks a little suspicious, but you promise you're not going to yell at him about his report card.

You're almost through with your meal before he finally brings up his grades by saying, "You know, my marks weren't that bad."

You're a little disappointed. You were hoping the two of you would be able to talk, but he sounds defensive. He's not going to make it easy for you. But you promised you wouldn't yell. And you decided that most of all you want to get closer. You ask, "How do you really feel about those marks?"

"OK," he shrugs.

"Really OK?" You're trying to widen those still narrow channels of communication. And listening does that better than talking.

"Well, I wish they were better."

He said it! He admitted that he has at least some desire for good grades. Now you're aware of something that's important to him—a need you can build on. But gloating or pressing an attack will do nothing for any relationship. So you only say, "Me, too."

Inside, you feel better than you have for days. You both sit there nodding; you're in agreement about something now. "Why do you think your grades were so bad?" you ask out of curiosity—not in order to blame, because blame will make it hard for your kid to talk to you and will hurt your chance to be helpful.

"I don't know," he says, responding to your genuine curiosity. "Maybe it's because . . ." and he mentions some problem he's having.

"Is there anything I can do to help with that?" you offer, instead of launching into a lecture that will make him feel you're trying to tell him what to do.

"I don't know." Then he talks about how totally uninterested he is in everything he's learning in school.

This upsets you because you wish he were different from the way he is. You get ready to lecture him about how he won't always be able to do what's interesting in life and so on and so forth, but then you consider that maybe it'll do more for your relationship if you talk about the time school was a struggle for you. *You remember that the essence of the relationship approach is always, always to get close first, to think about improving your relationship before you think about solving any particular problem.*

This story could end in a lot of different ways. Let's face it—it's very hard to take a poor student and set the clock of maturity ahead and realign his motivations to turn him into a good student. But at the very least, at the end of this conversation you'll understand your teenager better, have a better sense of what he needs, and, because of your improved relationship, you'll have a lot more leverage with him.

You've just found out from a friend that in a few days your seventeen-year-old daughter will be going to a party where there will probably be drugs. Now you're waiting for her to come home from school. What do you say to her?

First thoughts: She can't be allowed to go to that party. This is an emergency! I must act immediately!

But while you're revving your motor to go into action the minute she comes home, you remember the relationship approach. You remember to stop. Nothing is supposed to be more important than your relationship with your daughter . . . but wait a minute, not even keeping her away from drugs?

It doesn't matter *how* scary the problem is. The fact is that your relationship is all you have going for you. Blow your relationship with your teenager and you blow your chance of having any influence. Whether she listens to you, talks to you, and cooperates with you or totally shuts you out— everything depends on your relationship with her. So you have to turn off your panic and start to think.

You realize how lucky you were to have found out about this party. What about all the other parties she goes to? Her visits to friends' houses? The times she says she's going to the library after school? It starts to hit you how little battling for control can accomplish now that her day-to-day life has slipped out of your grasp.

There's so much you don't know. How does she feel about drugs? What does she know about them? How has she handled situations where drugs have been around in the past? Has she already experimented with drugs? If so, what happened? How would she feel if you told her how much you fear drugs? What role does she want you to play in all this?

Information is critical. Without it, problems get worse. Only with such information are solutions possible. And only with the caring and closeness of a good relationship is it possible to get information. Remember: *a good relationship is one where people talk to each other freely and tell each other things that people in poor or distant relationships don't tell each other.*

As you sit waiting for your daughter to come home, you realize this is really a great opportunity. Even in small towns, nearly every teenager is exposed to a person or a situation that in turn offers exposure to drugs. You have very little control over this exposure, and you have no direct control over how your teenager will respond to this exposure. *All you can control is whether you make your teenager feel you're a concerned partner or an obnoxious and ridiculous jailer.*

The more you think about it, the more you realize that the most important thing for you to do when your daughter comes home is to create a time when you can really listen to her and she can really listen to you. That way she'll find out how important it is to you that she not get involved with drugs.

This probably doesn't seem like much, compared to the control you'd like to have. But then perhaps you remember how irrelevant your own mother became to you when you were a teenager and she tried to persuade you not to drink. She just never knew what was going on, did she? Suddenly you and your daughter really listening to each other sounds like a big accomplishment.

As you wait for your daughter to come home you look back nostalgically on the days when you really did have control over her. It's too bad, but the fact is that those days of control are gone forever. The important thing now, worried though you are, is that you not lose what influence you have in a futile effort to bring back those days of control.

So what do you do and say when she actually walks in the door?

Remember: the less you try to control your kid by telling her what to do and by warning, lecturing, and threatening, the more she'll be able to hear how you feel and the better she'll be able to listen to solid information. In other words, there's a crucial difference between saying, "Don't do drugs" (which sounds like control and provokes rebellion) or "If you take drugs you'll ruin your life" (which sounds like a lecture but really is just more control) and your saying, "I think drugs are terrible and I'm scared about the effect they have" (which sounds like something you might say to a friend).

The relationship approach is not a science. It's not like the set of instructions that comes with your VCR. Instead, it's a way of thinking. So what you do when your daughter walks in the door depends on how close you are and the special kind of relationship you have.

If you're already very close maybe all you have to do is tell her how you feel directly. But most parents and teenagers could be a lot closer. If that's the case with you, then when she walks in the door *your energy first must go toward getting the two of you close enough for her to hear how you feel.*

If you're still not sure what to do to get closer, try this. Imagine you're lost in the woods. It's the middle of the night. There's no moon. You can't see a foot in front of your face. All you know is that you're on some kind of slope and at the top of that slope is a ranger station. What do you do?

You may feel scared, but even without compass, map, or light, it's surprisingly easy. You just feel around you. You take one small step in the direction that feels a little more up than down. It may not be the best step. But at least it's taking you closer to rather than further from the top of the mountain. And all you have to do is keep taking steps like that. Maybe if you're lucky you go straight to the top. Or maybe your route zigzags. But you get there. As long as each step is a little higher you will get there.

Well the relationship approach works the same way. No matter what problem is in front of you, you don't have to worry about doing the best thing or a wonderful thing or even a very good thing. You just have to take one small step that's more in the direction of strengthening than tearing down your relationship with your teenager. Eventually, you will become a successful parent.

So, to repeat, what do you do and say when she actually walks in the door? It's up to you. As with the mountain-climbing image, you already have all you need to get where you're going. No two people will take exactly the same path. The only thing that's important is the direction. And with your teenager, anything that builds closeness, caring, and communication will get you where you want to go.

How to Get *Your* Needs Met

7

Let's face it, being the parent of a teenager doesn't only mean taking care of him: Sometimes you have to take care of yourself. You have needs and wants that have nothing to do with making your teenager a better person or protecting him from danger. Drugs might be a problem because they affect him, but his making a lot of noise can be a problem because it affects you.

This is a chapter for you the person, not just you the parent.

Suppose you're worried because your thirteen-year-old daughter is an hour late coming home from school, even though she'd agreed to call you if she was going to be late. Your need for yourself is not to be worried. Or suppose you're upset and angry because your sixteen-year-old son won't clean up after himself in the kitchen. What you want is for him to stop foisting his messes on you. What do you do?

With any other person in the world you might know just what to do. But right now you're drawing a blank. Few people can make you feel more powerless than your teenager. This feeling of powerlessness runs like a wide, fast-moving river through many aspects of the parent-teen relationship, eroding your love and hope. The more powerless you feel, the more you want to take control. The more things you do to try to take control, the more your kid fights you. And then the more powerless you feel.

What's the solution?

We've said that you can have influence with your teenager if the two of you are communicating and if there's caring between you. And if you have all that going for you and you still need some leverage to get what you want for yourself, nothing works better than the magic question: "What do you need to give me what I need?"

But when it comes to parents getting their own needs met, some additional ideas are useful. Here's how you can use the relationship approach to stop feeling helpless and start feeling powerful with your teenager immediately.

Make sure that what you're asking for is something you want for yourself and not something you want because you think it will make your teenager different or better. Focus on your needs and not on what you think his needs should be.

How simple life would be if you liked quiet in the house and your teenager did too. How smoothly everything would go if you and your teenager shared the conviction that good grades are important.

Alas, you and your teenager usually don't want the same things. Whether it's because your kid is young, because he's different from you, or because he's experimenting with becoming his own person, he all too often likes noise and doesn't want to get good grades. And so the stage is set for a thousand and one battles.

How do you deal with this? It's crunch time: you want action, and inside you feel like screaming, "I want my kid to . . . and if he doesn't I'm going to explode." Now what? This is when you're most tempted to fight for control, and yet you know control won't work.

If you're going to get your needs met, you have to understand the situation. Remember: teenagers are getting ready to leave home; they want to get out and become their own persons. And what do parents do? They come at their kids from all sides, constantly saying, you should do this, I need you to do that, you should be this way, you should want to do things that way. From your teenager's point of view, there are too many shoulds and needs and wants piling on top of him, burdening him at the very time he most wants to be free. So all these demands do is add to your teenager's already intense desire to get out.

That's reality, and your ability to get what you want—to have some peace and quiet, some order in the house, some predictability in your life—must begin with your accepting that reality. But this doesn't mean that you have to give up trying to get the things you want from your teenager. After all, you can't be in a relationship with someone where she always gets what she wants and you never get what you want.

So what's the solution?

When crunch time comes and you want action, make sure that what you're asking for is something you want for yourself and not something you want because you think it will make your teenager different or better. Focus on your needs and not on what you think his needs should be. Don't contaminate getting what you want with trying to make your teenager a better person.*

This is how you can greatly increase your chances of getting what you want. Telling the average teenager what or how he should be, what he should need or want, feels a hundred times more controlling than simply asking him to do something. Teenagers feel far less controlled by *your* needs than by your telling them what *they* need.

Let's take a very simple example: household chores. You want your kid to help with the housework. After all, it's not fair for you to have to do all the work, and it's particularly unfair for you to have to clean up after your kid—you have a legitimate desire not to have to clean up someone else's mess. OK. But then you take the fatal step of saying your

---

*Yes, we know. In spite of everything, you still wish you could use your influence to actually make your teenager a better person. Well, don't worry. There's a chapter coming up that shows you how to use the relationship approach to be helpful and protective. But for good results you still have to separate getting the things you want from making your teenager be a better person.

teenager needs to learn not to make messes, needs to learn habits of tidiness and responsibility.

So you confront your teenager, bearing a whole stack of issues. The things *you* want (not to be saddled with his mess) are all tangled up with the things you think *he* should want (to be a neat, responsible person). As a result, trying to get your teenager to help clean up the kitchen after a big meal turns into a confusing effort to deal with all these issues.

The key to a solution is the fact that the same teenager who will fight like the devil against your telling him that he needs to learn to be tidy might easily be persuaded to clean up after dinner. So if you say something like, "Help with the kitchen, because you have to learn to clean up after yourself," your kid will probably feel attacked. But if you say, "I want you to help with the kitchen. I don't want to do it all myself," your kid will see that you're not trying to make him be or feel anything. *Your not trying to control him will make him feel more willing to help than anything else you could do.*

This is true regardless of the situation. No matter what your teenager may be doing to drive you crazy or scare you witless, your leverage will increase when you scrupulously struggle only about your own needs. Let's talk curfews again, for example. Your kid can be getting into all kinds of trouble every minute he's away from the house, not just those minutes when he's late. Telling him when he has to be home "to protect him" will just make him say, "I don't need protection." (Remember his drive to become self-reliant.)

But you could try saying something like this:

Look, I know that in the cosmic scheme of things it doesn't make that big a difference whether you get in by midnight or one. And I really do trust you. But I worry anyway. Whether I should worry or I shouldn't worry isn't the issue. Let's not tell each other what we ought to feel. Right now you're fifteen years old and when you're out past midnight I worry. That's why I want you to be home by midnight.

If you say this, then you're addressing the part of your teenager that cares about you without stimulating the part of him that's ready to rebel. (We understand that you wish your kid were more responsible, that he wouldn't want to stay out until all hours risking who knows what dangers. But if you want results instead of fights that go nowhere, stay focused on your concerns for yourself.)

Here's another example. Let's say you don't have much money, and that means you can't afford to shell out big bucks for college. You want to hold on to the little you've got. And if your kid gets really good grades she might get scholarships so you can hang on to your life savings. Yes, we're talking about the selfish part of you here, but that selfish part is real. Sure, because you're a caring parent, you wish your kid had a burning desire to be successful. But your experience with the control approach tells you that pushing her to study is a recipe for frustration. You can yell yourself blue in the face, but you can't make her want to be a good student.

So it's essential to separate out your problem—not having much money—from what you think is her problem—not seeming to care about being successful. How your kid feels about success has to do with her life, not yours. When you separate these different problems, when you separate what you want from what she does or doesn't want, you can deal with this situation effectively by making it clear how important your teenager's getting a scholarship is to you.

Unfortunately, many parents have both spoiled their relationship with their teenagers and failed to motivate them to work hard by telling them they "have to get good grades" and then getting into fights when their kids don't respond.

Instead, you can have a good relationship and take care of your concerns at the same time by saying something like this:

Listen, Mary, we've got to talk. I know that right now you don't know what you want to do with your life. And I certainly don't know what you're going to do with your life. In any case, it's up to you. And I'm sure you'll make decisions that are good for you. But I've got to talk to you about reality. I've got practically no money to send you to college. Whatever kind of education you get, you are going to be the one who makes it happen. I do know that the better the grades you get, the more choices you'll have. If you want to have those choices, then you'll just have to get the grades. Whatever you want to do is up to you; I'm just explaining the reality of the situation. I need to hold on to my savings for my old age.

Here's another example. David went nuts when he found out that Danielle, his college-freshman daughter, was smoking. First he gave her the antismoking lecture. Then came the threats, pleas, rules, demands, and so on. Danielle very quickly started feeling annoyed and harassed. Smoking became an issue of her independence, the way most issues do for teenagers. She'd gone to an out-of-state college precisely because she wanted to get away from this kind of thing. All she could do now was try to avoid her father, by not talking to him on the phone or coming home for vacations. Why shouldn't she avoid him? No friend would treat her the way he did.

When we talked to David we asked him whose problem it was if Danielle smoked. He was surprised by the question. At first, he couldn't separate out whose problem was whose. "It's the whole family's problem. Smoking is very unhealthy," he said. Yes, but if it hurts her health, who suffers? "Obviously she's the one who would suffer," he said, "but we're the ones who would be grieving if she died of lung cancer." So, we told him, if she's out of breath when she walks up stairs at age forty because of having smoked for years, it's sad—but it's her problem. *You're* not out of breath. Your problem is your fear of grief, of losing her. "Yeah," he said, "but it's also that I don't want any smoke in my house. I don't like it and it's not healthy for me."

What David wanted, then, was not to fear losing Danielle prematurely because she smoked and not to have cigarette smoke in his house. Once David figured out what *he* needed, the solution to the smoke-in-the-house problem turned out to be a simple negotiation between father and daughter, done as if they were friends. And the solution to David's fear of

losing Danielle prematurely was for him to simply tell her
how he felt. He didn't yell or threaten. He just talked from
his heart. This turned out to be much easier for her to hear
than the demands he'd been making.*

It was much harder for Danielle to make a snappy come-
back or just to turn him off when he wasn't trying to control
her. "I'm sorry," she said. "I'm not smoking to hurt you. I
know smoking is bad for me. Maybe I'll stop soon. But that's
just not something I want to put myself through now." This
wasn't a huge concession, but they felt closer—and it was
much more than David had gotten from his acting as if his
daughter's problem were his problem.

But how can a loving parent let go of worrying about her
kid's wanting the wrong thing or not needing what she thinks
he should need? Remember, you can do your job as a parent
best by helping your teenager do his job—and his job requires
him to learn to rely on himself. Self-reliance means solving
your own problems. It is precisely the difference between a
baby and an adult that the baby's problems *are* the parents'
problems, while an adult's problems are his alone. When your
kid was a baby he had to be weaned from the breast or bot-
tle. Now *you* have to be weaned from playing the parent role.
So, difficult as it is, you have to keep saying to yourself, "If
my kid screws up, that's his problem. He's got to be the one
to solve his own problems."

Now your mind may be reeling. You're the mommy, or the
daddy! How can your kid's problems not be your problems?
Your teenager isn't an adult yet!

Well, remember that trying to "set good patterns" usually
comes to nothing. Other than by the example they set, parents have almost no power to make their kids turn out to be
a certain kind of person. That's really why his problems aren't
your problems. Either your kid won't feel he needs to stop
being messy or lazy or, much more likely, with life and ex-

*Why isn't this just manipulation or a guilt trip? Because the purpose isn't con-
trol for the sake of control. Your feelings and needs are real, and they should have
an impact on people you have a relationship with. It becomes manipulation when
you use those feelings and needs (or even manufacture them) just to have your own
way without recognizing the other person's feelings and needs.

perience, your kid will start feeling he needs to do the things you think he should. In either case, there's nothing you can do about it.

Some Reassurance

Of course, it's hard not to worry about what your kid takes or doesn't take responsibility for. But this fact should help: if right now your teenager doesn't seem to need things like neat rooms or good grades and does seem to need things like loud music or wild parties, this only means that your teenager is like other teenagers. Right?

Why should this comfort you? Because the best evidence for the likelihood that your kid will be like other forty-year-olds when she's forty is the fact that as a sixteen-year-old she's like other sixteen-year-olds. *If she's like other teenagers when she's a teenager then the odds are she'll be like other adults when she's an adult.*

Many parents know this intellectually. But when they see their kid not doing things the adult way, the part of them that says, "He's just being a teenager," gets overwhelmed by the part that says, "That really isn't appropriate, and *some* other teenagers don't act that way, and I didn't act that way when I was a teenager, and I'm really scared that he'll keep acting that way." And then they're back into battling for control.

But the first response is the right one. Normal teenagers— no matter how different they are from what you'd like them to be—become normal adults. There's nothing you need to do except keep the relationship with your teenager strong and focus on what you want for yourself.

Make sure you say how you feel when you ask for what you want.

Parents are always sure they've used this idea. "Don't I *always* tell him how I feel?" parents ask. But in fact parents usually leave this out. Inside you may feel, "I hate this," or "This scares me," but somehow it comes out, "You're irresponsible," or "Do this," or "Don't do that." When parents think they've said how they feel, what they've usually done instead is criticize or make a demand.

If you want to do what works, don't say, "It would really be nice if you cleaned up the kitchen." It's better to say how you feel, so your teenager knows how important it is to you: "I'd like you to clean up the kitchen because it really makes me angry when you don't do your share around here," or ". . . because I'm really tired and I need the help." By saying how you feel, you become a person he can relate to, rather than a parent giving orders. You take your request out of the control game and put it into the person-to-person game.

Some parents find all this hard to believe. "I've tried everything," they say. "My kid can barely tolerate me. So he's certainly not going to do anything because I've told him how I feel."

Sure, telling your kid how you feel is not going to make him turn on a dime, and it's not going to turn him into an angel. But *nothing* could do that. And at first telling him how you feel may not do anything at all that you can see. But it will help bring you one bit closer to your teenager. Suddenly you're a person, not just a demander or a criticizer. You're someone to help, not fight. You're someone who elicits caring, not resistance.

For example, does your teenager's refusal to talk drive you crazy? Does it make you want to scream? Fine. But whether you actually scream or not, what's really important is that you tell him what his behavior is doing to you. The point is that you have to let him know what impact he's having on you. Maybe you feel you can't help screaming and maybe screaming lets him know just how intensely you feel, but when you scream, all that he hears is screaming. He hasn't learned anything. In fact, he probably just hears your screaming as an assault, as your attempt to get power, as control. But when you tell him what you're feeling and why, chances are he's hearing things he's never heard before. And then he has a chance to change.

Here are some other examples of how parents ask for what they want by telling their teenagers how they feel:

- "When you go around the house not talking and not answering when anyone talks to you, it makes me feel crazy [*not* "it makes me think you're crazy"]. I feel that you hate me, and that I must be an awful parent."
- "When you start yelling at me, it just makes me sad that that's how you'd treat me [*not* "you have no right to treat me that way"]."
- "When you show up with a bunch of your friends and you haven't called to tell me you're bringing them, it makes me very angry [*not* "you're a jerk"]."
- "When you keep saying, 'Don't worry,' I just feel you're trying to shut me out, and I get scared that there's really a serious problem that you don't want to tell me about [*not* "you're a liar"]."

Now if you're very upset, it's perfectly fine that your teenager sees it, because that's part of his learning about the impact he has on you. There's nothing wrong with your acting sad if you feel sad or acting mad if you feel mad. If you want to improve your relationship with your teenager, you have to let him know how you feel.

Make sure your teenager knows exactly what you want from her.

If you've been struggling with your teenager, you might be surprised: For all the energy you may have spent blaming, complaining, nagging, and worrying, it's very possible that your teenager still doesn't know what you want. And that's because she doesn't know the specific action or behavior you really want from her. It's also likely that for all the demands you've been making, you haven't really focused on what's most important to you.

It may sound like a horrifying thought, but if there were some kind of tape recorder following you around taking down the things you say to your teenager, far too many of them would be, "Straighten up and fly right," "Get your act together," "When are you going to start taking some responsibility for yourself?" "You've got to start caring about your future," and "I know you could accomplish a lot more if you just put your mind to it." What does any of this accomplish? Other than making your teenager want to resist your control, statements like these only create confusion.

Until you're clear about what you want, and until your teenager understands exactly what you want from her, it will be very difficult for you to get it. So just as the first thing to do to get started with the relationship approach is to stop before saying all the old kinds of things that weren't useful, the first thing to do in getting your needs met is to get as clear in your mind as you can about exactly what you want.

Let's say you want your teenager to be "more responsible." Ask yourself how you'll know that he's starting to be the way you want. What specific things can he do that you'll see to make you feel that he's changed? Once you have those observable, specific things in mind, ask for *them* and bypass the more general request.

You only have to make sure that what you're asking for is

- Clear
- Specific
- Understandable
- Doable
- Observable

For example, you may feel your teenager has been selfish and irresponsible about helping around the house. In fact, the angrier you've gotten about this, the more likely you are to yell at him to "be responsible." But this satisfies none of the criteria we've just mentioned. On the other hand, if you ask your kid, for starters, to wash any dish he uses as soon as he's through with it, this request satisfies all of the criteria.

So the specific ideas that will help you use the relationship approach to be more effective in getting what you want are:

- Don't contaminate your efforts to get what you want with an effort to get your teenager to want what you think he should want.

- When you ask for what you want, make sure you say how you feel.
- Make sure your teenager knows *exactly* what you want from her.

You can use these ideas to start getting results now and to put an end to the resentful, deprived feelings so many parents of teenagers have.

How to Protect Your Teenager

8

It's late. Your daughter is out driving around with some boy you've never met. You're sitting there worrying about things like drunk driving, date rape, and teen pregnancy. You need to know your daughter's OK.

But you need more than that. After all, if she doesn't care about whether her room's messy or not, she'll still survive, but if she doesn't care whether her boyfriend drinks or not, she could be in a terrible accident. As you sit there worrying about her, you realize that you also want her to care about her own safety. You want to protect her, and you want to know that she's protecting herself.

How can you use the relationship approach to protect your teenager?

You're not helpless. When you stop trying to control your teenager, he will be more willing to listen to you, and he'll be more able to let in your words of wisdom and experience. What's more, because the respect and caring between you haven't been damaged by battles for control, most problems that arise will be things the two of you can talk about and resolve. And since you're partners rather than opponents, your teenager will be more likely to go along with your suggestions.

But you can go further. Here are some specific ideas for

using the relationship approach to protect your teenager and make sure he can protect himself.

When you're tempted to start controlling, discover your underlying fear.

Far too often, parents' desire to protect their teenager leads to a terrible wreck before the train even leaves the station. Here are the steps to this crash.

1. Your teenager does or says something that alarms you.
2. You immediately go to battle to try to get him to stop what he's doing or to do something different.
3. Your teenager feels your control and not your concern, and so resists rather than responds.

The crash begins after step one because of something parents don't do: they don't take the time to get in touch with what they're really afraid of. They try to control their teenager instead of finding solutions to what's making them afraid. It's ironic: parents act out of fear but often do not deal with whatever is causing their fear.

For example, one fine spring morning Lenny announced to his parents that he'd decided to put off going to college for a year, maybe more. By the time they came to see us, the family was in an uproar because the parents were desperately pushing Lenny to start college and Lenny was loudly asserting his right to do whatever he wanted whenever he wanted.

What's the issue here? we asked the parents. We just don't think Lenny should take time off, they replied. It took a while before we were able to get the parents to say what their underlying fear was. It turns out they were afraid that if Lenny didn't go right to college, he'd never go.

Maybe they didn't say what they were afraid of because they hadn't taken the time to figure it out. Or maybe they didn't say what they were afraid of because they were embarrassed that their fear would be seen as not warranting their getting so upset. Whatever the case, naming their fear was the key to solving the problem of how to protect their teenager. Once they could say *this* is what we're afraid of, they could begin to work things out with Lenny. In fact, Lenny was able to reassure them of his commitment to going to college. And once they saw his commitment, they felt better about his taking a year off.

So when you're tempted to try to make your teenager do something or stop doing something, first take the time to figure out what you're really afraid of. The more clearly you can focus on a specific fear, the more effective you'll be in protecting your teenager.

Use information to protect your teenager.

It's tough to protect a teenager. Take sex, for example. How do you deal with an ignorant, rebellious teenager whose hormones are raging and who has plenty of time and opportunity to get into all kinds of sexual trouble?

Well, you'll probably feel your teenager is a lot better protected if he takes seriously the kinds of things you take seriously. And if he doesn't, *information is the only way to get your teenager to begin to think and act the way you would like.*

Here's how this works. Much, perhaps most, of teenage irresponsibility can be traced to a lack of information. It's much better if you, the parent, think of your teenager as similar to you but more ignorant, instead of as a different kind of creature. In fact, when your teenager has the same information you have, the odds are that he'll have the same map of the world you have, and then he'll be as much like you as it's possible for someone his age to be.

But how can you be *sure* your teenager will act responsibly once he has as much information as possible? Unfortunately, you can't be sure. (Ultimately, you can't even be sure *you'll* always act responsibly if you have as much information as possible. We all do our best, but . . .) Making mistakes is an inevitable part of growing up. Yes, it's scary to consider how great is your teenager's ability to get into trouble. But think for a moment about how he'll use his ability.

First of all, will he use it to deliberately destroy himself?

This is every parent's nightmare. Teenagers are heedless; they think they are going to live forever, and they are ignorant of many of life's dangers. *But teenagers are rarely deliberately self-destructive.* Teenage suicide, to take the most extreme example, is a serious concern, of course, but the incidence of teenage suicide is small compared to the total number of teenagers. And here we're talking about how to deal with the overwhelming majority of teenagers who are not disturbed. Healthy teenagers simply do not self-destruct.

Certainly it can be a serious mistake to ignore repeated danger signs. But it's a much more common mistake to over-react to normal teenage behavior as if it were a danger sign. As experienced physicians tell medical students, when you hear hoofbeats, think horses, not zebras.

Even if he doesn't deliberately create a disaster, your normal teenager can still get into real trouble, can't he? Sure. But let's look at some facts:

- The better informed teenagers are, the more responsibly they act.
- The more teenagers listen to their parents, the better informed they are.
- Teenagers listen best when they feel their parents aren't trying to control them.

When teenagers make mistakes, parents often say they are acting irresponsibly. But while some irresponsible actions are inevitable, information can help keep them to a minimum. And the reason is that, although it may not look like it from the outside, the overwhelming majority of teenagers want to stay out of trouble as much as their parents want them to. It's just that their experimentation makes them look as though they are courting disaster.

Take driving, for example. You know that speeding can cause the car to go out of control. And you know that there are cops out there waiting to give you a ticket for speeding. Your teenager knows the same thing—but only up to a point. He also wants to know how fast he can go before the car will start to go out of control or how often he can risk speeding without getting a ticket.

There's nothing you can do about this need for experimentation. And trying to win a battle for control will just poison your relationship with your teenager and deprive you of the information you need to really know what's going on in his life. But if your relationship is good, you'll get to hear hair-raising stories about things your teenager has done. And that will provide you with the opportunity to tell him why his behavior was dangerous. Your good relationship will not only give you this chance to inform him but will also make it more likely that he'll listen to you.

But what about total protection? Sorry, it doesn't exist. *Maintaining the flow of information back and forth is the best you can do.* And it's far more than parents who are stuck battling for control can do.

How to Inform

How do you go about the business of passing on information to your teenager? Let's go back to sex.

One way of informing that works is telling your teenager about reality. For example: What it takes for sex to feel good. How women get pregnant and how to prevent pregnancy. How sexual diseases are transmitted.

If you want to prevent this kind of informing from backfiring, then you must leave the spin out of it. There will be a place in this process for your agenda—your values and beliefs—and we'll get there in a moment, but when it comes to informing about reality, you have to leave your agenda out of it. Add no rhetoric that turns information into warnings and propaganda. A teenager notices immediately when you slide from informing to propagandizing—and then stops listening to the stuff you're telling him. He hears the propaganda, thinks you're trying to control him (which you are), and starts to resist you.

For example, it's a fact that a teenage girl can get pregnant the very first time she has intercourse. You may be horrified at the thought of your fourteen-year-old daughter having sex. But the minute your attempt to provide information ("Yes, it's true, it's as easy to get pregnant the very first time as any other time. There's nothing magical about the first time that prevents pregnancy.") slides into propaganda ("Sex is a terrible thing when you're too young. All kinds of bad things can happen. Some girls are ruined for life."), your teenager shifts from listening to resisting because she hears *you* shifting from informing to controlling. *If you put your agenda aside, your teenager has a chance to learn what's necessary to protect herself.* Informing comes through loud and clear only when the "noise" of control is taken out of it.

But while facts are essential, they're not enough. The cold, clinical conveying of information can't be satisfying to either of you if, for example, you really are horrified at the thought of a young girl—your daughter—having sex. Such feelings will contaminate the part of the process in which you give your kid information, but they still have to be dealt with. And they can be. You can go beyond talking about how the world works you can also talk about yourself, about the things that have happened to you, about your feelings, your thoughts, and, yes, your values.

What's most important is to be honest and real. Prefabricated fables accompanied by neat little morals just won't fly. Propaganda doesn't work here either, even when you're talking about your values; your teenager will smell your attempts at gaining control from a mile off and you'll blow it.

Conversely, even a personal story that seems to contradict the message you are trying to convey to your teenager helps your cause—if your story is authentic. The more personal you are, the more you'll strengthen your relationship with your teenager, the more effectively you'll be able to communicate your values, and the less what you have to say will sound like control, with the result that he'll be able to listen to you.

For example, maybe there was a period before you were married when you slept around. Or maybe you did something you don't feel good about. Or maybe you were a virgin when you got married and sometimes you think about what you missed. If you can talk about what you did and didn't do and about the impact it had on you in some kind of real way, then your teenager can really learn from you.

Now suppose the two of you have gotten close and your teenager's really listening to you. This is the time to talk about your values. But if you want to be effective, you can't heat up the branding iron of your convictions and try to burn your values into your kid's flesh. All you can do is tell him, "These are my values and this is why I hold them."

But you could still blow it. Since the best way to protect is to inform, the best way for you to communicate your values to your teenager is for you to inform him about what your values are, rather than insist that he share your values.

Do you believe that teenage sex is just plain wrong, for example? Fine, but laying down the law and saying, "You can't have sex before you're married," just won't work. You don't have control over your kid's behavior, and your demand is likely to call forth resistance. Suppose, however, you say, "This is the way I feel; these are my values. I just don't approve of having sex before you're married. I'd like it if you shared my values, but whether you do or not, this is what I believe." This is a lot easier to hear than simply "Don't." Controlling isn't going on here, but informing is. And without the attempt at control there's no resistance, and so the message gets through: "My mother doesn't approve of premarital sex. She feels strongly about that."

Now, because your teenager cares about you and respects you, this message carries some weight. One reaction might be, "If my mother feels that strongly about it, she must have a good reason. I'd better think about what I'm doing." Another reaction might be, "If this is so important to my mother, maybe I'd better act the way I know she'd like because she's important to me."

Will informing your teenager about your values work like magic and get her to share your mature adult needs? No. It will never work the way you thought control would. Nor is it a backdoor way of getting control. The control game is not a good game, period. On the other hand, informing just informs; the relationship between the two of you does the rest.

Now let's say you're trying to give information and to avoid control, but your teenager still isn't paying much attention to you. How can you protect your teenager?

How to Get Your Teenager to Listen to Information

Lying on the table in front of you is your teenager's first report card from his junior year in high school—and it's truly pathetic. Your dream of your kid going to Harvard dies then and there. And you're furious as you remember all the time he spent not studying.

The words are already on your lips. Doesn't he know what's going on? You have a lot to tell him, but how can you get him to listen? The answer is that *the best way to get your teenager to listen to you is for you to ask questions to find out*

What your teenager knows already
and
What's important to him

The benefits of this are enormous. Your teenager will listen when you ask questions because you're not boring him to death by telling him things he already knows. Think how great your relationship will be when you remove not only control but boredom!

How do you inform by asking questions? Let's go back to the example.

This time, as you see your kid sitting there with his lousy report card, you stop yourself from talking. You remember what works. So you ask some questions—real questions you don't know the answer to. You stay away from questions that are merely disguised attempts to drive your message home, questions like, "How are you going to get into a good college with grades like that?"

Instead, you build yourself a map of your own—because you need a map of what's going on with your kid just as he needs a map of the real world. You may think you know everything there is to know about your kid, but you probably don't. So ask as many questions as you need to build up a detailed map. Don't take anything for granted. For example, ask:

- "How do you feel about these grades?"
- "Do you want to improve them?"
- "Do you know how to improve them?"
- "Where were you thinking of going to college?"
- "What do you think you want to do with yourself when you're an adult?"

Now your kid may be wary. After all, he's waiting for the punishments, the handwringing, the lectures. He's waiting for you to pounce on him for giving the "wrong" answer or a "stupid" one. He may feel raw—guilty, upset, angry—the way you'd feel if you'd screwed up.

So maybe you have to wait until he's not feeling so bad. You can also reassure him directly: "Listen, honey, I really want to know a few things. I'm not going to yell at you or lecture you. I just want to see if maybe I can help."

Maybe he still doesn't want to talk. You can say, "Listen, I know it's a pain to talk about this, but I'll feel better if you answer these questions. Will you answer them? It's important to me." Your need for answers to these questions is not the same thing as trying to control who your kid is and what he wants. You're just asking him to do something for you.

Teenagers are also likely to answer "I don't know" to a lot of questions. If you're used to your teenager resisting you, then "I don't know" can feel like more of the same resistance. It's also true that teenagers really don't know the answer to a lot of questions about how they feel and what they want. But whether they are resisting or they just don't know, your pushing for answers won't work. All you can do is say something like, "Well, I'm really interested in how you feel about this. When you know, please let me know." If time goes by, you can ask again—as long as you remember not to push and not to make such a big deal about his answer that he's sorry he told you.

Of course you can ask questions all the time, not just when

the issue is grades. Ask questions to get a map of what your kid knows and how he feels. You won't get anywhere without one. And prepare to be surprised. In the example we've been using, you may be amazed to find that your son genuinely doesn't know that a C – average will keep him out of Harvard. Or you may find out that going to a "good" college isn't important to him. Or that he truly doesn't understand why his grades are poor.

We've found that when you really listen to teenagers you make genuine discoveries. A lot of the time you won't discover that your kid is ignorant. Instead, you may find out that you're the one who is ignorant—you didn't know, for example, that he's been thinking recently about becoming a chef instead of a doctor.

And a lot of times you may find that your kid is just ignorant in one specific area—which presents you with an opportunity to inform him. Now you're not throwing boring or irrelevant or controlling information at him. Instead you're supplying a real missing need, because by asking questions you've found out what is missing and what is needed.

He may not know, for example, that grades like his will keep him out of even State U. To use some other examples, he may not know that a girl can get pregnant even the very first time she has sex. He may not know that if he gets a speeding ticket he'll not only have to pay for the ticket but also the surcharges on your auto insurance—and that all that expense adds up to over four hundred dollars. He may not know about the long hours a chef has to work or about the mediocre pay most of them get.

OK. So you tell him. And only once, if possible. The point is that the more the two of you talk, the more you know what he knows—and does not know. Now you really can be helpful, because you know what's missing and you know what's needed.

Another benefit of asking your kid questions and really listening to him is this: he can't say his parents don't understand him. Think of the influence a parent has on a teenager if he can say to his friends, "My parents are OK. They understand me in a parent kind of way. They're cool." This gives you authority. You're no longer someone to be resisted automatically. Your understanding creates a bond of affection.

A word of caution: for some reason, even people who listen to one another often fail to check that they've understood correctly. This has got to come near the top of any list of Things People Most Often Fail to Do in Relationships. And it's particularly important with your teenager.

When you ask a question, the first answer you get is like a diving board. Just because there's a diving board doesn't mean you can automatically dive off it. First you have to make sure that there's water in the pool. And the way to do that with your kid is to make sure you're right about what you think you've understood. The simplest thing to do is to repeat what your teenager says in similar words: "So what you are telling me is . . ." This isn't a time to interpret or explain, just to show what you've understood.

For example, in a fight over her curfew, Carla asked her daughter Cathy, "Why is it such a big deal for you to stay out so late?" Then she got her answer: "You never let me do anything I really want to do."

Now Carla's at a turning point. Carla can dive into an empty swimming pool by answering before she checks out what Cathy means. She might respond, "How can you say that? You *always* get your own way." Then Cathy will say, "I never get my own way," and Carla will say, "You always get your own way," and Cathy will say, "I never get my own way"—and so on until they're both screaming at each other.

But if Carla checks things out to make sure she really understands—*before* diving into her response—she could ask, "So are you saying I really never let you do anything you really want to do?"

"Yeah."

"You really mean never?"

"Well, not never."

"So tell me about your feeling I never let you do anything you really want." Carla says this to show she really wants to understand Cathy.

"It's just that I don't want to be treated like a baby," Cathy says.

OK. Now Carla has an important clue about what's been bothering Cathy. Now the swimming pool's been filled up and Carla knows what she's diving into: the issue of her treating her daughter "like a baby." This is something the two of them can discuss like friends. They're not stuck arguing about whose view of reality is correct.

Here are some key phrases to use to make sure you really understand correctly what your kid is saying:

- "Are you saying that . . . ?"
- "How do you really feel about this?"
- "Just how important is this to you?"
- "What are you thinking of doing about it?"
- "What do you want to happen?"
- "How do you think things will turn out if they go on as they are?"
- "Is there anything else I should know about this?"

So far, so good. Still, there may be times when giving information isn't enough, when there's some problem or defect or deficiency or immaturity so glaring that you feel you must try to improve something about your teenager anyway. You just can't help yourself. How can you do it without damaging your relationship with your teenager? Rest assured, there is a way to do it that will even improve your relationship.

The Permission Technique

OK, you've done your best to separate your needs from your teenager's needs. You've tried to provide her with information. And you've asked questions to make sure that the information is relevant and useful.

Most of the time this will do wonders. But sometimes your teenager continues to do something you know is bad for her. The two of you have the best relationship in the world, all kinds of information and sharing is going back and forth, and she's *still* blowing her chance of getting into a good college or eating poorly or not practicing birth control or whatever. What can you do about it?

What works is something very simple: the permission technique. *You ask her permission to work with her on changing what you want to change.*

You say, for example, "We've talked about your grades, and I know you say you're doing your best and that I shouldn't bug you. But you've also said you wish your grades were better. I'd like to work out some kind of deal where I help you get better grades. Is that OK with you?"

What's amazing is that your teenager will often give you permission to *let* you bug her about the very things she wouldn't even let you talk to her about in the past. Isn't this the kind of thing you might do with a friend? You could have endless fights with your friend about her always showing up late and forgetting things. But that's boring, painful, and useless. What probably has the only chance of working is getting your friend to agree to let you work with her on this problem. While it's possible that won't work either, it's certain that nothing else will.

"What!" one parent shouted indignantly when we told her about the permission technique. "I've got to get permission before I can yell at my kid? I'm the *parent!*"

Our response is, yell all you want to—just don't expect it to accomplish anything. The *reason* you need permission has to do with the essence of being an adolescent. In some sense a child is still part of his parents. He's in the process of separating from them, but he hasn't done it yet. But it's different with adolescents. Engrave the following in your soul: *"My teenager is a separate person."* Your old battle cry—"But I'm the parent!"—just doesn't work anymore.

By using the permission technique you show your teenager respect, accept his separateness, and acknowledge his feelings—and this improves your relationship. You're also working with what's real (his sense of himself as a separate individual), and this improves your chance of success. It may feel like an indignity for you to have to ask permission, but

endless defeats in the battle for control are far worse. Without your teenager's permission, you can't succeed. With it,
you can't fail.

How do you get this permission? You ask. Why you want
permission doesn't matter. You love him, you care; that's all
you need. Much more important to your teenager than why
is the fact that you're not trying to impose control on him.
Then if he says yes, you ask, "What's the best way I can help
you?" The two of you talk about this and you listen to each
other and get close and make an agreement. And that's it.

One of the great things about the permission technique is
that you can use it either to meet one of your teenager's needs
(she wants to be more popular but doesn't know how, for
example) or to meet one of your needs (you want him to take
better care of his health).

Here's an example of the permission technique in action.

Deborah had a problem that most parents of teenagers have
had to wrestle with. Her fourteen-year-old son, Joe, was suf-
fering from that widespread teenage malady, sullenness. Most
of the time Joe had nothing to say to his parents; when he did
have something to say it was often something miserable or angry. Deborah felt she needed a better sense of what was going
on in his life and she wanted Joe to treat her better. Needless to
say, Deborah had spent years trying to control the uncontrollable by complaining, punishing, demanding, yelling—but
none of this got Joe to change. In Joe's mind, Deborah's nagging
only gave him another reason to be sullen.

Then Deborah put the permission technique into effect. She
waited until Joe was in one of his more talkative moods—
he'd just uttered two words in a row. The first thing she did
was talk to him. "You've been hearing me complain for a
long time about your being sullen around the house." Joe
nodded. "I guess this hasn't been much fun for either of us.
Do you mind if I ask you how you feel about the fact that
you don't talk very much and when you do it's often sort of
negative?"

By saying "Do you mind if I ask you . . . ?" Deborah was
letting Joe know that she was trying hard to be respectful of
him as a person. She was giving him the gift of acknowledg-

ing his separateness, of acknowledging that she had no right to violate his privacy at will.

Joe shrugged. "Not talking doesn't bother me." This wasn't a lot, but it wasn't a brush-off either. Asking for permission had given Deborah the green light.

"But you don't seem very happy."

"I'm OK. It's just hard for me to talk about stuff."

"So tell me—would you be willing to let me help you?" Here Deborah was making the key move of asking permission to get involved in changing something that she, not her son, wanted him to change.

"I don't care. Yeah, if you just wouldn't be *at* me all the time. If you really want to help you could . . . I mean, whatever I say is not enough. You always come at me with a million questions. If you could just, well, if I say something, you just would listen and be interested and stuff, but that's all. Then I'd feel like I did something good instead of something bad that got me in trouble whenever I opened my mouth."

"OK," Deborah said, trying to make the agreement clear. "You're saying that I have permission to try to help you talk more to me, and the way I can do it is by not making a big deal of what you say or asking a bunch of questions every time you open your mouth. Right?"

"Yeah," Joe said.

She'd done it. In a few minutes of conversation Deborah got more by asking Joe for permission than she'd gotten from years of nagging.

Here's how she described it to us.

I found if I just sat with Joe and didn't bug him and didn't keep talking at him—just as I would do with a friend—he'd start to tell me stuff. At first there weren't any big revelations; I guess he wanted to see if I would criticize him. But since I'd agreed that I wouldn't bug him if he was going to talk to me, I kept my mouth shut. I guess I sort of just grunted a lot, the way he used to.

I'd thought it would never happen, but actually it wasn't long before Joe started to open up. He told me this long story about something that went on at school where he got into trouble with some teacher—I couldn't follow all the details. I was so proud of myself though. Guess what I said? All I said was, "That's some story." And then he said, "Unbelievable, isn't it?" It was amazing. He was so happy just to have me listen to him.

You can even use the permission technique with a kid in late adolescence who's about to make a major decision that you think may be a mistake, even when that kid is living on her own and is totally out of the parental orbit.

Ellen, twenty-two, was planning to get married to someone her parents were convinced was a poor choice. What to do? Nothing? Criticize and risk antagonizing their daughter? It was actually very simple. Claire had a long conversation with her daughter in which they basically chatted like friends. She asked Ellen how she felt about the young man. Claire sensed that Ellen was ambivalent in some ways. Instead of using this as a pretext to jump in and attempt to control her by giving advice and opinions, Claire said, "You know, it's strange—we make some of the most important decisions of our lives when we're youngest and have the least experience."

"It's true," the daughter said.

"If you wanted to talk to me about this decision you're making, I'd be happy to listen," Claire said. "I'd like your permission to get involved in this decision."

There was a long silence. Then, "No, really, I'm fine about this."

In other words, Ellen refused permission. But, as we'll see, the permission technique is so valuable that it has tremendous benefits even when permission isn't granted.

For a long time Claire didn't hear much more about Ellen's marriage plans. Then a couple of years after their initial conversation, mother and daughter were talking and Ellen said, "You know, you almost blew it. I kept waiting for you to tell me why I shouldn't marry Phil. I mean, let's face it, I knew he wasn't the kind of guy you were dreaming of me marrying. Not that you wanted me to get married at all so young. But I really, really appreciate your just letting me . . . not just trusting me to make the decision myself but also that if I really needed to I could ask you for your advice. I would've, you know."

Ellen lived with Phil for two years before they broke up. But she didn't marry him. By using the permission technique (even though she was denied permission) Claire gave her daughter room to make her own decision. By showing her daughter this respect, she strengthened the bond between them. The moral: sometimes you have to stand back in order to get close.

How do you deal with it if your teenager doesn't give you permission to help her change in ways you'd like?

The answer is, do as Claire did. Do nothing. Stay out. Keep quiet. Even if it's very frustrating for you to do this, you'll be winning a valuable victory. By respecting the fact that she hasn't given you permission you'll be showing your respect for your teenager as a separate person. This will make her feel warmer and more trusting toward you. And the better your relationship and the more your teenager thinks you're serious about respecting her, the more likely it is she will respect you and your needs. Then if you ask permission to work on the problem a few months later, she may very well say yes.

What if she never gives you permission? Well, you'll still be much better off than you were when you were battling for control. The anger and frustration will be gone. But the two of you will have a much better relationship, and you'll have much more influence.

The permission technique cannot fail. If you ask permission to work on changing something with your teenager, you will improve the relationship. The permission may or may not be granted, and the things you want to work on with your teenager may or may not change. But as long as your relationship is strengthened, you have that much stronger a basis for having some kind of influence than you could get any other way.

The permission technique is so important and powerful that it's the only way you can break through the walls of separation your teenager is putting up between the two of you and improve your relationship at the same time. In other words, it's useful not only for the most major changes you want to make, but any time and in any way you want to slip back even for a moment into your old role.

Here's how. Let's say you can hear the parental voice inside you. You can feel yourself needing to warn or remind or instruct or exhort. But you're afraid your teenager will resist you. What you do, paradoxically, is *ask permission to play the very role that you know your teenager would resist your playing if you didn't ask permission.* For example:

- Your teenager is getting ready to go off to college and seems to have forgotten to do dozens of things. Instead of either criticizing and nagging or helplessly biting your tongue, you can say, "Listen, do you mind if I play parent for a minute about your getting ready for college?"
- You can see that your thirteen-year-old is being used by her friends. Instead of putting them down (and mobilizing her loyalty to them) or criticizing her (and implying she's stupid), you can say, "Look, I know I'm being a mother, but I have to talk to you about your friends. Is that OK?"
- Your fifteen-year-old is about to go out, but not only does she seem to you to be dressed like a hooker, you're also afraid she's going to freeze to death. So you can say, "I'm sorry, but I really feel I need to do my job as a parent now. Can you listen to me for a minute?"

This use of the permission technique is another example of how everything depends on the state of your relationship with your teenager. The better it is, the more likely your kid will say, "Sure, go ahead."

The reason this works is that it's not your being the mother or father that gives your kid trouble. She understands that she's the kid and you're the parent. It's control that teenagers have trouble with, not parents. By saying, "Do you mind if I say some parent kinds of things for a minute?" you're taking the control part out of the parental role.

But you have to play fair. Even if you're burning to say the wonderful, helpful words that are dancing on the tip of your tongue, if your kid says no, don't say anything. There will always be another day when your kid will want to listen to you. And when you use the permission technique, that day will come sooner.

Even though you fully acknowledge the fact that your teenager's life is organized around leaving home and that the most you can do as a parent is to focus on having the best possible relationship with him, you can still be there to provide some of the protection he needs. All you have to do is offer this protection in the context of the relationship approach. And that means not using threats, lectures, and control. Instead:

- Protect by informing—because information is the best and only way to get your teenager to begin to think and act the way you'd like.
- Make sure your information gets through by leaving out your agenda—because your teenager will be likely to reject the information if he feels you're putting a spin on it.
- Communicate your values in a personal way rather than try to impose them—because that's the best way to get your teenager's attention.
- Get your teenager to listen to you by asking him questions to find out what he already knows and what's important to him—because that way you avoid boring him and you can focus on what he most needs to know.
- Use the permission technique (asking your teenager permission to work with him on changing something you think he should change)—because it will maximize his cooperation and your effectiveness.

Switching to the Relationship Approach

9

Once they get started parents find the relationship approach easy to use. But occasionally someone has gotten so much in the habit of battling for control that he has trouble switching over. If you find it's hard for you to let go of the control approach, this chapter will help.

Here are some of the stumbling blocks parents run into—and ways to overcome them.

"Having a good relationship with my teenager seems like a huge task. Is there some shortcut?"

Yes, there is. The fastest way to improve your relationship with your teenager is to go right to the heart of things: *spend more time talking to your teenager about your relationship.*

What do we mean by this?

Well, let's say your best friend calls you up. "How have you been?" she asks. "I haven't heard from you in ages. Let's get together for lunch next Saturday."

"I'd love to," you say. "I'm sorry I haven't called. I've been really busy. I've missed you. Lunch'll be great. Let's meet at Emilio's."

This is not as much a conversation about lunch as about your relationship. Your friend is saying she cares about you and that she's sorry the two of you have been distant. You're saying you care about her and you're apologizing for your part in having been distant.

Friends do this kind of thing all the time. Even men who are uncomfortable with the language of intimacy will say, "Let's do this more often," after a tennis game with their buddies. This may be indirect, but it clearly says, "I like you and I can see we get along."

So the best shortcut to feeling at home with the relationship approach is to talk to your teenager about your relationship. If you wish the two of you were closer, a shortcut is to say directly, "I wish we were closer. How do you feel about that? Is there anything I can do?"

This shortcut becomes highly valuable when you feel the need for control, because your feeling a need for control means that something is wrong with some part of your relationship. It could be that your relationship has come down with a case of miscommunication or anger. If you treat the miscommunication or deal with the anger by talking about the relationship itself, then whatever was making you want to seize control will probably dissolve. Here are some examples.

Instead of saying . . .	*Try . . .*
"Why can't you be easier to get along with?"	"When you're angry, it makes me tense, and then before you know it we've gotten into a big fight."
"You're always so lazy. You never do any of the things you're supposed to do."	"We've got to get out of this pattern where the less you do the more I push, and the more I push the less you do. It doesn't feel good to me, and you probably don't like it either."

"The next time you come home this late I'm cutting off your allowance. I'm just not going to let you run wild."

"When you come home late I feel you are out of control. All that does is make me want to tighten the screws. And all *that* does is make you want to get out from under my thumb. This is terrible for us. We've got to do something to change it."

"I just can't trust you. You don't do what you say you're going to do."

"We've got to find a way to rebuild trust. I need you to do what you say you're going to do. And I need you to tell me what I can do to make it easier for you to do what you say you are going to do."

"What part of 'no' don't you understand?"

"What do you need to say yes?"

"Everything we do, we're doing for you."

"Let's talk about the things we need to be doing for each other."

"You're a really good kid."

"We have a really good relationship."

The exact words you use aren't important. What *is* important is the difference between focusing on your teenager and focusing on your relationship with your teenager. When you focus on your teenager, you're basically saying, "Do this," "Do that," "You're a this," "You're a that"—even if you're being complimentary. And being told who you are feels just as controlling as being told what to do, particularly to the typical supersensitive teenager.

But when you focus on your relationship with your teenager, you change the way you look at things. Instead of looking at and judging your teenager, you step back and look at the big picture—how the two of you work together. It doesn't mean taking your teenager off the hook for the things he does that annoy you, but it does mean seeing your part in his doing those things.

For example, her son's rudeness and sullenness were making Ethel furious. There was no way she could overlook it, and yelling at Mike and telling him what a jerk he was were getting her nowhere. But when she looked at the big picture, Ethel started to see the part she played in his being rude and sullen. This didn't mean that she had to start blaming herself for Mike's behavior. It just meant that she had to look at what the two of them did together to create the problem.

"What can I do to get you to talk more and be more cheerful?" Ethel asked. (Notice that this is really a version of the magic question, "What do you need . . .") The power of this question is that it acknowledges that somehow, somewhere, Ethel was playing a role in Mike's behavior. It didn't mean she was blaming herself or denying her need to have a son with a better attitude, nor did it mean that Ethel was depriving Mike of responsibility for his behavior. All it meant was that she had infinitely more control over herself than over Mike.

Mike's answer was interesting. "Just leave me alone," he said. It sounded like a rebuff, but Ethel decided to take it seriously.

"So if I leave you alone you'll be more communicative?" she said.

"I guess so," he shrugged.

In fact Ethel's leaving him alone was the key. When Mike didn't feel she was bugging him, he could stop trying to resist her. Then whatever cheerfulness and communicativeness he possessed could begin to flow.

Here are some other examples of how this works.

When you tell your daughter she has to be home by a certain time, there may be something about the way you say it that makes her feel you are treating her like a baby and that she has to assert her grown-upness. But when you focus on your relationship with her you can say something like, "Let's see if the two of us can come up with some ideas so we can get along better over the issue of when you have to be home."

To take another example, the things you do to try to "help"

your teenager may, believe it or not, make her feel you don't like her. If you tell her that she has to study more, she may feel that you think she's stupid and that you're disappointed in her for not being the brilliant child she's sure you wanted. But when you talk to each other about your relationship, you can also talk about what she thinks you think of her. You can separate her thinking that you hate her from the issue of how much homework she does.

Consider, too, that the demands you place on your teenager may make him feel that you aren't interested in who he is as a person. If you ask him to help you with his younger brothers and sisters, he may think he exists for you only as a "mother's helper," instead of as a person with a life of his own. But if you talk about who you are to each other, then you get a chance to say, "I really do need your help, but I'm glad we talked. I want you to let me know when I'm being too demanding and preventing you from having your own life." Now your kid can feel you're on his side.

And for still another example, when you're just trying to get your needs met, your teenager may feel you're on a power trip. If you tell your kid to turn down her music, she may think you're trying to tell her how to live. She'll either resist you, or, if she does do what you ask, she'll be resentful. The solution is to talk to her about your relationship and ask her how the two of you can get along with one of you liking quiet and the other liking loud music.

Finally, recognize that when you're trying to improve your teenager she may think you're just being mean. If you say, "Why don't you do something about your hair, dear?" your teenager may tell her friends, "My mother's always putting me down." If, instead, you focus on your relationship with her, the issue that might immediately leap out is whether it's any of your business how she wears her hair. When you become aware of the relationship issue, you can ask, "Do you mind if I comment on your hair?" What this question *really* means is, "Maybe it's time for us to renegotiate your boundaries." And talking about boundaries feels great to a teenager because the very essence of leaving home is shaping your own boundaries.

Look at what you accomplish when you talk about your relationship instead of talking about your teenager:

- You draw your teenager into a collaboration with you to improve your relationship. This gives him the signal that you've stopped blaming him for everything that's wrong.
- You let him know that you really care about the relationship. This signals to him that you want to help him make his life in the family better.
- And you put yourself in the best possible position to make the relationship better. You can't fix the car's engine with the hood down. By actually talking about the relationship, you raise the hood and make it possible for the two of you to tinker with the way things work.

It's really a simple idea. All you have to do is stop using the word *you* and start using the word *we*.

"My kid keeps thinking I'm controlling even when I'm not."

Occasionally a parent plunges into using the relationship approach and guess what happens? Her teenager still gives her a hard time.

Why is this? Let's compare two situations.

A parent who's been using the relationship approach all along may find that it's easy for her kid to cooperate with a direct request. "I'd like you to go to the store for me when you have a chance." "Sure," the kid says. He's not been programmed to resist control, so his spontaneous feelings of cooperation are free to come out.

But a parent who has consistently been battling for control may find that her teenager has become supersensitized to anything that even remotely looks like an attempt to gain control. She may find that her kid blows up at even innocuous comments like, "I like your shirt," or "I'd like us to spend more time together."

Why would a normal kid blow up when you say you like

his shirt? Well, he'd blow up if he was used to fending off your attempts to control him. Suppose you've always been bugging him about his clothes or that you've been trying indirectly to get him to stop wearing torn jeans by telling him how nice he looks when he wears regular pants. How is he going to know that you're not trying to get him to do something when you tell him you like his shirt?

Here you are, determined to strengthen your relationship with your teenager. You've sworn on a stack of Bibles that you're not trying to control your kid anymore, and yet your kid responds as if you're still the same old controller as before. What can you do about this?

If your kid blows up, the best thing to do is to say something like, "Look, I'm trying to change. If you think I'm trying to control you, please tell me. But when I said I liked your shirt that's all I meant. I wasn't trying to get you to dress in any other way. Sure, I'd rather you wore the kind of clothes I like. But what you wear is your business. Let's make a deal. You let me know every time you think I'm being controlling. If I really was being controlling but wasn't aware of it, I'll tell you. If I really wasn't trying to be controlling, then I'll tell you and I'd like you to believe me. That way we'll rebuild our trust."

You can say the same kind of thing when your kid blows up because you've asked what time she's coming home, whether she's using birth control, how she's doing in school—anything.

The point is that if your kid has become supersensitized to control, you have to become supersensitized too. The two of you built up a relationship based on pushing and resisting, and it's going to take time and energy for the two of you to climb out of this well-worn groove. And at first that energy may take the form of your being open about not being controlling.

And think of how good that will feel. If you're talking about trying not to control, and your teenager is talking to you and giving you feedback, then you're talking and listening to each other, and you enlist your teenager as your partner in switching over to the relationship approach. It's also how you influence your teenager. So you win in every direction.

"But teenagers are all different ages. Sometimes they're not old enough to be allowed to do what they want—after all, you don't let fourteen-year-olds drive. Sometimes they don't even want their parents to give up control—they know they're too young. I can't just give up all control the minute my kid turns ten or thirteen. How do I deal with this?"

This is a good question, because it focuses on one reason why it's hard for parents to let go of controlling their kids. Throughout adolescence your kid keeps changing, and it feels like you have to make a million judgment calls. Sometimes it can seem as though the easiest thing is to keep battling for control. At least then you can say you never stopped trying.

The control approach gives the illusion that you don't have to feel overwhelmed by those millions of judgment calls. But with the relationship approach you don't have to be overwhelmed either, and you can avoid battles at the same time.

As early as the day adolescence begins, your teenager begins fighting for his independence. And at the same time he's clearly begun a time of transition between your being in charge of him and his being in charge of himself. That's one of the reasons that adolescence is so confusing and that parents and teenagers fight so much: it's never completely clear who's in charge of what. Teens are constantly saying, in effect, "You're fired. No one can tell me what to do." And parents are always saying, as they battle for control, "I am still in charge of you. You're clearly too young to be in charge of yourself."

This is a formula for endless unproductive struggle if ever there was one. The way most parents handle this, of course, is by constantly fighting to hold on to their power and authority. But that's a doomed strategy; it always puts parents on the losing side.

There's no way you can avoid some confusion over who's

in charge as you go through this period. The only issue is this: is the confusion minimized or does it damage both your teenager and your relationship with him? And the only way to minimize the confusion between you is to keep talking and keep listening to each other. That's why it's so critical to keep improving your relationship with your teenager: a better relationship means better communication; better communication means less confusion; less confusion means less conflict.

There will always be some area where you feel your kid should be obeying you and he feels he shouldn't have to. If the only thing that's important to you is who ends up in charge, then your relationship is in trouble. But if strengthening the relationship is what's most important to you, then you have something to refer to and something to gain when, inevitably, one of you has to give up some claim of authority. And, just as inevitably, the person who's giving up authority is most likely to be you, because that's the natural direction things are moving in.

So acknowledge openly that there will inevitably be conflicts between the two of you over who's in charge of what. Then make it clear that you want to work out a process for solving this kind of problem.

The process is simplicity itself. Since you're the parent, it's your responsibility to say, the moment one of these power struggles begins, "This is one of those times when we're having a fight about who's in charge of what. Instead of yelling back and forth about what time you have to be home from school, let's talk about who should be in charge of making this decision at this point in your life."

In practice what will happen is that you and your teenager will, over and over during the five thousand days of adolescence, have to keep on making new agreements in both old and new areas about who's in charge of what. For example, Jimmy's in the seventh grade, it's seven o'clock, and Mom says, "Time to go do your homework, Jimmy."

"Oh, Ma, do I have to?"

"Yes, you do."

And off goes Jimmy, reluctant or not, to do his homework.

Flash forward two years. Now Jimmy's in the ninth grade. It's seven o'clock and Mom says, "Time to go do your homework, Jimmy."

Now Jimmy says, "I'll do my homework when I want to."

So Mom says what?—"You can't talk to me that way, young man"? "You'll do what I say or else"? "Hey, if you want to ruin your life, that's your business"? Or maybe Mom says nothing out loud, but to herself she thinks, "I just can't control that boy anymore. I'm so worried about what's going to happen to him."

In fact, Mom can do much better than that. Jimmy's saying "I'll do my homework when I want to" is just one of the thousands of turning points in his transition from child to adult. There's no single right answer to who should actually be in charge of this issue at this point. There's no book where you can look up and find, "Male, age 14.4, ninth grader. Issue: homework. Person in charge: _____."

The right answer to how Mom and Jimmy work this out is for two people with a good relationship to talk about what they want and to exchange information. Mom might say, "I think it's time for us to discuss who's in charge of your doing your homework." Then Jimmy might say, "Every time you tell me to go do my homework, it makes me not want to do it." Mom might say, "The thought of you just sitting around not doing your homework just makes me feel crazy inside."

Here are some other things you could say in similar situations:

- "I think we better sit down and talk. This problem isn't going to go away by itself."
- "Look, let's talk about what you need and what I need and see what we can work out."
- "I think it's time for us to discuss who's in charge of this."

The point is to talk until you work out some kind of solution that comes as close as possible to meeting both of your needs for now. In a year Jimmy will most likely be demanding still more autonomy. And next week the two of you will be struggling about who's in charge of some other issue. But for now and with respect to homework, you and Jimmy can come to some kind of agreement.

The important thing to remember is that as authority inevitably shifts from you to your teenager, your relationship can either be a battleground or a setting that allows the two of you arrive at solutions. It's up to you.

"But if don't battle for control, what will I do instead?"

People who want to stop smoking have the same problem. What will they do with their hands and mouth without cigarettes?

During all your kid's preteen years you've been automatically saying things like "Change your clothes" and "Make sure you do your homework." Suddenly not saying those things leaves a huge gap. Your kid comes home from school and you say, "How are you doing?" He says, "Fine." Now what?

Actually you don't have to do *anything* to fill that gap. As you're switching over, the best way to improve your relationship with your teenager might very well be to back off. Instead of controlling, do nothing. Just be available. Say hi. Ask what's up. Ask if your kid needs anything when you go shopping. And that's about it. Don't try to force an artificial togetherness. Just be available when your kid comes to you.

How can mere availability improve your relationship? It will send out a very powerful signal: "I'm respecting your need to be your own person" and "I'm giving up the control game." After all, limiting your involvement to mere availability is a big thing when the whole point of adolescence is learning not to need your parents.

Many parents are afraid that their teenager will never come to them if all they are is passively available. These parents have the mistaken belief that a relationship with a teenager is like a plant and that you have to keep pouring water on it to make it grow. That's not even true for the philodendron, and it's certainly not true for your relationship with your teenager. The best thing to do is to assume that by the time your child enters adolescence he loves you already. The roots of love have taken hold. Now his job is to become his own person. He'll continue to love you—in fact, his love will grow—if you just let him do his job.

So don't knock mere availability. It can be the foundation of a beautiful relationship with your teenager. Instead of being busy trying to gain control, you can just feel good about giving your teenager room to be his own person.

What is there beyond mere availability? Don't be surprised if at first it doesn't look like there's much. Lecturing, complaining, and scolding can take up a lot of time. But "How's school? Is there anything I can help you with?" takes almost no time at all.

Don't worry. The more your teenager believes in your commitment to ending the battle for control and to improving your relationship, the more he'll talk to you. In fact, the closer your kid moves to adulthood, the more his concerns will be similar to yours and the more he'll have to talk about with you. But this will happen only if you've abandoned the control approach.

Switching over from control also means you have time to do things with your teenager. When was the last time, for example, you took your kid out to lunch? One of the sad things about battling for control is that doing things with your kid feels like a chore. You feel you have to spend your mealtimes correcting his table manners. But if you let go of the idea of control, then you can enjoy the time you spend with him.

Making a decision to improve your relationship with your teenager means finding things you can do together—like shopping for clothes, going to a baseball game, jogging, making a meal, going out for ice cream, or just talking. It's sad that all many people remember of their teen years is their parents' attempts at controlling them and their own attempts at resistance. Do something today to give your teenager much better memories.

* * *

To sum up, there are four issues that sometimes come up as stumbling blocks in switching over to the relationship approach:

- How do you deal with the fact that improving your relationship with your teenager seems like a huge task and you'd like a shortcut? SOLUTION: *Talk to your teenager about the state of your relationship whenever you're tempted to try to gain control.*
- How do you deal with the fact that your kid keeps thinking you're controlling even when you're not? SOLUTION: *Make sure your teenager knows that you're trying to switch over to the relationship approach. If you emphasize your intentions, you'll get a break when it comes to your results.*
- How do you deal with the fact that teenagers are all different ages, and you can't just give up all control the minute your kid enters puberty? SOLUTION: *Understand that you're going to have to keep on making and remaking agreements about who's in charge of what as the adolescent years go by.*
- If you don't battle for control, what will you do instead with your desire to be involved? SOLUTION: *Realize that you can be tremendously effective just by being available when your kid comes to you. Also, find activities to do with your teenager.*

UNDERSTANDING TEENAGERS, UNDERSTANDING PARENTS

PART

Why You Can Stop Worrying about Your Teenager

10

Teenagers scare parents. How many times have you thought something like, "I'm afraid of my kid making her own decisions. She's too careless and thoughtless. Right now, it's discipline that will save her from herself and make her a responsible adult."

As family therapists, we've seen over and over how fear causes parents to fall off the wagon of the relationship approach into a drunken orgy of battling for control. Over and over, we've seen parents do a beautiful job of turning a bad relationship with their teenagers into a good one, and then that one situation turns up . . . their teenager makes that one foolish mistake . . . and mother's or father's hand slams down on the parental panic button and there's suddenly a full-scale push for control again.

To let go of control permanently (not just put it in the closet for emergencies), what you need is reassurance—something to help you calm your fears when your teenager scares you. We have found that these parental fears fall into two categories. You're afraid there's something wrong with what your teenager is *doing* (because he's taking risks). And/or you're afraid there's something wrong with who your teenager *is* (because he seems defective).

Of course, we can't just tell you, "Don't be afraid." So we

wrote this chapter to provide specific reassurance. Now you'll know *why* you can let go of most of those fears that keep parents stuck using the control approach.

It's Not as Risky as You Think

Most people think that teenagers tend to be crazy, mixed-up kids, ignorant and irresponsible risk-takers who don't have a proper appreciation of the costs and consequences of what they're doing. And because teenagers don't know what they're doing (people think), their decisions should be supervised. Most parents see nothing wrong in theory with their teenagers learning self-reliance, but when they think about the price their kids might have to pay for screwing up, parents feel self-reliance must take a backseat.

Parents use the control approach, in part, because it worked when their kids were little. Yes, you're happy your six-year-old is learning to ride a bicycle, but he has to use training wheels and ride under the supervision of a loving and watchful parent. And so parents try to do the same kind of thing in adolescence. They try to surround their teenagers' attempts at self-reliance with cushions and safeguards, which in most families mean warnings, threats, and lectures.

But this is a mistake. Parents wage terrible, costly, losing battles as they fight to control the risks their teenagers run. But the risks your teenager runs of "ruining his life" are slim. And the relationship approach provides a more effective way of dealing with the risks your teenager runs than battling for control.

Here's a family who decided that the parent-teen relationship was too valuable to jeopardize for the sake of eliminating risk. Mary Beth's grades in high school were so bad she squeaked into only one of the ten colleges she applied to. Her parents had told her that she would need good grades in order to have a choice of colleges. But Mary Beth had wanted to try things her own way, and throughout high school she had been more interested in writing poetry than in being a good student.

Fortunately, Mary Beth was allowed to learn what it felt like to screw up. This was *real* knowledge, rather than a debatable theory learned secondhand from her parents. Her own experience of not getting into the college of her choice taught Mary Beth that the world sets up its own measures and judges you by them.

On her own, Mary Beth made the decision to do much better when she got to college. Because her own experience led to this decision, Mary Beth left college with far more than good grades: she also came away with a good relationship with her parents and the strong feeling that she could rely on herself and her own judgments. The years of writing poetry didn't go to waste. Her good grades in college turned into a really distinguished performance in a graduate school. She's now a professor of English literature.

But while you know how Mary Beth's story turned out, you're still scared because you don't know how your own kid's story will turn out. He seems to take so many risks. You know what the safe, sensible path is, but he keeps wandering off it. If you could somehow make sense of some of the risks your teenager takes, you might be a lot less scared and a lot less tempted to battle for control.

What does it really mean when your teenager takes risks? Let's break teenage risk taking down into a number of different categories. The fact is that

- Some risks are appropriate to the context.
- Some risk taking is the way your teenager makes sense of the world.
- Some things teenagers do are far less risky than they seem.
- Sometimes when your teenager takes a risk he's trying to satisfy goals that are different from your goals.

Let's take these one at a time.

Risk Taking May Be Appropriate

There are tremendous advantages in being "just a kid," and one of the biggest is time. If you screw up when you're a teenager, you have time to fix your mistake. That's why every family has some wise aunt or uncle who says, "Leave him alone, he's just a kid."

If your kid selects the wrong major in college, there's time to change majors. Even if this requires an extra year or two to finish college it's no big deal in the grand scheme of a person's life—although many parents agonize over it anyway. If your teenager starts out in the wrong career, there's plenty of time to switch careers.

This is why, for example, older teenagers feel it makes sense to take a flyer at becoming a rock musician, and younger teenagers want to see how little studying they can get away with. If it works out, fine. If not, what's been lost? Certainly not anything worth ruining your parent-teen relationship over.

When you make it hard for your teenager to take risks that are appropriate for someone his age, you're really making it hard for him to become self-reliant. Your teenager knows that self-reliance is a sham unless it can be tested. He also knows that testing his self-reliance by taking appropriate risks actually puts that self-reliance on a solid foundation.

And what if your kid doesn't take risks? If you look at the careers of real, as opposed to ideal, people, you'll find they change things about their lives at every age. Forcing your teenager to stay on the safe path only makes it a little more likely that he'll put off his risk taking until middle age, when taking risks is less appropriate because the costs of making mistakes are greater.

So one reason you can let go of fear is that teenagers are young enough to afford to take risks.

Risk Taking May Be Map Making

Some risk taking comes from your teenager's need to learn firsthand how the world works. He needs to find out where he fits in the scheme of things; otherwise his growing self-reliance is built around a core of ignorance. A teenager may know, for example, that show business is a risky career. You've told him that a million times, and he believes you. But what his map doesn't include is knowledge of how risky this career is *for him*. What if he's so talented that the normal probabilities don't apply to him?

This is why your handing him *your* beautifully drawn and completely accurate map of the world isn't enough. Wise and knowledgeable parents are great, but no parent's knowledge extends to *fore*knowledge of how his teenager will one day fit into that world. Your teenager's map of the world must include himself, particularly his talents and preferences. Risk taking is often no more than his way of adjusting the map you're handing him to his growing knowledge of how he fits in the map.

And teenagers learn from their mistakes. They need to, because their mistakes are an important way of making their map of how the world works *for them*. As the years go by, that map will go by the name of experience or sophistication or maturity. It consists of accumulated knowledge of what works and what doesn't and of what's real and what isn't.

Teenagers want to make their maps from personal experience, because such a map is much richer and much more reliable than one made up of what their parents tell them. When your teenager leaves the house so late that she risks missing the bus to school, she has to run that risk and miss that bus to learn in her bones how even that small part of the world works.

Here's an example of a parent's failure to understand her daughter's map making.

Jessica is a well-known writer on women's issues. She feels she's had to fight hard to liberate her own thinking and to gain influence in what she sees as a male-dominated world. Having a daughter seemed a wonderful opportunity to bring up someone who would enter adulthood already free and powerful. Jessica let no chance slip by to teach her daughter what she felt were valuable lessons about how the world works and what women have to do to realize themselves.

It was a struggle. There were lessons to teach the day her

daughter demanded a Barbie doll, came home from a friend's house wearing makeup, mentioned she was trying out for the cheerleading team, and went on her first date. But Jessica felt that she was engaging in a most noble battle, one well worth any sacrifice.

When her daughter Barbara came home for Christmas during her sophomore year in college, Jessica had a shock: Barbara was pregnant by choice and was dropping out of college to get married and stay at home with her baby. She hadn't yet made any other plans for her future.

Jessica was knocked for a loop. She took the news personally as an attack on her values and everything she'd tried to achieve in bringing up Barbara. Angry, hurt, and confused, Jessica fought with Barbara, in effect saying, "If you're going to reject me, I'll reject you."

Now let's flash forward a few years and many tears later. Barbara is divorced now, bringing up her son on her own, and working at home as a free-lance graphic artist. She is now a strong, wise, self-reliant woman. And she now knows how she fits into the world her mother had worked so hard to describe for her. There was a lot of accuracy in the map her mother had given her, but Barbara had added the crucial piece, which was how she herself fit into that world.

Now it was as if Barbara could say, "Yes, you were right all along—*for you.* But now I know the ways in which you were and weren't right *for me.*" Barbara had not done what Jessica had thought she was doing: taking an irresponsible risk with her future in order to make some stupid point in a fight with her mother. Instead, Barbara was making a new map of the world she would be part of.

Sadly, Jessica's lack of understanding led to so much anger between mother and daughter that Jessica simply missed the changes and growth that her adult daughter went through. In fighting a losing battle for control, Jessica lost more than just control; she lost a lot of warmth and closeness.

So think of a lot of teenagers' risk taking like this: suppose you were brought into a strange room blindfolded and suppose you had to make a mental map of that room so you could get around in it. You could let yourself be guided forever, but you know that's not a good, long-run solution. The good solution is to feel your way around the room yourself, taking the risk of bumping into walls and furniture. In the end you might have bruises on your head and shins but you would own an accurate mental map. No one could do that map making for you.

And it's the same with many of the risks your teenager takes. You may feel that he's about to walk into a wall. But what's really happening is that he's making his own map.

What Looks Like Risk Taking May Be Parents' Misperceiving and Overweighing the Risks

Forget about whether it's appropriate or serves the higher end of learning about the world—what your teenager is doing may simply be far less risky than you think and may put him in little danger. And so fighting for control in an effort to save him from a risk may not only hurt the relationship; it may also be a waste of time.

For example, your son announces he's dropping out of college to start his own small business. You're scared, because this seems like a very dangerous thing to do, a risk of time and money. You may even think of him as likely to "lose everything" or "ruin his life."

But if he gets good advice, he has a better-than-average chance of success. What's more, what has to be figured into the cost equation is everything he'll learn by this experience. Even if he fails, this learning is part of the total return on his investment and may in fact make for a much more valuable experience than the low-risk alternatives you were pushing.

One of the most common mistakes parents make is to overlook and undervalue the almost certain benefit of learning and experience that accompanies even the riskiest ventures. So when you see your teenager doing something that looks risky, don't immediately start building a worst-case scenario. Go beyond thinking, "What if he fails?" Instead, ask yourself, "If taking this risk doesn't pay off, what are the permanent costs and unfixable damages?" You'll find that most of the things that scare you and that you get into big fights with your teenager over aren't worth the breakdowns in communication and caring that result from those fights.

Of course, some things are unacceptably dangerous. If your teenager has the stupid idea of financing a summer trip to Europe by smuggling cocaine into Turkey, the danger can't be minimized. Clearly, you'll feel you have to protect him. And that's why we included the chapter on how to protect your teenager using the relationship approach. But even in this worst case, where the risks are real and high, you still can't afford to damage your relationship with your teenager. You have no ultimate control (short of locking him up), and only a good relationship will give you a chance of having the information and leverage to do something that works.

Risk Taking May Be a Teenager's Attempt to Satisfy Goals Different from Her Parents'

Look at what happened to Noreen. When she started her sophomore year of high school, she seemed like a totally normal kid to her parents. But within a month she'd gone punk. Her parents were beside themselves. The half-shaved head, purple hair, and black clothes were not the worst of it—the worst was Noreen's new friends. She was risking giving up all her "decent" friends and, in exchange, getting exposed to God-knows-what dangers and influences.

To her parents, the risks Noreen was taking seemed to have more to do with some kind of suicide than with Noreen becoming her own person, so they tried to get control over what looked like the unraveling of their daughter's life. And of course their fighting for control threw Noreen all the more self-righteously into the arms of her punk comrades.

It might have been different if her parents had thought more about their relationship with Noreen. Then they might, for example, have simply talked to her. And they would have found out exactly what going punk meant to her and what connection it had to her becoming her own person.

Her parents would have found out that Noreen was trying to accomplish something that had never occurred to them. Everything in their family had always been so "normal."

Daddy was a businessman, Mommy was a homemaker, Older Brother was captain of the football team. Even Grandpa was negating the family legend of his gangster youth by being a normal-seeming retiree.

Was this all there was to life? Noreen wondered. Was the normal world something her family was choosing or were they living that way because they were afraid of the "other side"? What was there to this punk world of bad kids and causeless rebels? Would she be tough enough to make it in that world? Could she learn not to be afraid of them? Noreen felt she had to find out.

If they'd talked to Noreen in a way that didn't put her on the defensive, her parents would have found out that her goal in life was not to go rotten. Amazingly, she fully planned to stay on course throughout her life. But in the short run, going punk satisfied many of her goals and was important to her effort to become her own person.

By not talking to her, Noreen's parents missed this, and they thereby surrendered the influence they might have had when it came to dealing with some of the real dangers Noreen was exposed to.

What You Can Do about Your Teenager's Risk Taking

Remember when your kid was little and started to climb up a tree or jungle gym? You were scared then, too. But some voice inside of you told you to let him climb. Yes, if he fell maybe he'd get hurt. And sometimes he did fall and he did get hurt. But as Dr. Benjamin Spock said, "Better a broken bone than a broken spirit." So you did let him climb, and you saw him grow almost before your eyes from a fearful, earthbound child to a near-adult, able to rely on himself to climb as high as he wanted. You understood that his climbing was about his developing strength, coordination, and judgment.

But what happens now when you feel that your teenager is doing (or is about to do) something very risky? You could go down the wrong path, where your fear leads to his resistance, which leads to the two of you being in opposition, which leads to distance and misunderstanding, which leads to your not being available as a resource for your kid if it should happen that one of those risk-taking ventures *does* turn sour.

Still, the odds are that your teenager will take those risks anyway. *So your real choice isn't whether to try to control the situation but whether to be available to your teenager as a resource.*

As the parent of a teenager it's easy to feel helpless. But trying to gain control won't end the feeling of helplessness. It will only lead you back to where you were stuck, unable to turn your good intentions into good results. You can break through the barriers that have prevented you from being effective if you follow this path:

- Your desire to improve the relationship will lead to
- Your listening to your teenager, which will lead to
- Closeness and you both understanding what's involved in the risk your teenager is taking, which will lead to
- You being able to convey real information that he'll be able to hear, which will lead to
- You being welcomed to participate in some of the decisions your teenager is making.

Think of it this way: a teenager is a creature devised by nature to tempt parents into reaching for the panic button, throwing the relationship overboard, and laying down the law. At least it can seem that way. We know that control doesn't work. We know the relationship is a far more effective tool. And when all else fails, it's most important to remember that a lot of risk taking actually is good for your teenager and very little of it is truly harmful. Yes, your heart will be in your mouth, but you must let your teenager take the risks he's driven to take in his desire to leave home.

Your Teenager Is Not as Defective as You May Think

The other big thing parents worry about is not what their teenager does but who he is. He *acts* lazy, so you think maybe he *is* lazy. He *acts* irresponsibly, so you think maybe he *is* irresponsible. He *acts* like he doesn't care about anything, so you think maybe he never *will* care about anything. He acts in a way that's unacceptable to you, so you think that he's always going to act in unacceptable ways. You wanted Superkid, but you got a lemon!

How do you deal with this? We've found that what parents need most here is to feel reassured and to understand what's going on when they see something that makes them think their teenager is defective.

Let's begin by providing that reassurance. Parents often make unwarranted comparisons. They compare their flesh-and-blood teenager to an ideal, not to the average. And they do this for two reasons. First, they want their teenager to be ideal. Second, most parents don't really know what the average teenager is like. Thus, most parents compare their teenager to an unrealistic ideal—and they end up feeling there's something wrong with their teenager.

What's the way out of this? How can you make sense of this imperfect being who is your teenager?

Many of the things your teenager does that make you think she's defective have to do with becoming her own person with her own identity. *The job of an adolescent is to learn to leave home. And this means not only leaving with your body, but with your very self, your very identity. You can't really say you've left home until you can say you've become your own person.*

No matter what it seems they're doing from the outside, and even if it seems they're doing nothing, all teenagers are trying to achieve an identity. Part of leaving home means setting yourself up as being different from the people at home, or to the extent that you're the same, feeling that you've chosen that sameness.

Identity is all the answers you give when you ask yourself, "Who am I?" And this covers an awful lot of territory. Here, in no particular order, are just some of the things that your teenager has to determine in achieving an identity:

- Occupation ("Do I want to be a doctor the way I always thought? Or do I really want to move to LA and try to make it as a songwriter?")
- Style of dress ("Should I risk going punk? Or try to create my own style? Or should I just stay preppie since I'll probably end up that way anyway?")
- Religion ("I'd be happy never to go to Mass again. And yet it's hard to imagine turning my back on the Church.")
- Politics ("I hate the way things are now in the world. But do I care enough to do anything about it?")
- Preference in music ("If the other kids knew the kind of music I really like they'd laugh at me. So do I just keep going along with the crowd or what?")
- Sexual orientation ("Sometimes I think I'm attracted to guys instead of girls, and that scares me shitless. God, what if I'm gay?")
- Where you live ("I'm definitely leaving this hick town as soon as I can. But where do I want to go?")
- Whether you're basically crazy or sane ("Seriously, sometimes I think if people knew what was going on in my head they'd lock me up. Do I want to stop keeping it to myself?")
- How ambitious you are ("Dad keeps saying, go to West Point, go to West Point. But he's just a sergeant and he's happy. Who needs the hassle of being an officer?")
- What kind of person you want to spend your life with ("Guys like that are sexy and exciting but something tells me I wouldn't be happy with them in the long run. Probably a nice guy like Bob would be better for me, but I'm afraid I'll be bored.")
- What kinds of things you want to do for fun ("Is this the year I stop drinking and partying? But I don't know what else to do!")

This means it takes an awful lot of work to go from being "just a kid" with a kind of generic, off-the-shelf, kid identity to being a unique individual. It takes experiments, mistakes, confusion, and sorting out. And before an identity comes together, parent and teenager may have to suffer, because some of the things your teenager does to achieve an identity will seem weird and troubling to you. Sometimes your kid will seem all over the place, sometimes he'll seem nowhere. He'll make tentative choices (which probably won't seem tentative) that upset you. Sometimes the kind of person he's turning into will feel like a slap in the face.

It's no wonder that parents feel the call to battle over what seems like their kid's out-of-control process of achieving an identity. But you know by now that battling for control is a loser's game. Whenever parents interfere with their kid's trying to achieve an identity by trying to take control in any way—from criticizing his experiments with hair color to flipping out over her latest choice of occupation—they create distance and anger at best. And most likely they also slow down and confuse their teenager's natural and inevitable process of achieving an identity.

This last point is very important. Nature programs teenagers to achieve an identity. All you have to do for your teenager is keep the doors and windows open to the real world. You only have one choice: are you going to get out of his way or are you going to gum up the works?

There are actually four main ways teenagers work at achieving an identity, and each of these ways might make you think there's something wrong with your teenager.

Opposition

Your teenager will very likely take his first step toward defining who he is by defining who he is *not*. And often his clumsy and obnoxious first step toward becoming a special person is to set about *not* being you.

If it hasn't happened yet, it will. And it always comes as a shock. At some point your teenager finds a way to overthrow some cherished value of yours, to dash some long-held hope.

Sometimes you can accept this, because you can say, "Well, that's just adolescence." But it can feel like a series of slaps in the face.

Parents who love classical music find that their kids only listen to rock and roll. Religious parents find that their teenagers reject the church or synagogue. Politically active parents find that their teenagers are only interested in making money. Bookish parents can't get their teenagers to do anything but watch TV. Hardworking parents think their teenagers are lazy. Smart parents discover their kids are trying to cultivate mindlessness. Sociable parents realize their teenagers prefer being alone.

You could let this drive you crazy; many parents do. But the best way to think of your teenager rejecting something about who you are and what you stand for is to understand this: since there are so many possible identities, a teenager can make a little bit of progress in achieving his own by eliminating the identity closest to hand, which you represent.

It's important for you to understand that ruling you out this way, saying, "Anything but being like my parent," *isn't* a decision, *isn't* a slap in the face, and certainly *isn't* final. It's just one step in a process of your teenager's self-discovery, a burst of energy to get his rocket launched.

If it's any comfort, studies show that teenagers share more of their parents' values than they reject. What's more, by the time your kid is finally settled into adulthood, you'll find that he has quietly reclaimed most of those values of yours that you'd thought he'd rejected. *And as he gets a clearer sense of his own identity he can stop defining himself solely in opposition to you.*

Most parents understand this at least intellectually, at least most of the time. But inevitably, there's that one value, that one cherished area where your teenager suddenly seems driven to set himself apart from you. And you just go nuts. The other stuff you could understand. But this (whatever "this" is, from laziness to weird clothes) is just too much.

We've talked to many parents and asked them what it was about that particular thing their kid did to establish a separate, opposing identity that made the parent willing to sacrifice the relationship and go to war to change him. Two themes kept coming up as these parents talked to us.

- *Fear:* "If he stays that way he'll ruin his life." "She'll get terribly hurt." "He has no idea what he's getting into."
- *The slap in the face:* "How could she turn her back on us after all we did for her?" "He's only doing that to hurt us." "I must have done something terribly, terribly wrong for her to have turned out that way."

What can you do? All you can do is listen to what your teenager has to say. Find out what her values are. Look hard for something you can respect and understand in what she's doing. You don't have to give up your own needs and values, but you must remember the only way you'll be able to communicate these is in a solid relationship.

Take, for example, Howard, a distinguished professor of history at a major university. As his two daughters were growing up, the house was filled with books and with people talking about books. It came as a big shock to Howard that as his daughters grew up, they showed no interest at all in history. Even worse, they seemed imbued only with the crass values of the marketplace.

Howard fought this. But fortunately, before too much damage could be done to their relationships, Howard accepted his daughters' choices as not being an attack on him but simply their way of becoming their own people. Before long he found he was getting even closer to them by joking about the different paths they were taking. Maybe their paths were different, but they could get closer by talking about those differences.

Howard made an interesting discovery as he saw the kind of women his daughters turned into. True, they were never the bookish kinds of people he'd hoped and expected. But as the years went by Howard could see that in fact they'd held on to a kind of seriousness of purpose that they'd seen in their parents while growing up. All Howard could see when they were teenagers was their rejection of books. They were too young for him to see how they would eventually retain that seriousness of purpose.

In other words, what often happens is that the "being different from you" that you see in your teenager has most to do with the external trappings of your identity. The parts of who you are that successfully get transmitted to your kids are often the deepest parts, the parts hardest to see until a teenager finally emerges as an adult.

Experimentation

This is where you have fights with your teenager because you think he's drifting, or just fooling around, or wasting your money. This is where you find yourself saying things like, "What was wrong with [and here you name the previous thing your teenager did which he's now dropping]?" or "Why can't you make up your mind?" This is where you find yourself embarrassed when a friend asks what young Tom is up to now.

In a way, all the methods for achieving an identity are experimental in the sense that nothing is fixed or final, no matter how firmly held it seems at the time, and everything your teenager does is for the sake of getting information and seeing how things feel. But what's special about the particular method we call *experimentation* is that it actually seems as if your teenager were performing a series of experiments as he goes from one identity to another, sampling many different possibilities, changing college majors, jobs, friends, lifestyles, and anything or everything else.

And this can be very hard for parents to take. "He hasn't settled down yet? What if he *never* settles down?"

You can feel much more relaxed and be an easier person for your teenager to talk to if you think about this experimental method as a kind of bargaining or negotiating your teenager is carrying on with the world. By putting on one identity, he's making a kind of bid. Then the world makes a counteroffer. And then maybe your teenager makes another bid. Maybe he begins the bidding somewhere else. The point of all this for your teenager is to generate a lot of information. Nothing does it better than his actually wading in and getting his feet wet. And the only major cost is time, which is exactly what teenagers are rich in.

For example, Hilary went through high school loving English class. When she got to college she made a bid for an identity by majoring in English. The counteroffer from the world came in the form of boring classes, demanding teachers, and less-than-spectacular grades. Hilary could have made a new bid in the form of sticking it out until she got to the more interesting, advanced classes. Instead she made a different bid by switching over to the sociology department, where, she heard, the professors were really cool and the classes really interesting.

Things turned out the way Hilary hoped. But there was a different counteroffer here in the sense that the professors and her new fellow students were more politically interested and committed than it had ever occurred to Hilary to be. She responded to this counteroffer by raising her bid.

Political commitment *was* great. But why just sit around and talk about it? Why not actually go out into the world and do something, say by becoming a social worker? Now her new friends made a new counteroffer by their surprising response. They acted as though being a social worker wasn't at all a very cool thing to be. Hilary dealt with this by reconsidering and deciding that maybe she could do more "real" good as a lawyer. So now Hilary made yet another new bid by switching over to a political science major, since she thought that would be most helpful in getting her into law school.

If her parents had had a lousy relationship with her they would have seen this perfectly normal process as aimlessness and dilettantism. But Hilary's feeling and thinking gave the process meaning. And because they could talk to her, her parents were able to get in touch with this meaning.

No matter how much any teenager seems to be dithering from the outside, inside they all eventually want to tune in to a clear, definite image of themselves. The more you try to control a teenager because you don't understand the process she's going through, the more you stimulate her to put herself in opposition to you. And then you run the danger that she will do what so many teenagers do: construct some kind of sad identity from that opposition alone, like the young man who spent his youth flitting from one avant-garde artistic enthusiasm to another just to annoy his buttoned-down, desk-pounding businessman father. What started out as experimentation for the sake of finding an identity had become the pursuit of "freedom" for the sake of being in opposition to his father's "narrowness." This is exactly what is meant by the "rebel without a cause."

Understanding all this made it a lot easier for Hilary's parents. They could accept that what she was doing was healthy and normal and certainly not worth hurting their relationship over. Of course, they had needs too. And dealing with their needs was also a crucial part of strengthening their relationship with her. The fact was that they didn't feel they could afford to pay for more than four years of college. Any more than that would have to be Hilary's expense. Because the lines of communication were open, they could explain they weren't setting this limit as an indirect form of control, but that it was based on real needs that had nothing to do with trying to control her. This is why we say it's so important for you to separate your needs from what you think your teenager should need.

As long as you and your teenager are talking and listening to each other, you'll know what's going on and your teenager will know what you need. But with experimentation, there's one more thing you need: patience. As a teenager gathers information she can seem to be wandering all over the place, like Hilary. Getting all this information is often the very last part of adolescence to be completed—but, rest assured, it does get done. Impatience only hurts the process *and* your relationship with your teenager.

Keeping Your Options Open

When Tracy was a senior in high school, she seemed not to have any hobbies or interests. Her mother got so upset she called Tracy a blob. Poor Tracy, you might think. But Tracy was really doing something, and what she was doing was another strategy for achieving an identity. Instead of getting her hands dirty like the experimenters, instead of engaging in a kind of rough-and-tumble bargaining process with the world, Tracy's strategy was to commit to nothing, to stand back, observe, and wait.

The previous strategy, experimentation, can take a lot of time, but it generates a lot of information. The options-open strategy doesn't generate as much information but it usually doesn't take as much time. No one strategy is necessarily better than any other; it's only a question of what works for your teenager. It's best to assume that your teenager has chosen the strategy for achieving an identity that works for her.

Sometimes parents are disappointed in teenagers who follow the options-open strategy. Tracy seemed like a blob to her mother, and your teenager might seem very blah or blobish to you if it looks as if she's doing nothing but keeping her options open. And while impatience is very corrosive, it can be hard for you to keep it to yourself. To make matters worse, it's not likely that a teenager with the options-open strategy will be able to explain what she's doing, because teenagers don't choose their strategies by conscious deliberation.

At best, if your communication is good, she might tell you about how she's impatient with herself, how perhaps she feels confused and lost. This often leads parents to try to gain control by making "helpful" comments like, "I really think you should settle down," or "It's taking you an awfully long time to find yourself, isn't it?" But this just makes your kid feel worse and makes talking to you feel painful and dangerous.

There's really only one way to deal with your concerns here and that's to use the permission technique. But first you have to find out if your teenager thinks there's a problem. If she thinks so, and only then, you could ask, "How would you feel about our having a talk about it?" And then leave it up to your teenager.

Premature Closure

This is the strategy where teenagers decide firmly and early just who they are and what they'll do. It's one strategy for achieving an identity that usually makes parents happy, but it's also generally the one poor strategy.

Martin, for example, had started first grade as a very bright little boy. Other than that, he wasn't particularly special. As the years went by, however, he became special, all right. Because he was overweight, with a squeaky voice and poor interpersonal skills, Martin, unlike most bright kids, had no friends and ended up becoming an outcast. So throughout grade school his identity was mostly negative: he was someone disliked by others.

Throughout these same years he also knew he was smart. When he was thirteen he took the exam for Mensa, the organization for people with very high IQs, passed the exam, and became a member. Suddenly, Martin found people who would accept him. Suddenly, at age thirteen, he went from having a negative, unpleasant identity to having a positive identity that brought him rewards. "I knew who I was finally. I was a genius," he told us.

And that was it. At age thirteen, Martin closed the books on any further identity questions. He would simply spend his life being a genius, doing genius things, and earning a living in a genius way.

Now here's the problem. Achieving an identity as a smart person was a good thing for Martin. The problem was that he stopped there. Either as a rebel, or an experimenter, or someone who is keeping his options open, Martin could have found out a lot more about the fit between himself and the world and gotten a lot further. Having decided he was a genius got him out of the hell of his childhood fast. But by going no further, he arrived at age thirty with a huge amount of unfinished business. He was still a genius, and he'd had some academic success, but he didn't know who he was, what he wanted, or what he could do.

What's the moral of this story for parents? Making a seemingly final choice at a very early stage without much information can be a recipe for disaster. The earlier a kid "knows" who he is, the less basis he has for this "knowledge." So don't be too happy if your kid seems to have solved all his identity problems at a nice early age. And if your kid is going through the agonies of trying to achieve an identity, don't be so eager to wish he'd put the job behind him.

We wrote this chapter to show you why you can stop worrying about your teenager. The answer is very easy to sum up: adolescence is a natural process, and therefore the stuff your kid does as an adolescent is natural. Yes, we understand, the process can scare the hell out of you. But if you keep remembering that this is all nature's way of getting your teenager ready to leave home, then you can relax. When you're relaxed you can stop trying to control him. Then he can stop resisting you, the two of you can start listening to each other, and then you'll be able to know what's going on for your teenager and be a resource for him.

The Inner World of Parents of Teenagers

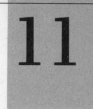

11

Many of the ways you deal with your teenager are colored by your feelings about yourself and your life. But maybe *color* is the wrong word. The word Pam actually used was *infect* when she talked to us about what happened to her in trying to deal with her fourteen- and seventeen-year-old kids.

> I'm telling you, I don't understand it. You'd think I would know better. I'm an educated woman. I'm a high school teacher, for God's sake, so don't tell me I don't know about teenagers.
>
> What you can tell me is why with my own kids it's like I'm infected with some disease and I'm always finding myself pushing and bullying or criticizing my kids in this really mean way. . . . It's like I'm seeing myself in a horror movie and I'm doing these things I know better than to do. What is this disease that I have? Why am I doing a bad job of parenting when I know better?

Pam was onto something here. There *is* something going on with parents that's like an infection or something you'd find in a horror movie that features someone's body getting taken over by an alien. As parents we're often taken over by things that are happening to us as people.

For lots of people their kids' adolescence defines their own middle age. The life cycle of adolescence, which is all about your kid's leaving home, gets tangled up in your own life cycle, which is marked by your coming to the end of your time as a parent. So your feelings about your teenager and the ways you deal with him get tangled up in your feelings about yourself and the things you're trying to deal with in your own life.

That's how parents like Pam can end up feeling somehow infected and out of control in dealing with their teenagers.

You'd think that nature would have made things easier for us, so that even with their urge to protect and control, parents, just as much as their teenagers, would want their kids to become self-reliant, achieve an identity, and leave home. You'd think that nature, so wise in providing teenagers with a healthful agenda, would have done the same for parents.

Alas, many of the things that are happening to you internally are giving you a very different agenda from your teenager's. And any time two people with radically different agendas meet, they are likely to get into trouble, as happens, for example, when

- The substitute teacher who just wants to keep order meets the class who just wants to have fun.
- A new boss who wants to cut costs has to deal with a staff who want to maintain professional standards.
- A husband sees the vacation as a chance to rest and relax and the wife sees it as a chance to have fun and explore the sights.
- A parent sees her teenager's upcoming birthday party as a chance for the whole family to get together and her teenager sees it as a chance to have a party with her friends.

Things get even more confused when people don't understand and can't even imagine the other person's agenda. For parents, this begins with the helplessness you feel in dealing with your teenagers. Here you are—older, wiser, and more knowledgeable than you have ever been—but all too often you just don't know what to do when your teenager is sullen or disrespectful, when he's not doing his schoolwork, or when you suspect scary things, such as that he's taking drugs.

You want to be smart. You want to be effective. But you find yourself reacting automatically to things your teenager says and does. Your kid does things to make you so angry and upset that you turn into an out-of-control robot, saying things you don't mean and doing things you know don't work.

Where do these automatic parental reactions come from? How does it happen that a smart, well-intentioned adult can be made to feel helpless by a teenager?

All of us adults have an inner world, a collection of thoughts and feelings we carry around, a selection of tapes we play in our heads, a bundle of expectations and desires we are filled with, an agenda. It's this inner world—mostly unconscious—that takes control of you when your teenager is at his worst. His worst brings out your worst.

Let's take a close look at the inner world of the middle-aged parent of a teenager pushing to leave home.

The inner world of parents of teenagers is remarkably universal. Liberal and conservative parents, younger and older, strict and neglectful, rich and poor—all tend to say many of the same things to themselves. If there were a typical, composite parent of a teenager and you could somehow extract and summarize what goes through his head, it would be something like this:

> I want my kid to be someone special, someone more successful than I am. . . . I want to do a better job with my kid than my parents did with me. . . . I want my kid to be a more successful teenager than I was. . . . At least I want my kid to be as good a kid as I was when I was a teenager. . . . I want my kid to benefit from all that I've learned and experienced, . . . I want some evidence that will make me feel that my kid's a good kid and I'm a good parent. And when I get evidence to the contrary, I feel I'm a bad parent and he's a bad kid, and that makes me feel terrible. . . . I simply can't take one more problem or dif-

ficulty or struggle. . . . My kids are all I've got; I don't know what I'll do when they leave.

For you to achieve a real breakthrough with your teenager, you need to be aware of the way your inner world sometimes sets your automatic pilot on a crash course, so that your parenting has nothing to do with who your kid is or with what he needs or with how you can make the two of you start feeling good about each other again. You need to understand the parts of yourself that keep you battling for control even though you know it can't work and even when you know what does work.

Let's explore what goes through the mind of a typical parent more deeply.

"I want my kid to be someone special, someone more successful than I am."

Parents having high expectations for their kids is one of those things that seems like a great idea but usually turns out badly, like taking small children on a four-week-long cross-country drive to see America.

Here's an example. Hugo's high expectations of his daughter Kate ultimately drove them apart for more than seven years. Read what he wrote in a letter he showed us, which was an attempt to explain himself to Kate in one of his periodic efforts at reconciliation:

What really turned you off is what you perceived as my high expectations, my exaggerated demands in trying to make you live up to the image I had of you, of what I would like to see you be. You must understand that these demands were not motivated by the egotistical wish of a father of an outstanding young woman, but by my conviction that it is essential to our happiness that we make the fullest use of our potential. I always felt that one cause of the sadness of the last couple of decades of my own parents' lives is that my father did not have the self-discipline to use his unusual intelligence and culture to become an excellent journalist and that my mother did not pursue her outstanding ability as a restorer of paintings but indulged her two husbands' appetites for social life. Well, you have the self-discipline, and I am sure you would not allow anyone to distract you from your goals in life.

Hugo's letter is a portrait of the father-protector, a loving, kindhearted man, whose good intentions drove his daughter away. It captures the way high expectations combine with good intentions to make a poisonous stew.

Hugo said that he wasn't trying to be egotistical but only to make sure that Kate "make the fullest use of [her] potential." The problem is that he's trying to tell her what her potential is. Hugo's imagining some kind of large potential and then trying to place it on Kate's back.* Notice how he sees his own father as a potentially "excellent journalist" and his mother as a potentially "outstanding restorer." This man even places high expectations on his dead parents. It was these high expectations that drove Kate away. That Hugo's intentions were good didn't help.

Why do parents put these high expectations on their kids?

It's a sad fact of modern American life that ambition is more widely distributed than are the rewards of ambition. Most adults find that wisdom comes from a wrestling match between hope and reality in which reality wins. Gaining this wisdom is necessary because otherwise it's too hard to feel good about yourself; if you must be a superstar to have self-esteem, you're in big trouble.

But people can't forget their dreams. A middle-aged legal secretary sees young women coming up as lawyers and realizes she could have been one of them. And lawyers see their

---

*In fact, potential is always imaginary. It's always a story about what might happen. It may be more or less grounded in reality, but it's still a story. It's bad enough to assume this story is a reality, but it's even worse to use the assumed-but-nonexistent reality of that story as an excuse for pushing the other people in one's life.

colleagues get the top partnerships or the big cases and think about how they missed the boat.

And while your own dreams may be sitting on the shelf, it usually doesn't seem like a bad substitute to think of your kid fulfilling those same dreams. So you're realistic about yourself but idealistic about your kid. And as your kids move through adolescence it feels perfectly natural to teach them how to avoid your mistakes. Learn the basics, you say to them. Play the game. Aim higher. Get to know the right people. Make sure you get into the right school.

This transfer of hope and ambition from parent to kid starts before birth. The mother's belly swells like a giant egg with the promise of a mysterious stranger about to enter her life. It feels as if a miracle is about to happen. It's easy to imagine that something far more wonderful than just another baby is growing in there.

Then comes the discomfort and pain of childbirth, or the difficulty and expense of adoption, and finally you're holding that little bundle of joy in your arms. Have there ever been parents who haven't talked about how one day their baby might grow up to be someone very special?

For parents it's always "Maybe she'll be a great writer," not "Maybe she'll write direct-mail advertisements for a small midwestern ad agency." It's "Maybe he'll be a great scientist," not "Maybe he'll be a lab technician in a community hospital." It's "Maybe she'll be CEO of IBM," not "Maybe she'll be assistant employee benefits manager in a branch factory." It's "Maybe he'll be President," not "Maybe he'll come in a respectable second in the election for school committee."

Of course, parents also say, "Well, as long as she's happy and healthy that's all I care about." But great expectations always creep back in. After all, life can be drab, but hope is free. The lines between hoping and wanting and between wanting and expecting are easily erased.

The dangerous thing about expectations is that they tend to feed on themselves and to infect the parent-teen relationship. Parents who expect their kids to be brilliant will ignore a thousand signs of intellectual mediocrity and seize on the one clever solution their kid came up with once in the second grade as confirmation indeed of underlying brilliance. After all, nothing has happened yet to really dash those expectations.

But then comes adolescence, and the teenager, in an effort to assert his own identity, demands that his parent recognize the real modesty of his IQ. And then the parent will say, as millions of parents have already said, "I don't think you give yourself credit for how smart you really are. I know you can do anything you want if you just try. You just don't work hard enough. I know you won't be happy if you don't give yourself a chance to be the best that you can be. You just have to push yourself. [And if you don't push yourself I'll be there to push you. For your own good, of course.]"

By the time your kid is a teenager, you've convinced yourself that your expectations are totally based on reality. If your kid doesn't share your expectations that means *he* has a problem and you have to help him with it. You have a chance to play the role of "beneficial parent," whether your kid likes it or not. You can be so convinced of the magical nurturing powers of your high expectations that it's literally unbelievable to you that those very expectations could do damage. If your kid resists, you feel there must be something wrong with him.

The problem isn't whether a parent's expectations are justified. It's not whether your kid is as destined for success as you think. Problems come because it's just not a parent's place to load his kid with high expectations, *whether justified or not*. Sure, you hope your teenager will do his best. It even makes sense to encourage him to do his best.

But parents with high expectations go further and so infect the parent-teen relationship. They say, "No, I really don't think you're doing your best. I think you could do better. You just need to try harder."

"But I'm trying as hard as I can," the teenager says.

"I don't think so," the parent says, "because if you were you'd be more successful. And," says the parent who's trying to "improve" his teenager, "I know you'd be happier if you were more successful, because then you'd be living up to your potential. You'd be who you really are. Do you really want to settle for less?"

The sad and destructive underbelly of high expectations is a constant message of disappointment. *When you impose your expectations on your teenager, it's as if your praise and appreciation are only for what you think he will one day become, not for what he is today.* Even worse, you're telling him that many things about him today are bad—everything about him, in fact, that results in his accomplishments and efforts being so puny compared to what you expect of him. Parents with high expectations may *say* that the kid can be great tomorrow, but the message—what actually gets conveyed—is that the kid is lousy today. He hears only that he's lousy.

It's very hard for some parents to recognize this. If you're one of these "high expectations" parents, then your good intentions and the love and faith you feel for your teenager may be so real to you that you can't imagine anything bad coming from them. But bad things do come from them. Not only does the message of disappointment damage your teenager, it damages your relationship with him. Your disappointment makes him angry. The fact that he gets disappointment messages when he's with you makes him feel vulnerable and scared and makes him want to avoid you.

This may still be hard for you to believe. No, you may be saying, high expectations encourage a kid to do better. Isn't that really all I'm doing, encouraging him?

Parents who think this confuse cheering a kid on with having high expectations. For the record, then:

- *High expectations* happen when someone is trying and you attempt to push up the level of his effort by saying, "I know you can do better—you should try harder—what you've just done isn't enough for somebody like you."
- *Cheering on* happens when somebody is putting out effort, at whatever level, and you say, "You're doing it—go team! Go for it—I'm with you—you're doing great."

In other words, high expectations happen when you get ahead of your kid. Cheering on happens when you get behind your kid. Here's an example of cheering on. Your teenager's report card is mostly C's. What do you say? *It depends on what your kid says. Ask him how he feels about his report card.* If he's happy, congratulate him. If he feels sad, commiserate *and ask him if there's anything you can do to help.* That's all you have to do.

Here's an example of how *not* to do things. Hal tried to add energy and direction to every ambition his son Willie mentioned. When Willie talked about becoming a lawyer, Hal immediately told him how much money top lawyers made, about how he should take different courses, about how Willie should aim to get into a top law school because he'd be sunk if he didn't graduate from one. In other words, Hal tried to tie a booster rocket onto Willie's already-existing ambition, instead of accepting it and cheering it on at the level it was. Eventually Willie stopped talking about becoming a lawyer. Then Willie mentioned becoming a doctor. This time Hal immediately talked about which specialties made the most money, about how Willie would have to get straight A's from then on if he was to have a prayer of getting into medical school. Eventually Willie stopped talking about becoming a doctor.

This pattern went on until Willie stopped talking to his father at all. What Willie did become was a librarian, because there no one would bother him about clawing his way to the top.

So cheer on your teenager by all means. Say, "That's great!" and "Good for you!" But leave him alone about where he's going and how hard he's pushing to get there. Where he's going has to do with his identity, how hard he's pushing has to do with his self-reliance, and both have to do with his getting ready to leave home. You can't interfere with that without causing problems, and your high expectations are a serious interference.

Very few people can become huge successes. The real decision for the majority of people is whether to be a happy or an unhappy less-than-huge success, not whether to go to the top. Your contribution to your teenager's happiness depends on your not having higher expectations for your teenager than he has for himself.

When we tell parents about the dangers of high expectations, they often say, "Well, what do you want us to have— *low* expectations? Don't kids need pushing and encouraging sometimes?" Our position on this is very radical. Even though it might be hard in practice, we recommend you have *no* expectations. Expectations of *any* kind—high or low—are harmful and totally unnecessary in bringing up a teenager successfully.

We're not saying you should encourage your kid to become a couch potato. We *are* saying you should just trust him to become the best he can be. Why wouldn't he become the best he can be? Adolescence is naturally a time of optimism and high hopes. The future feels wide open for most teenagers.*

But you may not get to see your kid's ambition, because teenagers often keep that kind of thing private. Because he's ignorant about what the world has to offer, his ambition may be too amorphous for him to talk about. But private and amorphous as it may be, it's still there. Pushing has the same effect as yelling at a turtle in a turtle race: it just makes him crawl back in his shell.

So suppose your kid does seem to be heading in the couch potato direction. Will pushing help? Will tying booster rockets to him help? Will high expectations and loud exhortations help? You might think they would work for you. But believe us, you'll be the very first parent who has gotten them to work for his teenager.

If you really want to help your teenager, you can do it very simply. Drop your expectations, and use these questions:

"How can I help you?" and *"What do you need?"*

That's all it takes.

---

*It's part of the nature of adolescence that coexisting with optimism and hope are moods of nihilism and despair. Sometimes these dark moods even briefly become a life-style. But teenagers' dark moods usually pass, while optimism and hope remain the premise behind most of their actions.

You can use these questions all the time. They work when your teenager is hopeful and when he's discouraged. They work when he's pushing himself and when he seems to be slacking off. They work when he's just succeeded and when he's just failed. They work when he thinks he knows what he's doing and when he doesn't have a clue. They work when you see him being a couch potato and when you see him headed for *Who's Who*. And they work when he's going in the right direction and when you're sure he's going in the wrong direction.

In fact, "How can I help you?" and "What do you need?" are like those all-purpose cleansers: they're useful in just about any situation. They will give you everything you could reasonably hope to get from having high expectations, with none of the bad effects.

Last, but not least, asking these questions will help the two of you get along. Since one of the basic dynamics parents and teens get into is polarization, your pushing (even if you think of it as merely "encouraging") will generally result in your kid resisting by seeming lazier or less interested than he really is.

But if, instead of pushing, you ask "How can I help you?" or "What do you need?" then you may be able to start a dialogue. You set things up so that what you're trying to do is listen and understand (which means respecting your kid for who he is) rather than push (which means not accepting him for who he is). Then you will get to hear some of his hopes and dreams. Most kids have them.

If they should happen not to fit your expectations (and they probably won't; it sometimes seems as though teenagers were put on this earth just to surprise and confuse their parents), just remember that even as young adults most people haven't progressed far enough to be able to formulate their expectations of themselves clearly. Most successful people in business, science, and the arts were already working adults in their twenties, thirties, forties, or even later before they could define their dreams.

We really do understand how hard it is for many parents to accept what we're saying about the damaging effects of their high expectations. They're sure that they're merely being helpful; they're sure that what's meant to be encouraging will be taken as encouragement; they're sure that their kid will be grateful for their push once the kid experiences the momentum—they're so sure of all of this that it's hard to see the evidence right in front of their eyes that their pushing doesn't work. But the fact is that there's no evidence that high expectations (as opposed to cheering on your kid's own efforts), wherever they come from or however they're expressed, will have any positive effect on a teenager's success. On the contrary, there's plenty of evidence that imposing your high expectations on your teenager will only damage your relationship.

"I want to do a better job with my kid than my parents did with me."

Remember the story of the boy whose mother sent him to market to buy some butter? On the way home he put the butter on his head under his hat. By the time he got home the butter had all melted down his face. His mother scolded him and told him he should have kept the butter in a cool bucket of water.

The following week she sent him to market to buy a puppy. The boy, remembering what he'd learned about the butter, took the puppy home by putting it in a cool bucket of water. Of course, the puppy had drowned by the time the boy got home. His mother scolded him and told him he should have tied the puppy to the end of a string and let the puppy follow him home. The following week she sent him to market to buy a loaf of bread. The boy tied a string around the loaf of bread and dragged it home on the ground behind him.

This went on and on. The boy kept learning his lessons, but he didn't pay any attention to the fact that circumstances kept changing.

It's the same thing with bringing up your kid. Let's be honest. You don't just want to be a good parent—you want to be better than your own parents. Even if you feel your parents did a great job, you are sure you can make improvements. You're determined to do some things differently from the ways your parents did them.

There are many examples. If your parents yelled at you, you're determined to be mild and patient with your own kids. If your parents tried to involve themselves in every detail of your life, you might want to give your kid a lot of breathing room. It might be that if your parents were too traditional, you try to be cool. If your parents didn't seem to care about you, you could be eager to show your kids how much you can do for them.

What does all this do to your relationship with your teenager?

It means that even though your kid's right in front of you, you may be more involved in a relationship with your own parents (even if they're dead) than in a relationship with him. It means that you keep trying to correct in the present something that should have been corrected in the past. It means that you may be complicating the job of bringing up your teenager by bringing in extraneous material and at the same time overlooking things that are right in front of your eyes.

As far as bringing up your kid is concerned, *you can ignore what your parents did and how you feel about it.* Both you and your kid are different people.

Here's an example. Sheila's mother had personified the parent who battles for control. Her mother's theory had been that everything imperfect and unseen in Sheila had to be brought to light and bent under the weight of her authority.

Sheila was determined to do things differently with her own daughter, Mandy. She was absolutely committed to "not being overinvolved" in Mandy's life. So when Mandy did things that bothered her, Sheila did nothing about them. She never asked Mandy if there was any way she could help her. She never tried to get her daughter's permission to work on anything with her. She neglected to get involved enough to make sure that her own needs got met.

The point is that the past is often a confusing guide to the future. It's all too easy to learn the wrong lessons and to apply them blindly. Things between Sheila and Mandy didn't improve until Sheila stopped applying to the problem of how to bring the puppy home the lessons she'd learned about bringing the butter home. It was difficult at first, because Sheila no longer had the simple guideline, "Think about what my mother would do and do the opposite." But once Sheila got over trying to redo the past, she found that focusing on who Mandy really was was almost as simple as what she'd been doing and much more effective.

"I want my kid to be more successful as a teenager than I was."

This is another way parents use their teenagers as an opportunity to redo their past.

According to one study, even the tiny minority of kids who were the high-school quarterbacks, cheerleaders, and class presidents often felt insecure, awkward, lonely, and ill at ease deep inside. In fact, most people don't feel they were very successful as teenagers. You either didn't study hard enough or else you didn't know how to make your studying pay off. You didn't know how to be popular. Or you didn't know how to translate your popularity into self-satisfaction. You made all kinds of bad choices and got stuck in a variety of unrewarding situations.

But now you've learned. Adulthood has given you knowledge and perspective. You know what you should have done differently. A surprising number of adults have a fantasy of going back to high school and being a huge success the second time around because of what they know now as adults.

So when you see your teenager having problems you're sure you know how to save him from making the same mistakes you did. It can be almost physically painful to watch him struggle without coming to his rescue. Why shouldn't you help him feel better about his teen years than you did about yours?

Let's face it, part of the nightmare quality of adolescence is that it's such a painful mixture of ignorance, awkwardness, and frustration. How good *can* you feel as a teenager? A teenager is just a rough draft of an adult, subject to many revisions. It's good that we feel better as adults—it means there's something to look forward to when we're teenagers.

What's sad is that many parents try to make their teenagers do things the parents believe will make the kids feel better about their adolescence. So kids get pushed into doing sports or being popular or taking courses that are too difficult for them, all based on the parent's superior wisdom about how to do high school and college right.

What gets sacrificed are the good feelings between parent and teenager. And this is something you do have control over, something that will make a big difference in how your kid feels about his adolescence when it's all over. Few things make people feel better about their teen years than being able to say, "No matter what, I could always talk to my parents."

"At least I want my kid to be as good a kid as I was when I was a teenager."

We've seen it happen dozens of times. The parent says, "Hey, I'm not asking my kid to do anything I didn't do. If I got straight A's in high school he can too."

It's not that we doubt your word, we say, but sometimes the memory plays tricks. Are you sure you always got straight A's in high school? More often than not, when they look up their old report cards these parents find that things are not quite what they thought. Maybe there was a semester of straight A's, but the rest of the year was more mixed, and two years earlier their grades were really poor.

When you use your memory of the way you were to create a set of expectations for your teenager, it's the rule rather than the exception that the bad things were never quite as bad and the good things never quite as good as you remember. Memory tends to turn shades of gray into black and white.

If this is true of grades it's even more true of personal qualities like ambition, energy, community spirit, and so on. In fact, memory creates fables, even for the most scrupulous of us. And it's terrible to derive expectations for our children from fables.

But let's say that you were the rare person whose memory of himself is crystal-clear and who truly was a teenage paragon. It's still unfair to use yourself as a source of comparison, because your teenager is a different person from you. He needs to measure up to himself, not to you, and the "self" he has to measure up to won't really be known until he's been an adult for some time.

And the issue of fairness aside, comparisons designed to motivate your teenager just won't work. Since part of becoming self-reliant and achieving a separate identity means becoming different from you, what possible reaction can your teenager have when you say, "Be like me"? What's supposed to motivate him will only make him resist. Your attempts at gains will create losses.

Still, parents can't resist talking about themselves when they were teenagers, and it's good for teenagers to hear some of this talk. Strangely, the talk that will be most useful for your teenager will be where you tell him about the difficulties and problems you had, the things you struggled with, your confusions, mistakes, and fears. Then if the timing and atmosphere are just right, occasionally you can talk about some solutions that worked for you when you were a teenager.

But note the difference. "I tried this and it worked" is much easier to hear than "I was terrific and you can be, too."

"I want my kid to benefit from everything that I've learned and experienced."

It's frustrating, even shocking for most parents. When it happens you're sure that your kid is stupid or crazy. Here you've been an adult longer than he's been alive and when you try to tell him what's what, he simply tells you you're wrong.

Yes, that's exactly what your teenager is doing. He's telling you you're wrong. When you say something doesn't work, he tells you it does. When you say something is dangerous, he tells you it's safe. When you say something is bad, he says it's good. You've suffered in the process of learning your lessons, and now your kid tells you your lessons aren't worth much. For example:

- It's obvious to you that you have to study hard and get good grades in high school and college to have a leg up on life. The longer you've lived, the more you know this is true. And then your kid comes along and tells you about businessmen and rock stars who were dropouts and became huge successes. "All that matters is your personality," he tells you.
- As the years have gone by you've learned how important it is to take care of your health. Eating right, getting enough sleep, and laying off the booze have become high priorities. Now your kid tells you it's "stupid" for her to worry about her health because she's probably going to die young anyway.
- As you've experienced the slow growth of your career, you've learned how important it is to get along with the right people. If you want to be successful, you have to be popular with people who are successful. Now your teenager tells you that the successful kids in high school are nerds and dweebs. He tells you that it's much better to hang out with the cool kids, who, unfortunately, are punks.

It's hard not to take things like this personally. It can feel as if you're being attacked. Many times, because of the thoughtlessness and exuberance with which your kid expresses himself, it can feel as though you're not only being attacked but are being given evidence there's something wrong with him. So what do you do about this assault on your psyche?

The two things *not* to do are take it as a personal attack ("You're just saying this to drive me crazy!") or take it as a sign of brain damage or low intelligence in your teenager ("How could he even *think* that?"). It's neither of these things.

Instead, when your kid casually overturns a lifetime of your hard-earned lessons, it's important to understand that all he's doing is insisting on seeing things for himself. Yes, your lessons were true for you, but your kid can't be sure they're true for him unless he checks them out personally.

For your kid to develop self-reliance, he's got to fine-tune just the right mixture of things he takes on face value and things he checks out for himself. The more he cares about the issue, the more likely he is to feel he has to check it out personally, because he feels he brings to the issue something different from what you brought.

So let's rethink what it means for you to do a good job here. It doesn't mean trying to force him to learn your lessons. That just won't work. He'll see you trying to push your wisdom and experience on him as an attempt to control, and he'll try to resist. Instead, doing a good job means that, with all your knowledge and experience, you become a resource and a support.

As a *resource*, all you have to do is be available to your kid. If and when he asks for information, tell him what you know. If he doesn't ask, then you offer to give him information. Say something like, "Would you be interested in hearing something you might find useful?" If he's not interested, you just have to be prepared to be a patient bystander as he goes off and either does or does not get the information for himself.

For example, while he's shamefully neglecting his health, he may also complain about feeling tired and out of sorts. So you can offer to explain to him what he can do to feel better. If he's not interested in your offer, there's nothing you can do to help him at that moment. All you can do until he's ready to accept your help is take care of your own needs by, for instance, putting a limit on how much complaining you're willing to listen to if he's not willing to listen to your suggestions.

Don't worry: your teenager knows you're available with all kinds of information. If anything, your kid has been staying away to avoid being buried under the avalanche of information you're ready to dump on him. On the other hand, the less you're an information-pusher, the better your relationship with your teenager will be, and the easier he'll find it to talk to you, and the more opportunities you'll have to pass on what you know.

The other thing doing a good job means is becoming a *support* for your teenager. As a support, it's more important to you to help him get through his difficulties in his own way than to prove what an idiot he's being by not relying on your wisdom. For example, maybe his poor grades have gotten him into trouble and you feel you've proved your point. But saying "I told you so," even if you're sure this will help him by getting him to rely on you in the future, is a mistake.

Whatever you can accomplish in the way of passing on what you know can only happen in the context of your relationship with your teenager. Madison Avenue, for example, knows very well that we listen to and believe people we like. That's why they choose a Bill Cosby and not a Richard Nixon to sell products on TV. The better your relationship with your teenager, the more believable and the easier to listen to you become.

"I simply can't take one more problem or difficulty or struggle."

This problem is often overlooked, because in their battle for control many parents are reluctant to admit that they're tired and overwhelmed just by leading their own lives, much less trying to perfect their kids' lives. So this problem is usually not stated directly. The battle for control just gets more tense and grim and shrill. Now it's not just "Be the way I want you to be," but "Be the way I want you to be *or I'll scream.*"

Anyone struggling through his or her thirties, forties, fifties, or sixties will have sympathy for parents with this problem, because everyone is more or less overwhelmed by the demands of life. The big difference is in what parents do about feeling overwhelmed.

The danger is that the more parents feel overwhelmed, the more they intensify the battle for control. With things flying off in all directions, they desperately try to get all the hatches battened down tightly. But eventually, as battling for control proves ineffective, they grow discouraged and exhausted. They start to give up. They stop caring.

But you don't have to choose between fruitless struggles and sad surrender. You don't have to let the things that are overwhelming you in your life damage your ability to be a successful parent. This is one area where using the relationship approach pays particularly high dividends.

There's a simple two-step solution to the problem of feeling overwhelmed. Let's say it feels as though one of your kid's problems is the last straw.

First, try to relieve the pressure on yourself by giving as much of the problem as you can back to your kid. Your teenager's problem is only a burden if you put it on your own shoulders. When he forgets to do something important in his life, this is where you say, "There's nothing for me to scream about because this is his problem to solve. It doesn't have to make me upset unless I let it."

For this step to work, you have to convince yourself that in the overall scheme of things you can't let yourself go crazy. Sure, your kid's not doing as good a job as you could. But his doing a mediocre job is far better than your going crazy trying to do his job.

Take applying to college. Suppose you're harassed and burdened with a thousand and one things going on in your life. Even so, you're sure you could do a much better job of managing the application process than your sloppy, scatterbrained kid. But the real issue is whether it's worth the relationship-destroying anger and tension that come from your making him do his job when you're under a lot of pressure anyway.

All the evidence is that it's *not* worth it. No matter how much better you can do his job than he can, the damage to the relationship will seriously diminish your ability to be a positive influence on him later. The temptation to give yourself one more reason to feel overwhelmed can be strong, but you have to resist it.

Now for the second step. Use this step if the first hasn't worked for you. If you've given the problem back to your kid and he's dealt with it so poorly that you still feel burdened by it, the next step is to let him know the impact this has on you. "Look," you might say, "I know I shouldn't let it bother me, but every time I hear that you've flunked another test in college I just lie awake at night getting upset about it. So listen, if you don't want me to get upset, either don't flunk any more tests—or don't tell me if you do. If you have to, transfer to an easier college. But we have a relationship here, and we have to take care of each other. That means you have to take care of me sometimes."

Instead of solving the problem by either battling for control or giving up, you solve the problem by bringing it into the relationship and dealing with it as an issue of how two people can get their needs met.

"My kids are all I've got; I don't know what I'll do when they leave."

Few of the normal experiences of adulthood are sadder or more difficult for people to deal with than their kid's leaving home. All that caring and love you gave, all that time and attention—yet somehow your kid blithely walks out of your life, leaving a big hole. This makes some parents feel as if they've lost a loved one; they go through a period of mourning. For other parents there's a feeling of bitterness, as if they've somehow been ripped off. And for other parents there's a feeling of panic, as they wonder what to do with that huge empty part of their lives. Sometimes there are all of these feelings.

At the same time, it's also true that many parents feel relief, pride, and joy at their kid's leaving home. After all, the house is quiet again, you have more time, and you aren't always getting problems thrown at you. In addition, you feel good about the adult your kid has become. And if you've been smart, you've also done what you can to feel good about the relationship you have with your teenager.

The proportions of bad and good feelings vary from parent to parent. But for too many parents the sense of loss dominates. Let's look at how this works.

In the beginning, you saw bringing up a child as a hands-on job. You wanted to get in there and really do something: to care for someone, shape him, mold him, guide him. Then along comes adolescence with its message that your job is being phased out. In a way, this makes absolutely no sense. You didn't have a kid so you could not have a kid. You didn't take care of somebody so that you could stop taking care of him.

So the hidden message of adolescence feels like a huge betrayal. The only way to fight back is to pretend that nothing has changed. You decide that this getting-bigger stuff, looking-and-acting-like-an-adult stuff, this leaving-home stuff is just an illusion. It covers up the "real" child who still desperately needs you to be in charge. And thus is born the over-involved controlling parent that is part of us all. So also is born the teenager who can't wait to get away.

By the time a kid's in late adolescence, his parents are well into middle age, and their horizons don't feel quite as limitless as they might have once upon a time. But a teenager . . . now there's a source of new horizons. And new horizons mean new investments. Adolescence may actually seem like an ideal time for a parent to invest in his child.

"Hey, kid, make me a partner in your life and I'll help you go places," many parents seem to be saying to their teenagers. But, of course, any substantial investor wants more than just the privilege of giving unasked-for and unlistened-to advice. Let's face it, if you own a big enough piece of the action you want *control*.

But parenting a teenager has to do with psychology and relationships, and so things work differently than they do in business. They work backward, in fact. Instead of your investment giving you control as it does in business, with a teenager control gives you an investment—in the sense that your battling for control gives you the feeling that you're invested in your teenager. "That's *my* kid," parents say. As a result, parents try to increase their sense of control so they can increase their feeling of investment. In other words, the more a parent can make his kid do a bunch of things, the more he feels he's holding on to his kid.

The problem is that while *you* want control and investment, *your kid's* desperately trying to leave home. Your investment is in fact trying to run away. All the hours you put in, all the time you gave to your kid that you took away from yourself, all the pearls of wisdom you poured on his head, all the worry you endured . . . all this turns out to be for a kid who can't wait to say good-bye.

We all know what people say to the father of the bride: "You're not losing a daughter; you're gaining a son-in-law." Of course this is meant to cheer the father up, but it has an ironic, bittersweet quality. What son-in-law can make up for the loss of a daughter? So this line captures a kind of truth. You can't avoid the loss that's involved when a teenager leaves home, when the cute little kid who climbed into your bed on Sunday mornings turns into the adult who too often forgets to pick up the phone.

What turns loss into tragedy here is that while some loss is inevitable (because all kids leave home), the panic over this loss that drives parents to battle for control only makes their ultimate loss greater.

What's the solution?

The solution is to accept some loss as inevitable but then to cut down on the extent of the actual loss as much as possible. *That's what the relationship approach is for.* One of the best reasons to use the relationship approach is that the thirty- or forty-year relationship you have with your adult son or daughter is at least as important to both of you as what happens during the five thousand days of his or her adolescence.

With all its emphasis on helping your child leave home, the relationship approach is actually a recipe for minimizing your loss and maximizing your gain. While your adult child can never give you the passionate love or fill your life the way he did when he was little, he can be somebody you talk to and are close to. Both of you, in fact, can turn to each other for friendship—providing you're not still caught up in battling for control.

So the real comparison isn't between what you had when your kid was little and what you lose when he leaves home. It's between what you can have now and in the future if you mismanage your relationship with your teenager by battling for control and what you can have if you make that relationship the best it can be.

THE PROBLEM SOLVER

PART **4**

If You're Having Trouble Getting Along

12

Nobody's perfect. And we've found that even parents with terrific "people skills" feel they can do more to have better relationships with their teenagers. Why don't we get along better? they ask.

The issue probably isn't how skillful you are but the strange way teenagers have of making parents forget their skills. We've found that there are a few key things parents forget to do in their relationships with their teenagers. Doing them will help you break the patterns of anger and distance you've fallen into.

Show You Care

The problem: If you're like most parents, you take it for granted that your teenager knows you love her. But sadly, in day-to-day life, filled with fights about who failed to do what chores, nothing gets lost more easily than the feeling that you're loved. Instead of feeling loved, far too many teenagers take it for granted that their parents hate them.

The control approach makes this worse. As you battle for control—even though you're only doing so because you care—your teenager feels he's a constant target of your anger and disappointment. You're always making him feel that there's some other teenager you would prefer to have as your kid. When you say, "Why aren't you studying harder?" your teenager hears you saying, "You're not good enough." He thinks that you really care only about some ideal teenager, and that you'll kick him around until he becomes more like that ideal. So he feels all the more uncared for.

Parents often say, "But he should *know* that we say those things because we care. We're just trying to help him."

It doesn't matter. Teenagers still hear, "You're not good enough."

The solution that works: The simplest solution is to begin by assuming that your teenager feels *unloved* by you.

You don't have to feel guilty about this, you don't have to start buying him expensive presents, and you can keep on working at getting your needs met. You can still struggle about the things that are important to you. But while you're dealing with your teenager, recognize that making your kid feel loved is not something that you can do once, like putting a new roof on the house, and then forget about it. It's something you have to keep doing, like filling up the car's gas tank.

All that's required is for you to say clearly, directly, and often how much you like your kid. And explain why. Tell him what you particularly like; praise him for even small things he's done. Tell him you're glad he's your kid. Think about the ways he's a good kid and tell him about that. Tell him you love him.

And remember, sometimes the best way to make a teenager feel you care is just to listen to him.

You'll still get angry when he doesn't do his share of the household chores, and you'll still struggle with him to get him to do his share. Showing you care doesn't mean lying down for him. It's just something you add to everything else to make the relationship work.

Of course teenagers are all different and, just as important, they're trying hard to confound your expectations. So you have to realize that some of the ways you'll find to show your caring will backfire. "I hate it when you say that," he'll say in response to some loving remark you spent three days preparing to say to him.

Try not to let your feelings be hurt. All he's saying is, "I can never let you forget that I'm me, a separate person, and not someone you can take for granted." It's nothing personal. It's all part of his leaving home.

What you can say:

- "I really like it when you . . ."
- "You know, I feel really lucky to have you for a kid."
- "I feel really proud of you when . . ."
- "I really love you."
- "What can I do to show you how much I love you?"
- "You're a good kid, and I know you're under a lot of pressure, but you still can't leave the kitchen like that."
- "I'm annoyed that you screwed up, but I want you to know that I still really love you."

Prevent Miscommunication

The problem: Most people think that talk means communication the way summer means heat. But that's a mistake. Even in the best of relationships, screwed-up communications are as common as they are on a battlefield. In fact, miscommunication is *worse* in relationships, because although you expect snafus in wartime you don't when you're pouring your heart out to a loved one.

For example, your parents probably said things like the following to you: "You're going to really have to buckle down now." "You're too old for that kind of behavior now." "From now on it's your responsibility." "You have to respect your body." "You've got to get good grades." "Decide where you're going with your life." "If you keep up that way, you're going to end up in big trouble." "I want you to start coming home on time from now on."

Did you ever know exactly what statements like these meant and what to do about them? Probably not.

When you say things like these to your teenager, you may think you've spoken very clearly and that your kid knows exactly how you feel and what you want. "What do you *think* 'buckling down' means? It means buckling down," you say.

But your kid probably doesn't understand. And the reasons are probably not that he's stupid or obnoxious. It may be that he genuinely doesn't have a clue what your words mean. Or he doesn't know what you want him specifically to do. Or he's just not heard you. Or he doesn't know what to do about it. There are a million causes of miscommunication, and they'll all pop up in your relationship with your teenager.

But you know how teenagers are. They don't say, "Would you mind telling me precisely what you mean by that?" Instead, because they don't know what else you mean, they just hear the control in your voice and say, "Leave me alone."

The solution that works: If you have trouble getting what you want, assume first of all that you have not made yourself understood. And don't assume that your teenager has maliciously or stupidly failed to understand you. Perhaps *you've* been too vague, or too general, or too contradictory. Or perhaps you've omitted crucial parts of your message. Maybe you've said something one way but it's been heard in a completely different way.

If you focus on strengthening your relationship with your teenager, you can acknowledge the fact that you could be the one causing the problem. It's better to assume that your teenager is well-intentioned but doesn't understand you than that he's out to get you.

Tell your teenager what you want and how you feel as directly and simply as possible. If you think there's a problem, ask him what he's understood. You'll be amazed at how often teenagers misunderstand. If he didn't understand, don't repeat the same words. Keep using different words until he does understand. One of the best ways to improve communication is to talk to your teenager about how you're communicating and what can be done to make it better.

What you can say:

- "Help me with this. I'm trying to get my point across, but I don't seem to be making myself very clear."
- "What do you think I'm trying to say?"
- "Let me try to put what I'm saying in different words . . ."
- "What I am specifically asking you to do is . . ."

Treat Your Teenager the Way You'd Like to Be Treated

The problem: Let's say your teenager's sitting at the dinner table. His manners are more atrocious and his attitude is more sullen than usual. Naturally you're annoyed. So you snarl at him, "Sit up, for God's sake; stop shoveling food in your mouth, and change your damn attitude."

Now it makes sense that you'd want your kid to show some consideration toward you. You're entitled to consideration. But what many parents don't realize is that the best way to get consideration back, or to get any of the things you want from your teenager, is to treat him the way you would want to be treated.

Your teenager is a real live human being sitting there. You yourself might be a lousy dinner companion if you'd had a bad day or something were bothering you. And if you were being obnoxiously uncongenial, you wouldn't want to be snarled at; you'd either want to be ignored or to have people ask how you are.

You probably don't even know how your teenager feels, to say nothing about respecting how he feels. When you're angry, upset, or disappointed with your teenager, do you stop to ask yourself how he's feeling? When you need him to do something, do you stop to think about what he needs? No wonder teenagers don't feel their parents care about them.

Maybe—and this is teenagers' contribution to the tragedy of so many bad parent-teen relationships—he can't tell you how he feels; he may not even know. Sometimes teenagers are just angry and miserable for no reason whatsoever. They can be so inarticulate that even if they know why they're upset they may not be able to put it into words. And they can behave so obnoxiously that you think they're just awful people.

You don't have to tolerate an obnoxious teenager. But it's easy for you to get so wrapped up in your problems and your feelings that your kid becomes invisible, you don't take into account his feelings and needs, and you fail to pay attention to how he's going to take whatever it is you're saying or doing. And all that does is make things worse.

The solution that works: Treating your teenager the way you would like to be treated has more to do with smart politics than with morality. Ask yourself how you would feel if you were sitting there, angry and miserable, and your parent said, "Sit up and stop acting like a jerk." Would that work with you? Regardless of its effect on your posture, what would it do for your mood? Would it make you start acting like the ideal social companion, or would it make you sour and resentful?

The politics of relationships are that everyone's keeping count in their heads of "fairness." And everyone's count is a little biased because people are naturally more aware of the unfairness they receive than the unfairness they give. You can make this work for you, because if you increase the extent to which you're fair to your teenager, you'll create a strong pressure inside him to be fair in return.

Try to put yourself in your kid's shoes. Think about the details of his situation. Think about how you would feel in that situation. It's not good politics to do anything else. In other words, before you yell at your kid for coming home with a bad report card, ask yourself how you would have liked to have been treated when you were a kid coming home with a bad report card.

It can particularly be effective to ask your teenager what would work with him. When he does something that makes you angry or disappointed, for example, ask him how he'd like you to respond. He might say something like, "Look, I really don't need you to yell at me right now." If you go along with that, you'll strengthen your influence with your teenager enormously. His gratitude for being respected can only increase his desire to cooperate.

Remember, you can still get your needs met. Some parents resist treating their teenager the way they'd like to be treated because they think what we're saying is "Be nice no matter what. Always let your teenager off the hook."

We're not saying that at all. There are plenty of ways for you to get your needs met and deal with your concerns. And if you have a good relationship with your teenager, the simplest and best way is to ask for what you want and say how you feel.

But getting what you want must always rest on a foundation of treating your teenager the way you'd want to be treated.

What you can say:

- "How would you like me to respond to this?"
- "What do you need from me?"
- "You seem very unhappy. Is there anything I can do?"
- "If you were in my shoes, how would you handle this?"

When You Talk . . .

- Think about what you want to make happen by the end of the conversation.
- Organize what you say around that goal.

The problem: It's paradoxical, but while parents often feel helpless, they make things worse by failing to have a clear goal in mind when they talk to their teenagers. Parents either don't know what they want or they don't think of a direct way to get it.

Here's an example of how this works. Your twenty-three-year-old college graduate has been living on his own and you've been hearing disturbing things about his crazy and irresponsible life-style. Now you're expecting him to come home for Thanksgiving. Over and over you keep saying, "I've got to talk to him about the way he's living. I've got to tell him that he's headed for trouble."

The problem with this is that you've started at the wrong place. You've started with how you feel—"I hate the way he's living"—and what you want to say—"You're heading for trouble"—instead of how you want things to be *when all the talking's over*. It may sound logical: you start at the beginning with what you want to say and work toward the end. But the result is too often a huge and disappointing fight. Imagine that your vacation plans revolved around getting to the airport rather than where you wanted to fly to and what you wanted to do when you got there—you could spend your vacation stuck at the airport.

The solution that works: When you think about talking to your teenager, work backward! Start from what you want at the end.

If you're upset about the way your kid is living now that he's graduated from college, for example, first determine what you want at the end of a talk. His total conversion from being a messy, lazy, party animal to being Mr. Responsible? A tearful confession of the error of his ways? A feeble promise to do better? A halfhearted admission that you're right?

Play with the alternatives until you come up with what you'll accept—which will probably be some kind of compromise between what you really want and what you think you can get. Keep thinking about this until you're sure that what you're trying to make happen is realistic and will satisfy you.

Then, still working backward, ask yourself, "How can I get him to do [or say] that?" Don't do or say anything until you have a clear and realistic idea of how you're going to get what you want.

Let's say you're angry with your fourteen-year-old for coming home late. What do you want to have for yourself *after* all the talking's over? Do you want your teenager to understand how angry you are? Do you want him to apologize? To change his behavior? It's most likely that your initial unthinking actions will get you just what you *don't* want. The clearer you are about what you want at the end, the more likely a clear strategy for getting it will emerge.

And once you've put yourself on the right track, don't let your teenager knock you off it. Teenagers are masters of distraction. When you say, "Listen to me," they say, "What do you know?"—and the next thing that happens is that you're explaining what you know and how you know it instead of what you intended to say. So stay focused. You can always say, when they interrupt or distract, "If that's important to you, remember it or write it down, and I promise you we'll deal with it later. But right now what we're talking about is . . ."

What you can say:

- "What I'd like to have happen by the end of our talk is that you'll know how I feel about . . . You don't have to change anything or even agree with me."
- "I just can't cope any longer with . . . unless you do more to help. What I want to have by the end of our talk is some kind of solid agreement that will work."
- "I've felt really out of touch with you since . . . Let's go out for lunch, and hopefully by the end of an hour we'll know more about what each other has been doing. And we'll feel closer."

Let Your Teenager Know How to Take What You're Doing and Saying

The problem: Here we go again. Another opportunity for misunderstanding. More times than you can imagine, you think you're doing one thing, but your teenager thinks you're doing something else:

- You're "helping"—but you're also yelling, and so what your teenager thinks you're doing is "just getting mad."
- You're "worried" and you talk to your teenager about

his "problem"—but what he hears is that something is wrong with him, that he's defective.

- You're just "setting limits"—but you do it in the form of a punishment, and so your teenager thinks you don't really care about him, that you're just trying to get even.

In each of these cases, you do or say something that you want him to take in a certain way, but your teenager is sure that you're saying something very different. And to make matters worse, the two of you don't even know that you're on completely different levels.

The solution that works: We're not saying you have to send a telegram or hire a sign painter. We *are* saying that when you deal with your teenager you have to find a way to put some kind of label on or frame around what you're doing and saying, in addition to just doing and saying it.

If, for example, you're yelling at your kid because she seems obsessed with dieting and refuses to eat healthy food, you'll be much more effective if you also say, "Look, I feel you're hurting yourself. I'm yelling because I don't know how else to get through to you. But all my yelling means is that I really care." Then your teenager will know how to take what you're saying.

This is a solution that some parents say feels artificial and unrealistic. "What? Before I say anything I have to say, 'The way I want you take what I'm about to say is . . . '? Give me a break. I have to feel comfortable with my own kid. I can't watch every word."

But what's wrong with making sure your message gets heard the way you want it to be heard? What's "natural" about you and your teenager getting into incredible tangles because he doesn't know where you're coming from? Parents want this mutual understanding to happen automatically, but lots of things that are "natural" aren't automatic. You have to make them happen. This is one of them.

What you can say:

- "This is really important to me and I hope you'll pay a lot of attention to what I say."

- "I need you to hear me without making a big deal of it."
- "This is how I want you to understand what I'm doing . . ."
- "I know I've been bugging you a lot about doing your homework, but I remember how I felt when I didn't get into any of the colleges I wanted to go to and I don't want that to happen to you."*
- "I know I seem awfully worried about your problem and I always talk to you about it, so I want to make it clear to you that there's nothing wrong with *you*. *You're* fine even though you have that problem."
- "I know that my taking the use of the car away from you seems like a punishment, like I'm just being mean. But you've been driving very irresponsibly, and this is the only way I know to get the point across that this is a very serious matter."
- "This is how I want you to take this."

Reward Good Behavior Instead of Punishing Bad Behavior

The problem: We've never had a parent ask us, "What should I do when my kid does something right?" Most parents are punishment- and problem-oriented—they always ask us, "What should we do when our teenager screws up?"

This is natural. Most human beings notice things only when they don't work. When you're watching TV, you don't notice the set if it's working. You're just aware of the program.

In the same way, it's all too easy *not* to notice the times when your teenager is cooperative, responsible, and productive. It's not even that you want to ignore those times, but that usually you're not even aware of them. And on top of

---

*Of course your teenager will very possibly say, "Yeah, but I'm not you." All you need to say in response is, "Sometimes it's hard for me to remember that, but at least you know where I'm coming from when I bug you."

not being aware of them, many parents feel that there's something wrong with praising a kid for what he's supposed to do in the first place.

Some parents even think this praise is harmful. They feel that if you praise a kid for doing what he should be doing in the first place, then instead of taking it for granted that he should behave well he'll start thinking good behavior is something special. They're afraid he might even start refusing to behave well unless he's praised.

The solution that works: Since there are so many things the experts don't agree on, when they do agree it's worth paying attention. And one of the things experts are most agreed on is that rewarding good behavior makes more learning happen faster than punishing bad behavior.

What this means for you is very simple. During the five thousand days of adolescence your kid is going to do a lot of things right and a lot of things wrong. If you want to be effective in getting your needs met, if you want to be successful in having some influence over him, then *orient yourself toward searching for and praising good behavior and away from reacting to bad behavior.*

Obviously, there's no point in praising behavior that's already automatic. You praise a two-year-old for using the toilet, not a five-year-old. You praise a five-year-old for dressing himself, not a teenager. And if your teenager has had consistently good table manners, then there's no point in suddenly going out of your way to praise him for it, although any teenager will benefit from hearing you mention your appreciation once in a while.

Where praising your teenager becomes critical is at the cutting edge of improvements in your kid's behavior, when you see things that need to change. At that point emphasizing reward instead of punishment becomes vital. It's in the areas where he's most imperfect that praise is most important.

Here's an example. Let's say your teenager has been coming home late and driving you crazy with worry. You're not trying to control when he comes home, you just want to know when to expect him. Now comes the crucial incident. Your high school junior who drives has said he'd be home by five o'clock. Now it's almost six and you haven't heard from him. Suddenly the phone rings and there he is telling you he's sorry he didn't call, he lost track of time, and he's calling now so you shouldn't worry, and he'll be home in a few minutes.

What do you do?

Most parents would inadvertently punish by saying something like, "Why didn't you call sooner? Do you know how worried I was? Why can't you be more responsible? I really wonder if you're mature enough to take the car to school." When your teenager hangs up, his friends ask, "What did your parents say?" And his answer is, "Oh, they yelled at me."

Now this parental reaction is understandable; after all, you were worried and angry. But worry plus anger rarely equals effectiveness. If anything, your kid is congratulating himself on toughing out being yelled at.

To respond more effectively, find the good behavior and reward that. When your kid calls, you think to yourself, "On the one hand, I'm mad as hell that he didn't call sooner. And I really don't feel like rewarding him for calling late. There was no excuse for his not calling when he knew he wouldn't be home by five. On the other hand, *he did call,* and that's what I'm trying to get him to do. And his calling was certainly better than not calling. And it's calling that I want to encourage. And I remember that it's better to reward instead of punish."

So what you say to your teenager in this situation is something like, "I'm so glad you called. I was really worried but now I feel much better. It's always better when you call. Next time I'd appreciate it if you called as soon as you knew you were going to be late. But I'm really glad you called now."

Now your teenager can say to himself it's not a hassle to call home and say you're going to be late; in fact it's easy, and it's really only fair, and it's a lot better than getting into trouble for not calling. In other words, *you've made it much more likely that he'll call next time.*

Going from thinking in terms of punishment to thinking in terms of reward is a real shift. It means you often have to go against your spontaneous feelings and against your image of yourself as "tough." But if you want to be successful, you must make that shift.

You can use the technique of rewarding instead of punishing in every aspect of your kid's life. If your kid hasn't been doing well in school, then praise him if he brings home a report card showing he's done better in one subject, even if he's done worse in other subjects. If your kid's been uncommunicative around the house, then appreciate him if he tells you something, even if what he tells you is trivial.

Many parents are ready to burst at this point. "What about my anger, my disappointment?" they ask. You're definitely entitled to let your kid know how you feel. That's why you have to work hard to have a good relationship with your teenager. The better that relationship, the easier it is for you to find a time and place to tell your kid how you feel and the easier it is for your kid to hear you.

But praise him first. Later, after he's been rewarded and you've cooled down a bit, you can talk about how angry and worried you were. Then the discussion of your anger and worry becomes not a punishment but a problem the two of you are trying to solve together.

The point of this isn't to take your feelings away from you. Instead, we're trying to show you how you can reschedule when and how you express your feelings. If you praise the good behavior first and present your negative feelings in the context of problem solving second, then you will be successful at getting your needs met in the end.

You can even use this technique to encourage *behavior that has never yet existed in your teenager.*[*]

For example, suppose you think your teenager is lazy. In fact, you're sure your teenager has never been anything but lazy. Trying to control him, trying to make him want and need to be hardworking only calls forth resistance.

Instead, even though he's still not showing you any hard-

---

[*]We are indebted for this idea to Adele Faber and Elaine Mazlish's *Liberated Parents, Liberated Children* (New York: Avon, 1976).

working behavior, praise any behavior that seems even slightly less lazy than is usual for him. For instance, suppose your kid did a slapdash job of washing your car. But he washed it. You can say something like, "I appreciate your really working at washing the car," even though that's not strictly true. This won't give your teenager a swelled head. What it will do is make him feel good about working hard. And it will take him one step closer to changing his self-image from someone who is lazy to someone who works hard.

If you praise nonexistent behavior, you'll eventually change the way he acts precisely because you'll be changing your teenager's self-image. Parents have used this to turn their teenagers from being lazy to being hardworking, from being rude to being polite, from being selfish to being classy, from being sullen to being communicative.

If you're impatient, think about it this way. Suppose you had a headache, a really bad head-throbber. You might take some aspirin. Then what? Most people know that aspirin takes time to work. So you'd wait a couple of hours before you took any further remedies.

But imagine what would happen if those first two aspirins didn't immediately cure your headache and you just kept on taking more and more without waiting, thinking that you'd keep taking them until your headache went away. You'd probably get very sick from aspirin overdose, be very likely to suffer permanent damage, and quite possibly die. All because you could not wait for those first two aspirins to take effect.

No, your teenager won't change immediately. And his not changing often looks like resistance. But don't react to your teenager with the equivalent of popping aspirins until the headache is gone by yelling, complaining, demanding, blaming, and threatening in an effort to get your kid to change faster.

This is a terrible mistake. Teenagers must be given their own time. The reason your teenager may not be changing as quickly as you'd like could be immaturity: maybe your teenager is not ready to make the change you want. Or it could be part of his job of leaving home: if you're going to demand a change, he may be demanding the autonomy of making that change at his own pace.

What you can say:

- "I really appreciate your calling to say you're going to be late."
- "I think it's great that you always try to look good."
- "I'm so happy to see you studying."
- "I'm really impressed by how well you take care of yourself."
- "I think what you're saying is really interesting."
- "I know it was hard for you, but I can see you really tried."

Understand Your Teenager's Language

The problem: Actually there are two problems: when you don't understand your teenager, and when you think you understand your teenager but don't. Sadly, those two problems can cover a lot of territory. What they have in common is that they leave you feeling angry, hurt, or uncomfortable.

Parents really feel assaulted by many of the things their kids seem to communicate. They assume their teenagers *intend* them to feel bad. And, because they are feeling assaulted, parents naturally either want to withdraw or to strike back. This is really a tragedy, because most of the time, when your teenager's communication makes you feel bad, that bad feeling is the result of a misunderstanding.

The fact is that a lot of teen communication has one purpose, which is to help him do his job of getting ready to leave home. Teen talk is really intended to accomplish a very small number of perfectly natural and understandable goals. The misunderstanding happens because parents hear rude, obnoxious words instead of those goals.

The solution that works: Next time your kid says something you find upsetting, instead of blowing up or breaking down,

translate. Assume that your teenager is trying to do something positive for his own growth and that, sadly, he's doing
it in a way you don't like. If you want to deal with the *way*
your teenager is communicating, it will help if you first deal
with *what* he's communicating. To figure that out and to
translate *from* his unpleasant words *to* his buried message,
you have to take what your teenager says and guess which of
five possible goals he's trying to accomplish.

Here are the five goals your teenager's probably trying to
accomplish:

- *Setting boundaries.* This involves teenagers asserting
  their right to take one more step toward independence—
  and to take away from you one more thing you used to
  be in charge of.
- *Asserting uniqueness.* Teenagers doing this are saying as
  strongly as they know how that they're not the way you
  want them to be, or the way you think they are, or even
  the way they used to be. Instead, they are now a special,
  undefinable, never-before-seen form of human being,
  and you'd better get used to it.
- *Claiming the freedom to choose.* To a teenager, the spe-
  cifics—the risks and costs—are not the issue. The only
  issue is that a decision is their choice alone. Anything
  that threatens their right to choose is a threat to selfhood
  and independence.
- *Expressing negative feelings.* When teenagers sound negative, it's important to keep two things in mind. One is
  that teenagers really do have frequent and deep bad
  feelings.* They may recover from their negativity
  quickly, but while they're in this state their freedom and
  uniqueness (see above) give them the right (they think)

---

*They also have frequent and extreme good feelings. It's normal for teenagers to
be moody from time to time, but normal teenagers *on average* feel OK. What
research shows is that teenagers feel their good feelings most often with their friends,
while parents are privileged to witness and even be the recipients of more than
their share of teenagers' bad feelings. But it's a mistake for parents to infer from
the bad moods they see that the overall proportion of bad moods their teenagers
actually feel is high.

to express their feelings. The other thing to remember is that they need something but have a difficult time asking for what they need and sometimes even knowing what they need.

- *Engaging in map making.* It may be your teenager has just said something very stupid or mentioned a hare-brained and scary plan. Rather than thinking he's doomed or defective, try to understand that assertions like these are part of your kid's figuring out how the world is put together.

There's no magic formula for matching what your kid communicates with the proper item on this list. You'll just have to play it by ear. But the good news is that you don't have to worry about getting the "right" answer. Most of the things teenagers communicate are intended to accomplish more than one of the things on the list. Whatever you guess will probably be close enough to the truth.

Now let's say your teenager has said something really obnoxious, but you've retained enough presence of mind to figure out that he's probably doing something like setting a boundary. You already know that taking what he said personally and getting hurt or angry is a mistake. Now all you have to do is accept his basic right to do whatever it is you guess he was really doing.

If you think he was setting a boundary, then support his right to do that. If you think he was asserting his uniqueness, then support his right to do *that*. Notice—you don't have to agree with either his content ("I can take the car whenever I want" or "I don't need to go to school anymore") or his tone (sullen or hostile). You just have to support his right to do his job of accomplishing his goal.

What that means is this. Take what you guess his real message is—boundaries, uniqueness, whatever—and talk about that. If you want your talking to be successful, make sure you begin by letting him know, for example, that you respect his right to assert boundaries. It's not easy to do this. You have to walk a fine line between taking care of your needs on the one hand, and, on the other, letting him know that he has a right to want what he wants (if not necessarily to get it).

What you can say:

- (If your teenager's setting a boundary): "I support your right to negotiate a new agreement about which one of us is in charge of this. Let's talk about it."
- (If your teenager's asserting his uniqueness): "If that's the way you'd like me to see you, then I'll be happy to see you that way. But there are also some things I feel we have to talk about."
- (If your teenager's claiming the freedom to choose): "Listen, of course you've got the ability to choose to do what you want."
- (If your teenager's expressing negative feelings): "It sounds like you feel awful. If you want me to listen, I'll be happy to. If you want me to leave you alone, that's OK too. And if there's something you need from me, tell me what it is. What's not OK is for you to just dump on me."
- (If your teenager's engaging in map making): "I hear you telling me this is the way you see things. Now what do you want? Do you just want me to know how you see things? Do you want to have a discussion about how I see things? Either way is fine with me."

So when you're having trouble getting along with your teenager, remember to:

- Show you care by letting your teenager know you love her and by telling her the specific ways you feel good about her.
- Prevent miscommunication by making sure your teenager really understands precisely what you want from her.
- Treat your teenager the way you'd like to be treated by making sure you understand how he feels before you criticize or make a demand.
- Organize what you say to your teenager around what

you want to have for yourself when the two of you are finished talking. Do this by beginning your talk with a clear goal in mind and making sure you keep your goal in sight while you're talking.

- Let your teenager know how to take what you're doing and saying by actually telling him your intentions and goals.
- Reward good behavior by paying attention to the times your teenager does things the way you'd like and by praising him for those things.
- Understand what your teenager is really saying to you by figuring out his underlying message, and then make sure you respond to that message.

How to Think about Rules and Punishments

13

Parents ask more questions about rules and punishments than about almost any other area. It's almost as if parents feel that if they could just master some secret code of rules and punishments, they'd have nearly magic powers of control over their teenagers. So parents often ask us questions like these:

- "Should we tell him that he can't have an after-school job if he gets poor grades?"
- "Should we forbid her from getting her ears double-pierced until she's eighteen?"
- "What should the rules be about who his friends are?"
- "Should I tell him that I'll throw him out of the house if I catch him doing drugs?"
- "She's always fighting with her sister over clothes. Should we make a rule that they can't go into each other's closets and take the other's clothes?"

And then parents want to know what to do about punishing their teenagers when they break a rule:

- "If I don't make the punishment strict enough, they don't respect the rule. But if I make it too strict I can't enforce it. What do I do?"
- "What kinds of punishment should I use with my teenager when she breaks a rule?"

What's really going on here? First, a lot of talk about rules and punishments is really a back-door way of talking about control, because parents control by making rules and punishments. But you already know the control approach doesn't work and that there are much more effective ways to deal with your needs and concerns than acting as legislator, judge, jury, and jailer.

And second, a lot of the questions parents have about rules are really questions about when teenagers are ready for certain privileges and activities. A question about whether a teenager should be allowed to go steady is in effect a question about how old a kid should be before it's safe to allow her to go steady. The same goes for many other kinds of rules, like going out on school nights, being home by a certain time, and having an after-school job.

As we said earlier, there is no book you can consult for definitive answers to these questions. In one sense this makes it hard for you because you never know for sure that you're doing the right thing. But in another sense the fact that there's no official Timetable for Teenagers is a very good thing. It means that instead of issues being decided by appeal to authority ("You have to do it because it says so in the book," or "This is the rule because I know it's right"), these issues have to be worked out between you and your teenager. You have to make agreements.

But while control doesn't work, it's certainly useful for you and your teenager to know what to expect from each other. We wrote this chapter to help you get the good things you want from rules and punishments—clarity, consistency, and predictability—without any harmful side effects. Here's what to do.

Think about Making Agreements Instead of Rules

There you are, a person and a parent with needs and feelings. This means there are things you want for yourself and things you're afraid of for your teenager. These can range from wanting polite dinner conversation to being afraid of your kid killing himself because he was driving drunk.

What do you do about all this?

If you want to lay down the law, you can. You're the parent. But if you want to do something that works, then the really effective way to solve problems, the way guaranteed to maximize your kid's cooperation instead of his resistance, is for you and your teenager to work together in hammering out agreements. Agreements are the guaranteed-to-succeed alternative to rules.

A rule says, "You have to do this." An agreement says, "Because of such-and-such, you agree to do this and I agree to do that." For example, a rule says, "These are your chores." An agreement says, "Because of all the different responsibilities people in this family have, we all agree it's fair if we divide up the chores this way." Notice: your kid still ends up having to take out the garbage.

Here's why agreements work. Rules are based on your unilateral decision about what's best. The problem is, first, that your decision might be wrong because you've made it in isolation and, second, that by making it in isolation you've failed to enlist your teenager's cooperation. But since your decision is going to have an impact on your teenager, he must be included in the process. The more he's included, the more information you'll have to assure your agreement is the best one, and the more cooperation you'll have to assure your agreement is maintained. By going through the process of making an agreement, your teenager will feel better about the agreement and is much more likely to keep to it.

So when you're making an agreement, you'll know it will be a good one and will work if you base it on talking to your teenager about things like

- Your needs and your teenager's needs
- Your sense and your kid's sense of who he is and what he's ready for
- Your values and your teenager's values
- Your fears and your teenager's fears
- How you live, where you live, and the things your kid's friends do
- What you and your teenager want to make happen

You won't know the answers to all these questions in advance. That's why you have to talk about them with your teenager. That's why making agreements is a process of discovery and gives you a sense of working together, a sense of sharing a joint project.

Agreements work because your teenager buys into an agreement. He has some ownership of it. He cares about it.

For example, if it's important to you that your thirteen-year-old not wear makeup to school, then to make an agreement you tell her why her not wearing makeup is important to you, and you try to get her to understand and accept your reasons. You say things to her like "Can you understand why it's important to me that . . . ?" You also listen to her telling you why she wants to wear makeup to school—in a spirit of caring and curiosity rather than of searching for facts you can use against her.

Then you work out an agreement acceptable to both of you, like "OK, you agree not to wear makeup to school for now and I agree that once you turn sixteen you can wear any kind of makeup you want and I won't bug you about it," or "All right, you won't wear makeup to school but I agree you can wear makeup around the house and when you go to parties," or "I agree you're old enough to start wearing makeup and you agree you're old enough to start doing your own laundry."

It doesn't matter what the specific agreement is. Remember, there's no book where you can look up where you should be giving in and where you should be holding firm. The important thing is that the agreement be acceptable to both of you.

There are rare situations in which trying to come up with an agreement isn't appropriate because your kid is too young or the issue is too serious. For example, you might make the rule that your eleven-year-old is too young to ride a minibike or that your teenager can't skate on the pond until the fire department has said the ice is safe. All you can do in these cases is make a rule.

But even in these cases, what's critical for making the rule work is that you talk to your teenager just the way you would have if you were coming to an agreement. That way, he will understand your reasons and will know that you're at least aware of how he feels and what's important to him.

We feel very strongly that almost every issue with a teenager should be an agreement instead of a rule. Throughout your kid's entire adolescence you should probably have no more than a handful of rules. Make more than that and it's likely that what you are really doing is trying to take control over things that are uncontrollable.

And even with the very most serious issue, you can turn rule making into agreement making. Take drinking and driving. Rules here are setups for evasion. But an agreement in this life-and-death area could go something like this. Your kid agrees not to drink and drive. You agree to pay for cab fare or to come pick him up yourself wherever he is even if he's had the car and has ended up drinking. And you agree to do this without getting mad and no matter what time he calls. With an agreement like this your kid has no incentive to drive home drunk in the hope of not getting caught.

In a situation like drinking and driving, the distinction between rule making and agreement making can seem subtle. After all, you don't have a lot of room to compromise about your kid driving drunk. But in practice the distinction isn't subtle at all. Even a simple question like "How does that sound to you?" or the magic question "What do *you* need, to give me what *I* need?" can turn an arbitrary-seeming, resistance-evoking rule into an agreement-making process that evokes trust and cooperation.

If it should happen to be one of those rare times in your

kid's adolescence where you feel you have to make a rule, you could say something along the lines of what Mary said to her fourteen-year-old son, Tim:

> I know how much it means to you to get a job. But this is just one of those times where I have to say no. You know I don't go around always telling you you can't do things, but this is different. It's not like I can prove to you that it's a bad idea. For all I know you're right and I'm wrong. But you've told me that school is important to you and I take you seriously. I just don't see how you'll have time to do well in school and do all the other things you want and have a job too. I know there are times when I should just let you learn from your own mistakes, but this doesn't seem one of them. Next year, we'll look at how you've done in school and think through this issue all over again.

As you can tell, this mother had gone through a process with her son before she reached this point. And it's this process that's important. You may never know for sure whether you made the right rule, but you can know for sure that you made that rule in the right way.

Only Push for Agreements You Can Enforce

"You're forbidden to wear makeup to school," a parent says to her thirteen-year-old. "You're forbidden to do any drugs while you're away at college," another parent says to his twenty-year-old son. The object, of course, is to get control over a kid's life that seems to be rapidly spinning out of parental control. But doing it this way is a mistake.

It's useful to think of your total influence over your teenager as something finite, like having a hundred strongmen, no more, no less, at your command. If you send them out to do a hundred different tasks, particularly tasks that are impossible for even strongmen to accomplish, then you're wasting your strongmen. But if use them in carefully chosen tasks on which they will be able to work together to use their strength effectively, then your own sense of power will be much greater than when their effort was wasted.

It's the same with agreements and rules. If there are too many rules about things you can't enforce, you're wasting your influence. And the end product is a tense parent-teen relationship and, ultimately, your kid's sense that his parent is a joke. After all, it's both futile and ridiculous to try to control things you really don't have any control over.

This guideline becomes all the more important when you think of some of the less obvious things that are very difficult to enforce. Take table manners. It's easy to say that you have rules about having good table manners: "Our rule is that you have to leave the table if you don't eat politely." But what if your kid only does something slightly impolite? Or is impolite by mistake or accident? What if your kid is impolite when you're about to have a very important dinner-table conversation you need him to be there for?

Making a rule is one thing, but making it work in the real world is something very, very different, even when your kid is sitting right in front of you. That's why before you even think of asking for something, you need to consider carefully how you would enforce it under the real, day-to-day conditions of your lives.

When parents start thinking carefully about how few things they can truly enforce, it's easy for them to get discouraged. Fortunately, there is something that will make you feel much better. That's the next guideline.

Struggle Only about What's Most Important to You

Want a recipe for going crazy? Struggle about everything.

Many parents fail to make crucial distinctions about which is most important: whether their kid takes out the garbage, gets good grades, or avoids using drugs. They try to have control over all these areas, and what gets fought over depends only on what comes up in the moment.

Effective parents think about this in a radically different way. Effective parents have some sense of how much more important the drug problem is than the grade problem and how much more important the grade problem is than the taking-out-the-garbage problem. Then they use their energies appropriately. If they think the drug problem is ten times more important than the grade problem, they put ten times the attention and time and energy into dealing with the drug problem than into the grade problem. The same for the grade problem and the garbage problem.

Of course, how important a problem is for you doesn't only depend on how damaging it is; whether your kid gets hooked on cocaine is *always* more important than whether he gets good grades. But your particular teenager may not be at much risk of using drugs, and he might be in serious danger of having to repeat a year of high school. So when you weigh the importance of problems, you also have to factor in the immediate risk to your kid.

Here are examples of things so important to parents that they struggle with their teenagers about them:

• Using birth control if a teenager is sexually active
• Hanging out with kids who are using drugs
• Having parties in the house when the parents are away

The fact that you take a firm stand on only your top priorities gives the message that you know what's important. And it's much easier for your kid to respect you and cooperate with you when your priorities are so clearly focused.

What's to prevent your kid from violating agreements? Most parents are convinced that they are in a weakened position if they don't have the threat of real punishments available. And yet as teenagers get older it gets harder and harder to punish them. What's the solution?

Think in Terms of Consequences, Not Punishments

"OK, that's it. You're grounded!"

Now you've got him, right? He's sure going to think twice next time.

Well, maybe. But probably not. Punishments usually don't work. You can impose them all right, or try to, but then what? The average teenager isn't frightened by most of the punishments you can threaten him with. If you do find a way to punish him, nine times out of ten his response is a determination not to get caught again rather than a decision not to commit the crime again.

And why waste your time with punishments when you have something that will make you much more effective? Adults live in a world of consequences, not punishments. Sure, if you rob a bank, you go to jail. But much more important for most adults is the fact that decisions have consequences, not that crimes have punishments. If you just do an OK job at the office, what's important isn't that you're going to be punished but that you're unlikely to advance.

For you to be successful as a parent, all you have to do is communicate about consequences rather than pushing punishments. Here's an example of how effective it can be to talk about consequences. The great young jazz trumpeter Wynton Marsalis was asked if his parents made him practice. What the questioner was getting at was whether the threat of punishment was necessary to turn out a musician of Marsalis's great technical ability.

Marsalis said no, he was never made to practice. Instead, his parents simply made it clear to him that the consequence of rarely practicing would be poor technique and that being a great player required long hours of practicing. Once he was aware of the consequences, he made the decision that was right for him.

When you talk to your teenager about consequences, you cut down on the number of agreements you have to make (remember the importance of limiting the number of things you struggle over?). This is particularly true for parts of your teenager's life that don't directly affect you. Take grades. After you've made it clear that not studying leads to poor grades and poor grades lead to fewer options in life, there's not a lot more you can do. Your teenager's level of ability, motivation, and maturity will do the rest.

Information is one of the best ways to get your teenager to begin to think and act the way you would like. And no kind of information is more important than knowing about consequences.

And what if your teenager does break an agreement? Translate your thinking about punishments into thinking about consequences. Think less about what you'll do to him if he screws up than about what inevitably will happen if he screws up.

For example, if your teenager has agreed to be home by a certain time but instead comes home an hour late, the natural consequence is a decrease in your ability to trust him. And so the price he should pay for failing to keep to the agreement should have something directly to do with that natural consequence of your losing some trust in him. You didn't have to impose that loss of trust; it happened by itself.

Grounding your kid (to take one very common punishment) probably has nothing to do with the natural consequences of his coming home later than he agreed. Grounding is just a way for you to try to use your power. When, for example, your kid fails to keep his agreement to come home at a certain time, it's much more effective to say something like "Look, I really trusted you to be home by one and you didn't come home until almost two. That really hurt my ability to trust you. You're going to have to work to regain my trust. I think next time you ask to borrow the car and you say you'll be home in plenty of time for me to use the car to go shopping, it's going to be harder for me to trust you and more likely that I won't let you."

When he does ask to borrow the car, it's important to say, "Look, I'm sorry. Maybe at some point in the future I'll let you borrow it when I'm feeling more trusting. But you have to rebuild my trust first."

That's living in the world of consequences instead of punishments. Not only is this more effective in getting your needs met and influencing your kid's behavior, it actually strengthens your relationship with your teenager. And the more you and your teenager build up a sense of being able to rely on each other, the closer you'll feel and the stronger will be the bonds between you.

Have a Trial Period during Which You See How the Agreement Works

Agreements are easier to make than to live with. Often an agreement gets made, it's soon violated, there's a big fight, parent and teen feel betrayed, confused, and upset—and the next thing you know the agreement's been abandoned and parent and teen go back to angry battling for control.

In the real world, every time you make an agreement, you are entering virgin territory. You can *hope* things turn out a certain way, but you can't *know* how they'll turn out. In fact, if anything's predictable it's that surprises are in store for you.

For example, Mary, who told her fourteen-year-old son, Tim, that he could not have an after-school job, made an agreement with him a year later that he could have an after-school job as long as it didn't interfere with his schoolwork. Tim duly promised he'd be home by six every day and start his homework by seven, "Which is when I've always started it anyway," he said. The agreement was that he'd quit the job if his school work suffered.

Within the first week it was clear that Tim wasn't spending as much time studying as he'd done before. Deciding she had to take control of the situation, Mary insisted Tim quit his job. Tim was furious. In the end, both mother and son felt betrayed.

If instead they'd accepted the fact that the first week was just a trial period, then they would have been able to tinker with the agreement to make it better. The original agreement had been too all-or-nothing. What did it mean that Tim was spending less time on his homework? Was this just a temporary adjustment until he got used to the job? Was the job making him more mature so he could use his studying time more effectively? Was the problem that he just needed to work an hour less on the job every day?

Mary and Tim could have found all this out and strengthened their relationship at the same time if they'd only built in a way of evaluating their agreement as time went on. The way to do this is simple. You just have to remember to say something about evaluating when you make your agreements. Don't enter into an agreement until you know how you'll evaluate it.

For example, some agreements take time before you find out how they're working. So you set aside a specific time period. Other agreements require a specific event, such as a kid's report card, before you find out how they're working. With these, the event marks the time for evaluation.

The point is that no agreement is final until you've given yourselves a chance to see how it works and, if necessary, a chance to revise it.

When Your Teenager Disappoints You

OK, it's happened.

You've just found out your teenager has done something really dumb or has behaved badly or has gotten into trouble. We're not talking about "noble failures" like your teenager not making the Olympic gymnastic squad in spite of trying very hard. Instead we're talking about situations where he has just screwed up, where he's either broken an agreement or disappointed an expectation of yours. For example:

- He's gotten fired from his part-time job at McDonald's for goofing off.
- She has three F's on her report card for the second semester of her junior year in high school, perhaps the

single most important semester so far. And it turns out she just didn't do any work in these courses.

- He has just been arrested for shoplifting. You find out this is his third offense.
- She tells you she's pregnant. She was fully informed about birth control and yet she took no precautions. She's far too young to have a baby.

What should you do?

Your first step should be to make your immediate response as nondestructive as possible. Unless you stop yourself, you'll probably say and do things you'll later regret. You feel punished and threatened by what your kid has done, and it's easy to say things that will hurt your teenager. At this point, any parent's sense of disappointment will be out of control.

Your feelings are inevitable. After all, it's an emotional situation and you respond emotionally. But while there's probably nothing you can do about your initial feelings, it's best to make the least damaging response you can. (An aside: even though emotional first reactions are generally destructive, there may be a redeeming feature to them. They let your teenager know how you feel. They let your teenager know just *how* important what happened is to you and just what *kind* of importance it has. If you were totally calm it might give your teenager a distorted picture of how seriously you take what happens to him.)

The way to make your first reaction as nondestructive as possible is to try (even though it's difficult) to take the blaming and labeling and name calling out of your words and instead focus on how you feel. It's much better to say, "I'm really disappointed in you," than to say, "You're really a screwup." And it's much better to say, "I'm scared witless to think about your having acted that way," than to say, "You're never going to learn."

In fact, you should never, ever, under any circumstances, calmly or in anger, tell your kid there's something wrong with him. You can always ask for what you want or say how you feel, but when you describe reality by making a negative statement about your teenager, you're essentially committing a form of verbal psychological abuse. The fact that you're furious and feel helpless doesn't excuse doing this.

All right. There you are with the feelings pouring out of you, minus the name calling and labeling. Now what?

The second step is to stop your first reaction as soon as you can. In other words, accept the fact that you're a normal, fallible human being who will overreact, but avoid going on too long with your first reaction. Feelings may be inevitable, but they don't have to go out of control.

Right now you may be angry, scared, and confused. But at some point in the future you'll be much smarter and more effective than you are right now. So by stopping yourself you're giving yourself an opportunity to handle this problem successfully later.

The third step is to wait. Your goal is to be smart in dealing with this situation, so it makes sense to wait until you have enough perspective on it to be smart about it. While you're waiting try to keep this in mind: even though your teenager may be toughing it out and minimizing what you see as a serious problem, he probably feels as badly as you do. So you don't have to keep churning out evidence of your being upset to "wake him up" to what a terrible thing he has done.

Time has a way of making people a lot more intelligent than they were when their emotions were exploding all over the place. Milly, for example, was in shock when she found out her son Rick had to repeat the ninth grade. But, after her first reaction, she didn't say anything for over two weeks. Finally, it occurred to Milly that the best thing she could tell Rick was that school was part of his life and that he'd be the one who would live with the consequences of whatever he did. She came up with a wonderful thing to say: *"You've entered the age when no one can protect you from the things you do to yourself."*

But in addition to wanting to be smart, in their disappointment many parents think about getting tough.

* * *

The fourth step is to think very carefully before you make plans for getting tough. It's natural to feel that if only you'd been more controlling, your kid wouldn't have done whatever disappointed you. Control always seems like the answer to things being out of control. And when parents are disappointed they think of getting control by getting tough.

So you have getting-tough thoughts like "You're on your own now," "Now we've got to crack down," "This only happened because I wasn't tough enough," "I've got to come up with some punishment to bring this home to her." What do you do about these thoughts? Make sure you get tough in the right way and for the right reason.

The best kind of toughness is when you let your teenager experience the real and appropriate consequences of his actions. More than this probably creates a backwash of bad feeling that poisons your relationship. Anything less than this is clearly not tough enough. Calling the manager of McDonald's and getting your teenager his job back is only telling the kid that he has an insurance policy protecting him from anything bad happening if he screws up. In the real world, people who goof off get fired.

By not insulating him from the consequences of his actions, you're fitting your toughness with the world's toughness. If your kid was driving irresponsibly and cracks up the car, the real consequences are the costs and hassles of repair, the increases in insurance, and not being able to use the car. And that's what your teenager needs to experience. You don't need to shout or ground him or anything else. He just needs to take full responsibility for paying for what he's done and reimbursing you for what you've suffered.

So why freak out when all you have to do is hand him a list of all the costs and work out with him when and how he's going to take care of them? In this way, the toughness of the world will do your work for you.

At the same time there's no reason for your teenager to suffer inappropriately harsh consequences of his actions just because you want to teach him a lesson. If your daughter gets pregnant, the real consequences are that she's going to have to experience having an abortion or giving the baby up for adoption or keeping the baby. That's tough enough, and there's nothing you can do about it. But there's no need to add to these consequences just to make your point. Throwing your daughter out of the house, for example, goes too far and inappropriately adds your punishment to her problem.

The difficulty is deciding which consequences are appropriate and which are inappropriate. Anything that comes out of your anger and your desire to punish is likely to be inappropriate. You're certainly entitled to your feelings. Anger and punishment by themselves only generate further anger and a desire to punish back.

But, if you're like most parents who've been seriously disappointed in their teenagers, there's still one more thing you're itching to do, something you feel cries out to be done. You want more than for your teenager to suffer the consequences of his behavior. You want to punish.

It makes sense, in a way. You feel used and abused. Somehow you feel something has been taken from you, and so your teenager must pay you for what he's done. The balance must be righted.

And that's the key to successfully responding to your disappointment: the idea of rebalancing the relationship. When your teenager has done something to disappoint you deeply, your relationship is seriously unbalanced, and the balance must be righted. The successful response can only be something that will right that balance.

How, then, do you respond successfully? Your response has to have something to do with the relationship. It has to give you something *you* need so that you can put an end to the anger you feel about what he's done. What's needed is some kind of consequence that will rebalance the relationship. When your teenager has suffered the consequences, the two of you will be back to where you were with each other before the incident.

In other words, the consequence should have to do with striking a balance and not with striking back. Here's how to do it:

- Don't impose a consequence while you're still in the first heat of anger. If you do, you're likely to go too far and create a new imbalance. The consequence should have something to do only with the real anger that's left after your initial fury has dissipated.
- Make sure the consequence is enforceable. If you have to spend too much time and energy making the consequence stick, you'll just get angrier and create a new imbalance.
- Try to make the consequence fit the crime. There is a specific reason for this: the closer the fit, the more quickly and easily the balance between you will be righted. And after all, making your kid suffer the consequences isn't an end in itself; it's for the sake of rebalancing the relationship.
- Make sure you understand how your teenager really perceives the consequences. Your teenager may complain about any consequence, however mild. At the same time some consequences really go too far and just shift the anger over to the other side so the relationship is unbalanced again. It's much better to impose a milder consequence that will achieve some real balance now than to impose a very strict consequence that you'll have to take back later on.

As an example of this last point, suppose your kid dented the car and you want to take away the use of the car for a period. That is a natural consequence, but because you live in the suburbs and a car is a kind of lifeline, losing the use of the car will be deeply humiliating to your kid. On the other hand, another consequence could be that your kid would pay for the part of the repair not covered by insurance. The payment might actually be a bigger burden, but because it's not humiliating it won't unbalance your relationship.

The fifth and final step in dealing with your disappointment is to try and get some perspective. Above all, you want to try to avoid the "that's it" mentality, where you sit around in your disappointment thinking, "That's it, my kid is a loser, fatally flawed, doomed never to amount to anything."

Disappointment squashes relationships like a steamroller. What makes it even worse is that not only does it create distance and anger between you and your teenager, but it also creates a terrible image of your teenager in his own mind and so hurts him as well. The mental and emotional abuse parents inflict on teenagers is rooted in disappointment, and that's why your disappointment can be so lethal.

Perspective is the antidote. Disappointment only makes sense when things really are all over. If you feel disappointed with the movie when it's ended and you're walking out of the theater, that's one thing. That movie is truly finished. But you can't judge a whole movie after the first ten minutes.

That's the point with teenagers. An adolescent is a new-born adult. A newborn infant is funny-looking, incompetent, and inarticulate—a mess. But very soon it becomes a beautiful child. Your teenager—however big a mess he seems to be now—will very likely go on to become a fine adult.

The evidence is very clear on this point. Your teenager's personal problems are a poor indicator of how well he'll do later on. Sure, if he's tone-deaf he won't suddenly become a musician, and if she can barely pass algebra she won't blossom into a nuclear physicist. But those extremes aside, lazy kids commonly go on to become hardworking adults, absent-minded goof-offs go on to become responsible, hardheaded adults, and teenage shoplifters go on to become law-abiding citizens.

It works if you look backward, too. If you examine the lives of some of the most successful people, you find that when they were teenagers many of them did things that made their parents' hair stand on end. One woman we know is now an architect, but when she was in high school she got pregnant and dropped out for a couple of years. A distinguished psychiatrist ran with a gang and was arrested several times before straightening himself out. An owner of a successful and fast-growing chain of women's clothing stores was kept back twice in high school and was unable to go to college.

What about the golden people, who were wonderful as

teenagers and went on to become wonderful adults? Yes, there are people like this. Many of them stay wonderful. And some of them go on to crack up, get into trouble, go bankrupt, commit fraud, or become alcoholics.

The ball game goes on for nine full innings, and it can even go into extra innings. And, yeah, if your kid is down three to nothing at the end of the first inning it's discouraging, but there's a lot of ball game still to be played. All your disappointment does is make it that much more likely that you and your teenager will both end up losing.

This is what we mean by gaining perspective: OK, your teenager has disappointed you. Your feelings are real. But they tell you nothing about the future. And that's why you have to give yourself as many days as you need to cool off and find some perspective before you react too strongly to your disappointment.

Remember, your success as a parent isn't measured by how successful your kid is. You have no control over that. The only measure of being the successful parent of a teenager is whether you and your kid have a good relationship with each other.

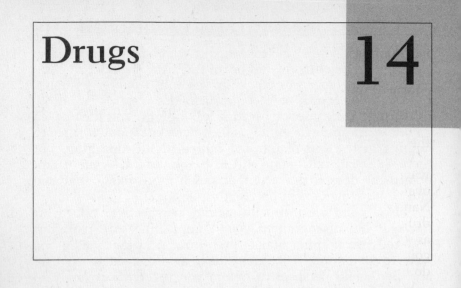

Drugs

14

Which would you guess is safer, a typical American city or Beirut?

How many of you answered Beirut? Well, one father we know did. He felt so desperate about the omnipresence of drugs in the United States and his own inability to protect his teenagers from them that he moved his entire family from the United States back to Beirut (where they'd originally come from); he thought even civil war would provide a safer environment for his kids than America's drug-filled streets.

Nothing scares parents more than the thought of their kids getting involved with drugs. Even the hippest, most liberal, most "modern" parents draw the line at drugs, even (perhaps especially) parents who used drugs themselves when they were growing up in the sixties.

If there was ever anything calculated to make you feel you really don't have any control over your teenager, this is it. After all, drugs are everywhere. And if anything was ever calculated to make you feel you *have* to fight for control, this is it.

In our experience, this mixture of helplessness and desperation leads parents to make two mistakes. Their helplessness leads parents into denial. Their desperation leads parents into battles for control.

Strangely, when it comes to drugs, our experience is that denial and battling for control go on at the same time for most parents. It's as if they had the motto, "If you think you can't control it, deny it; if you think you can control it, fight for control." What this means in practice is that most of the time parents are underreacting, and then from time to time they overreact.

When Nancy, for example, found out her daughter Wendy was going to a party where there'd be drugs, she agonized over what to do. Nancy wanted to forbid Wendy to go. But Nancy was also a parent who'd ignored possible signs of actual drug use. It's as if she'd been saying, "Why go nuts as long as I'm afforded the luxury of being able to pretend what's going on has nothing to do with drugs? And what else can I do besides go nuts when I'm forced to stop pretending?"

When it comes to drugs, most parents are doing the best they can with a problem that's frustrating and scary. And the sad fact is that drugs can defeat even the most skilled and best-intentioned of parents.

Still, if you've been dealing with the teen drug problem the way most parents do, you can do better. You can minimize your teenager's chance of getting involved with drugs, and you can guarantee that, whatever else happens, your relationship with him will be so good that the two of you will be able to deal with whatever comes up.

You only have two possible weapons in your arsenal: information and influence. Nothing else. Information includes both what you tell your teenager and, even more important, what your teenager tells you. Influence is the magical ability of your words and beliefs to have weight even when you're not around and have no chance of control.

Denial and battling for control, on the other hand, destroy information and influence. Let's look at how this works. The most important realities parents deny are that

- Drugs are being offered to your teenager at an early age.
- Drugs are attractive to your teenager because they're connected to peer acceptance and acting grown-up and because they make your teenager feel good.

- Your teenager has probably experimented in some way with drugs already.
- If your teenager is actually using drugs now, it is likely you won't realize that the first signs of his drug use have anything to do with drugs. You might see his having red eyes as fatigue. You might think he's "moody" or "just going through a stage," rather than going through withdrawal.

Because they tend to deny these realities, parents don't talk to their kids until it's too late. As a result, their kids are deprived of information that would have had all the more impact if the teenagers had gotten it when they were younger. And, you, the parent, are deprived of information because you're not creating an opportunity to hear about your kid's feelings and the realities he's dealing with. It's likely your teenager will not be the one to bring up the drug topic; he expects that if he does you'll either freak out or give him a long, boring lecture about things he already knows.

And this is where the battle for control hurts you, too. Far too many parents fall into what may be the single most harmful dynamic in the parent-teen-drug situation:

- Your kid tells you something that connects him with drugs. He may tell you he was offered drugs, or that he tried some drug, or that a friend of his is using drugs.
- You get upset. You're probably more scared than angry, but to your teenager you probably sound more angry than scared. So you warn, threaten, or punish. You act as if you feel this is a situation where fighting for control is more important than your relationship with your teenager.
- Your teenager responds by feeling, "She doesn't care about me. She doesn't want to talk to me, listen to me, hear how I feel. She doesn't think I have anything to contribute to this. She just wants to yell at me and boss me around. I can't talk to her."

- Your teenager decides to cut you out of the information loop. It's just not worth the hassle of telling you anything. All you do is freak out, tell him a bunch of stuff he knows already (" 'Drugs are bad'? So what else is new?"), and act like he was some kind of jerk. Your teenager figures he can deal with drugs himself.
- You start thinking things are OK because you're not hearing anything to the contrary.
- You've lost your influence over your teenager and so he's now in more danger than ever.

So what can you do instead?

How to Use the Relationship Approach to Deal with the Teen Drug Problem

Start with where you want to end up. You can't end up with "everything is OK," because drugs will always be a threat. So denial is not an option. You can't end up with control, because keeping your teenager away from drugs is not something you can control, and remote control doesn't work. So battling for control isn't an option.

The only things you can end up with are information from your teenager, influence over your teenager, and a good relationship with your teenager. And you want to end up with these because they are the only possible weapons you can have in the war against drugs:

- With a two-way flow of information between you, you'll find out from your teenager what he needs to know and then you'll be able to tell him what he needs to hear.
- Influence will allow your words and values to carry over into the truly dangerous situations—the ones where you're not around.
- A good relationship with you gives your teenager things that he doesn't have to get from drugs or druggy friends.

If you can accomplish this, you can feel successful because you'll know that you're doing the most a parent can do.

But how do you do it? You just do the opposite of denial and battling for control. Let's take these one at a time.

The opposite of denying things is dealing with them. Drugs are a fact of life in your teenager's world. So find out what's really going on in your teenager's world. Does anyone he knows use drugs? Are drugs available at his school? What kinds of drugs are available? Does he know any kids who are dealing drugs? *If your teenager isn't telling you things that scare you, then you're failing to do your job of making it easy for your kid to talk to you.* When (notice we say "when") your teenager does tell you something that scares you, the best way to interpret this is with gratitude that he trusts you and that you're learning real stuff, and with pride that you've managed to have a good enough relationship with him that he can tell you these kinds of things.

Does this mean you have to condone it if he tells you he "tried" pot or coke? Of course not. That would be denial, too. He doesn't expect to be handed bouquets for his admissions. It's perfectly fine—in fact, it's ideal—if you tell him how you feel about what he's doing.

The crucial difference is whether he experiences your response as a punishment. *Don't* say things like

- "If I ever catch you having anything to do with drugs, I'll kill you."
- "I'm so ashamed of you—you've broken my heart."
- "Are you trying to kill me, is that what you're trying to do?"
- "I'll tell you one thing, you can't hang around with those kids anymore. And if I catch you with them, you'll be in the biggest trouble of your life, mister."

You get the idea. These are words that come so naturally to parental lips. But, sadly, they backfire. Don't mess up your message with punishment, bullying, hysteria, and anger on your side, because if you do, you'll cause resentment, anger, distance, and a strong desire to oppose you on your teenager's side.

If you want to be effective, try saying things like

- "You know, I really get scared when you tell me you're hanging around with people who do coke."
- "I feel that doing drugs is stupid, crazy, and self-destructive. It just messes you up, period. I'm always going to hate it if you do drugs."

This communicates real information. You're doing nothing to contaminate your relationship with your teenager or his love for you. Your influence remains strong. Your teenager knows how you feel. You increase the likelihood that he'll do what you want him to because he cares about you, because the way you've talked to him increases his caring.

And when your teenager tells you scary things about drugs, you can prevent yourself from overreacting by reminding yourself that experimenting with drugs is not a sign that your teenager is inevitably heading down the road to addiction. Don't misunderstand us: experimenting with drugs is dangerous, and that's why you have to deal with it. But the average teenager stops experimenting with drugs as he gets older.

This, then, is how you start to deal with the drug problem. Instead of denying, you ask questions, you listen, and you talk. You increase communication by decreasing the pain and fear of communication. You don't condone drug use, but you say how you feel without ranting and raving. You don't have to be afraid that making it easy for your teenager to talk to you will be seen as condoning drug use, because you know that by talking you're dealing with the drug problem directly in the only way you can.

We also said that, in addition to doing the opposite of denial, you have to do the opposite of battling for control. Well, the opposite of battling for control is strengthening your relationship with your teenager.

The good news is that by dealing with the drug problem by talking to your teenager and keeping the lines of communication open, you're already strengthening your relationship with him. By talking about drugs openly, by making it possible for your teenager to feel comfortable talking to you, by letting him know your thoughts and feelings, you're making him feel that his relationship with you is a safe place to work on the teen drug problem.

In other words, serious and scary as it is, the teen drug problem only requires you to use what you're already using as part of the relationship approach. For example, some parents, building on an already good relationship, have found it very effective to make an agreement with their teenager based on the following kind of statement:

> I can't follow you around and it's physically impossible for me to prevent you from ever trying drugs. But I'd like you to agree to this. If you're ever in a situation where there are drugs and you're tempted to use them, then call me collect any time day or night and give me a chance to talk you out of it. Then if I succeed, I succeed; if I don't, I don't. What do you need to agree to something like this?

Of course some teenagers refuse to agree. Of course sometimes they don't keep to the agreement. But believe it or not, working out an agreement like this helps. It puts you a little closer to your teenager and to his decision about using drugs.

If you find out your teenager is already using drugs or keeps finding himself in situations where he's being tempted to use them, then, in addition to the free flow of information, feelings, and values back and forth, the permission technique is a valuable antidote to your feeling helpless.

Once you know how your teenager feels about the problem, you can gain tremendous leverage by asking his permission to help him solve it. You can ask, "Is this what you want to be doing to yourself? What is it giving you and are there other ways you can get that for yourself? Do I have your permission to find a program you can enter that will help you? Do I have your permission to help you in any other way?" You can only be helpful with his permission, and asking for it is the best way to get it.

Getting influence this way is all you can do. But it's the most any parent can do on his own. If you're convinced that your teenager is drug-dependent, then the relationship approach is more important than ever, but you'll also need professional help. You'll find useful suggestions in our Appendix—"What to Do if You Think There Might Be Something *Seriously* Wrong with Your Teenager."

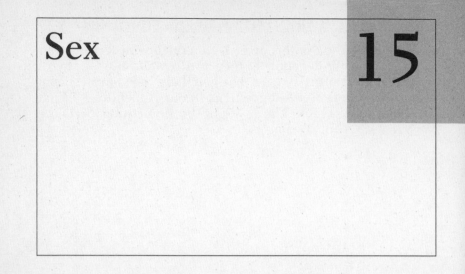

Sex

15

Louisa and Henry came from Europe when they were teenagers. They were seeking freedom in America. Years later, as their daughter Elaine went through adolescence, they surrounded her with restrictions, threats, and warnings about sex.

Louisa and Henry loved Elaine, but their fierce fight to protect her didn't make her feel loved. She said to us what we've heard hundreds of teenagers say: "My parents don't really care about me. They don't really know who I am. They have some image of who I'm supposed to be, like I'm a pedigree dog they're getting ready for a dog show."

Elaine's bad relationship with her parents, her feeling neither seen nor cared for, had serious consequences. It goes without saying that Louisa and Henry's endless restrictions were useless at preventing Elaine from getting involved in sexual activity at a relatively early age. In a way, they caused that sexual activity—Elaine sought out sexual encounters partly out of anger with her parents, partly out of ignorance (because of course she couldn't talk to them and get information), and partly because she didn't feel her parents saw her as someone special. All this made it easy for her to let herself be used by boys.

It gets worse. Elaine's need to feel loved and to feel that

she was someone special ended in her getting pregnant by age fifteen. It wasn't a complete accident. She wanted to get pregnant because she wanted a baby—someone who would love her for who she was, someone who would care for her unconditionally. Fortunately, Louisa and Henry didn't go so far as to kick Elaine out of the house. But their anger and disappointment were so intense that Elaine was determined to go off on her own as soon as possible after the baby was born.

The details of this story are dramatic, but the process is all too common. In an attempt to protect, parents of all backgrounds do and say things that make their teenagers feel stupid, sinful, ugly, hated, weak, and very much alone. Particularly in the area of sex, the battle for control, whether filled with fiery or icy anger, not only damages the parent-teen relationship but results in parents actually losing the influence they might have had—and so pushes their kids into the very things their parents were trying to protect them from.

Why is this?

Too much, too soon, and too fast—that's what it feels like for most parents as they see their sweet-cheeked kids flirting with sex. It feels like only yesterday that they were babies. And you know only too well how much they're still like babies. So as you see the evidence that your kid is ready to have sexual experiences of whatever kind, you want to take control and slow things down.

This is an issue for all parents, not just the more conservative ones who believe that intercourse should only take place after marriage. All parents have values they want to transmit to their kids; for example, no parent, liberal or conservative, wants her daughter to let herself be used as a sexual object. And all parents are concerned about issues of physical safety, like pregnancy, AIDS, and sexually trans-mitted diseases, and of psychological safety, like having trust destroyed.

At the same time, your concerns about sex and dating make you anxious because this is a major part of your teenager's life over which you have no control. After all, acting sullen or not studying happens right under your nose, but the things you worry about in the area of sex always happen when you're far away. This can be an explosive combination: you feel profoundly out of control and you desperately wish you had control.

Many parents deal with these feelings by trying to achieve *remote control*. They do this in two main ways.

One way is *restrictions:* the parental thinking here is that you can gain control over your kid's going too far too fast too soon by restricting his opportunities for getting into trouble. "I don't know what goes on at those parties you go to," some parents say, "but I figure a hell of a lot less will be going on if I can get you home by midnight."

Another way is *threats and warnings:* the thinking here is that if you scare your kid badly enough, then you'll build into her the kinds of controls you wish you could impose on her. "If you sleep around," some parents say, "everyone is going to know it immediately and you'll get the reputation of being a slut."

But you already know—don't you?—that you can't achieve remote control. It's as if these parents were saying, "OK, I don't have much control, but I'll fight for it anyway," and that really doesn't make any sense. Secretly, these parents may be hoping that, if nothing else works, at least their teenager will see how much they care and will cooperate out of respect for their caring. But in fact, this strategy of restrictions and threats is unlikely to make your kid feel you care, and is almost guaranteed to make him feel like a thing you're trying to control.

A much better strategy for dealing with sex and your teenager, of course, is the relationship approach. Instead of saying, "I don't have any control but let me fight for it anyway," you say, "Since I don't have the kinds of control I used to have when my teenager was a child, what can I do to maximize the kinds of real influence I do have now?"

The launching pad of this strategy is the strength of your relationship with your teenager. If your teenager isn't expecting you to try to control her with restrictions, threats, and warnings, and specially if she's not expecting to get yelled at, she'll talk to you. She'll tell you about the things she does and thinks and feels and wants. And the way to make it easy for her to talk to you is to remember that your priority is to listen, not to jump down your kid's throat because of what she said.

This last point is critical. The graveyard of parent-teen communications is parents freaking out when their kids tell them things. *The birthplace of good communications, a good parent-teen relationship, and your ability to influence your teenager is your being able to listen to what your kid has to tell you without being judgmental.* You can only shoot the messenger so many times before he gets tired of delivering messages. There will be plenty of opportunity for you to communicate your feelings and values. But if you don't listen and hear, and if you don't make listening and hearing possible, all you'll do is cut yourself off.

Now, the more your kid talks to you, the more two things will happen. One, you'll know more, and so you'll be in a position to have some idea of what's important to deal with. Two, the atmosphere of respectful listening that you create will give you tremendous influence when you respond to your teenager.

Here's how this works in practice. Your teenager has just told you something that you find very upsetting. "I've been sleeping with Bobby," she says. All your warning lights are flashing, all your too-much-too-fast-too-soon indicators are blinking. Your instinct is to try to grab for control—just as if you felt your car suddenly veer off the road—by restricting, warning, threatening, yelling, and so on.

But now you remember that that strategy will fail in the long run. By talking to you, your teenager was experimenting, asking herself: "Is this the kind of thing I can tell my parents?" The more negative your reaction, the more likely it is that, instead of hearing your reaction, your teenager will conclude, "I can never tell my parents this kind of thing again." *There is no more telling sign of parental failure than teenage silence.*

Decide you're going to go for real success. It may be hard for you, because you're very upset about what your kid said, and you don't like to think about her doing what she's told you she's done, and you're afraid for her future. But in spite of all this you are determined to listen. Really listen. First. Before anything else.

Ask questions. Most of all, ask how she felt, because that's both more important and less intrusive than grilling her about who did what to whom. Of course the easier it is for the two of you to talk, the easier it is for you to ask about specific things like just how far they went or whether they used birth control or whatever else you think is important.

Part of really listening is not jumping to conclusions. Many parents get tremendously wrought up and yet fail to ask simple questions like, "Is this something you think you'll do again?" or "Is this something you want to keep on doing?" Again, the friendlier the atmosphere between the two of you, the easier it will be for you to explore just what this has meant to your kid.

Finally, what about you? You've been sitting on all kinds of feelings this whole time. What do you do about them?

The key is for you to *talk about yourself.* If something about what your kid told you makes you feel angry, sad, or scared, you can say, "I felt angry [or sad or scared] when you told me that." It's fine for you to express your feelings; after all, your kid knew you'd be having them. The problems come when you turn your feelings against your kid and use them to control him. For example:

- It strengthens your relationship with your teenager when you say, "You know, I felt really sad when you told me what you did." It creates distance and silence when you say, "What the hell's wrong with you? Are you sick?"
- It strengthens your relationship with your teenager to say, "It made me angry to hear about your letting yourself do that." It creates distance and silence when you say, "I'm going to ground you completely if I ever hear about anything like that happening again."
- It strengthens your relationship with your teenager for you to say, "I'm really scared to think that maybe you don't respect yourself." It creates distance and silence

when you say, "How could you do this to me, after all I've done for you?"

You can respond as a whole human being with all your caring and concerns and at the same time respond in a way that strengthens your connection to and influence with your teenager. It's really much easier to do this than many people think. In fact, it's just as easy to go down the right track as the wrong track. Once you shift tracks, there's nothing to it.

It will be tremendously helpful in keeping you on track, particularly during supercharged conversations, if you spend some time talking about your relationship instead of just talking about your teenager. It can be tremendously helpful to say something like, "I notice that you're starting to act defensive, so I must be putting something out that looks like I'm blaming you. I really don't want us to get into that kind of thing, so let me know what I can do to help you not feel defensive."

Of course, just getting your kid to hear how you feel is not enough for most parents. No matter how you define "acting responsibly," you want your kid to act that way. This is when you use the magic question and ask for what you want directly, by asking your kid what he needs to give you what you want.

You do this whatever you want, whether you feel it's important for your kid to use birth control or to refrain from sex before marriage altogether. You have to recognize, however, that you're probably not going to get everything you want. After all, the whole point of your kid's struggle to leave home is for him, not you, to be in charge of himself. So all you can do is your best, while realizing that absolutely nothing is important enough to jeopardize your relationship with your teenager.

To make this point even clearer, let's talk about many parents' worst nightmare when it comes to sex: teenage pregnancy.* Next to drugs, this is one of the things most likely to

---

*Of course AIDS is much more serious than teenage pregnancy in the sense that AIDS is fatal. And for parents of teenagers who are at risk, AIDS will certainly be

goad parents into battling desperately for control. As they worry it's easy for some parents to say, "Yeah, my relationship with my kid's important, but it's worth her hating me if I can prevent her from becoming pregnant."

Unwanted teenage pregnancy *is* a personal calamity and a social disaster. And of course parents should do what they can to help their teenagers prevent unwanted pregnancies. This is why many wise parents say, "If you've made a decision to have sex, come to me and I'll arrange for you to get birth control. No questions asked, no lectures. That's how important it is to me to prevent pregnancy or sexually transmitted diseases."

Parents whose religion or values make them totally opposed to premarital sex have problems with this. These parents have to make a decision for themselves. If they believe they know what's going on with their teenager and have communicated their values successfully, they may not feel they have to transgress their own values by offering their teenager birth control. But even the most traditional parent still has to decide what's most important: preventing pregnancy or advocating values. That's why it's possible for a parent to say to her teenager, "I think premarital sex is a terrible sin. But it's not as bad as teenage pregnancy. So if you get to the point where you reject our values to the extent that you're going to have sex, I'll never approve of it but I will help you to get birth control and I will ask you to come to me so I can help you get birth control."

We believe that the parent-teen relationship is so important that for the average teenager even the consequences of getting pregnant, bad as they are, aren't quite as bad as the consequences of having a terrible relationship with her parents. The reason: a very bad relationship tends to hurt more and do more damage than even an unwanted teenage preg-

---

their number-one concern. But at-risk teens are a minority, and AIDS is rare among the non-at-risk population. That's why most parents worry most about teenage pregnancy. When it comes to dealing with at-risk teens, the relationship approach—more than anything else—will enable parents to know what their kids are doing and will create an atmosphere in which the parents' advice and warnings will be listened to.

nancy. In other words, if you really care about your teenager, if you really want to help instead of merely giving yourself the illusion that you're helping, then you won't let something even as scary as your kid getting pregnant interfere with your having a good relationship with her.

This doesn't mean that you indulge her or accept behavior you don't approve of. You can be as strong an advocate as you like for what you think is important. But if your concerns create an atmosphere of anger, silence, and distance, then not only have you blown your relationship with your teenager, you've probably failed to protect her against getting pregnant.

Don't allow the illusion of control to transform your caring for your teenager into a monstrous force that will destroy both your relationship with her and your chance of having influence with her. Instead, accept your lack of control and accept the fact that your kid will probably do some things you wish she wouldn't. But know that if you keep your relationship strong and the lines of communication open, then you'll be doing the most it's possible for a parent to do.

What Teenage Relationships Are All About

It helps parents deal with the issue of teen sex to understand something about teen relationships. Just the way becoming self-reliant and developing an identity are part of the process of getting ready to leave home, another part of this process is developing the capacity for intimacy. After all, part of the overall job of leaving home is learning how to be successful in intimate relationships. He's not leaving home to go nowhere—he's leaving your family ultimately to start a family of his own.

Almost everything that happens to your adolescent with others is part of developing the capacity for intimacy—everything from the giggle- and snicker-producing activities of junior high school kids to the quasi-marital arrangements of post-college young adults.

So as a step to your dealing with all this, you need to keep saying to yourself, over and over throughout your kid's adolescence, "He's just doing his job." If he doesn't do the job of developing the capacity for intimacy by having all kinds of romantic experiences, he could end up in trouble.

A good way to illustrate this is to tell you about a young man who did *not* do the scouting necessary to develop his own map of intimacy. John was a brilliant student, in part because he'd always worked so hard. He had been too busy studying—in high school, an Ivy League college, and then a prestigious medical school—to have much time for intimate relationships. Finally, in his second year of residency, vaguely feeling he "wanted a wife," John somehow managed to meet someone and get married. But his inner knowledge of the way intimacy works had all the gaps and mistakes of the average fourteen-year-old. He didn't have a clue about how to meet someone's needs or get his own needs met in an intimate relationship. He had grasped the rose of marriage unprepared to deal with the thorns. That his marriage would end in difficulties was all too inevitable.

During his entire adolescence, John had made no mistakes. To his parents he'd been a golden boy. But as far as intimacy went, he'd experienced nothing, and he'd learned nothing. John never got to the point of being able to imagine there could be problems. And so he didn't have a clue about what to do when the honeymoon was over. It's worth remembering this story as you see your teenager experiencing the risks and pains that come with learning about intimacy.

Intimacy demands an important trade-off that some parents don't appreciate. The capacity for intimacy is built out of the bricks of self-knowledge, understanding of others, and people skills. You have to buy those bricks, and the cost is getting involved in the heartache and confusion of a variety of intimate relationships.

This is why we say that many of the things parents do to "guide" their teenagers through the stormy seas of intimacy are a mistake, however well intentioned. There's no doubt that teenagers do things that seem to scream out for guidance. *But it's all about getting experience.* Sure, teenagers are going to make a lot of mistakes and do a lot of foolish things in relationships, but they need that experience even more than they need protection from those mistakes. In the long run, the costs of making mistakes are far less than the costs of not having experience. Remember John?

The point of adolescent experience with intimacy isn't to make teenagers successful in intimate relationships now. The point is trial and error. Every awkward telephone call, all the teasing and fooling around in the school cafeteria, each disastrous or blissful date, each broken heart or budding romance, is part of the necessary preparations for adult intimate relationships.

And intimacy involves map making. With respect to intimacy, your teenager is making a map that contains himself in the world of the opposite sex. He already knows how to have a casual relationship with people of the same sex—he's been doing that since before the first grade. But anything more than casual contact with the opposite sex is generally terra incognita.

Intimacy can be even more complicated for gay teens. Among the additional things gay teenagers need to figure out is how to go from having friendly relationships to having romantic relationships with members of their own sex. But the process is the same: exploring and experimenting in order to build a map of how to have an intimate, adult sexual or romantic relationship with another person.

When you interfere with your teenager's experimenting with intimacy—whether in the form of guiding, advising, prying, or commanding—you're trying to help out where no help is necessary. Your teenager is almost inevitably doing his job the best way he can, and you can do your job best by getting out of the way.

Occasionally, though, something comes up that makes you feel it's impossible to keep silent. Lulled by your being a great listener, your teenager pops out with some revelation like "I don't know why he dumped me, so I keep calling him about ten times a day, but he won't talk to me and I can't sleep or anything," or "You know, we're having sex and we're not using birth control." How can you still bite your tongue? What about your needs? Is there a way to get involved without blowing your teenager's ability to confide in you?

Yes. There's something at your disposal that will help you maintain intimacy with your teenager, take care of your need to protect him, and take care of his need to be free of parental interference. After he's dropped the bombshell on you and you regain enough composure to speak, you can ask this question:

"Is this one of those times when you want me to just listen, or do you want me to tell you what I really think, or what?"

And then you wait. Nothing works better at preventing parents from getting into terrible tangles with their teenagers than this question, which is really a version of the permission technique.

It's possible that your teenager will tell you he really doesn't want to hear anything from you about this. Then there's nothing you can do. But you've still accomplished a lot. For the mere price of holding back words your teenager would have ignored anyway, you purchase a tremendous increase in his ability to trust you to be there for him as the parent of the adult he will soon become. The two of you are now making a very good beginning in the forty-year relationship you'll have as adults.

Yes, it's painful to stand by as he's doing something dangerous or scary, knowing that all you can do is ask, "Is this one of those times when you want me to just listen, or do you want me to tell you what I really think, or what?" But you have to assume he's doing his job of learning by doing. Remember, if you're scared but all he wants you to do is listen, then you just have to listen and then say something like "I trust you to take care of yourself."

Every time you say this kind of thing, something about your trusting him lodges in his brain and makes him feel good about you. And every time you say this, something about taking care of himself lodges in his brain and makes it a little bit more likely that he'll be careful on his own.

Other Problem Areas

16

Sometimes it must seem as though as the parent of a teenager you'll never run out of things to worry about. Drugs and sex can generate some of the biggest worries, but so can many other things. In this chapter we show you how to use the relationship approach to deal with these areas:

- Friends
- Helping around the house
- School
- Money
- Moods and attitudes

In every case, what's important isn't mastering a tool or technique but using the relationship approach to rethink the problem and break through the difficulties that have prevented you from being as effective as you'd like.

Friends

According to one study, teenagers are happiest when they're with their friends. But you knew that already—your teenager seems to live to be with his friends. Of course there's no problem if you can say, "Jennifer has such nice friends." Unfortunately, teenagers often refuse to cooperate; they choose friends who are weird or disturbing or disruptive or even apparently dangerous.

Then what do you do? How do you think about it? It's easy for your teenager's friends to become one more irritant goading you into a battle for control. Is there a way for you to relax and concentrate on strengthening your relationship instead of attempting the impossible task of getting your kid to select different friends?

Yes, there is. You can do this when you understand all the things the gang provides your teenager.

Friends Provide Support and Acceptance

Your teenager and his friends complain about things to each other and reveal their failures and weaknesses. But then they avoid doing something that most parents do: they don't criticize or try to change each other; they understand and side with each other.

Say your teenager flunks math. Most parents say things like "How could you do that?" or "I thought you were studying," or "Don't you want to get into a good college?" But friends are likely to say something like "That sucks," or "Mr. Hanson's a jerk," or "Oh, my God, what are you going to do?"

Now, of course, the problem with this from the parent's point of view is that it sounds like your teenager's friends are giving him permission to screw up. Well, this is exactly what they're doing. But it's not quite as bad as you might think.

Do you think he *doesn't* have permission to screw up? Of course he does. Adolescence is precisely the period when he can make mistakes "for free," when mistakes can be rather benign learning experiences, compared to adulthood when they can have very real and sometimes terrible consequences. Even the courts recognize this; they expunge a youthful offender's record when he turns eighteen.

Friends Provide Temporary Identity

In the beginning, your teenager doesn't know who he is, nor is he ready to make final decisions about his identity. But he can be spared the agonies of nonidentity by being part of a teen culture. Whether it's the world of thirteen-year-olds or twenty-three-year-olds, your adolescent can always feel there's something real and safe about participating in that world.

This relieves your teenager of the burden of leaping from being a child with no real identity to being an adult with a clear identity. It provides a place where your child can say, "OK, I am now much more than just a piece of my family. I have an existence in the outside world that's even more important to me than my existence in the family. I don't know who I am specifically as an adult yet, but I do know I'm somebody."

Knowing this should allow you to be more accepting of teen culture; you don't have to see it as merely distracting and destructive. Yes, teen culture can seem like a cruise on a ship of fools, but it's not a voyage to nowhere. Adulthood is the inevitable destination, and that's where they all get off.

Friends Provide a Way to Try Out New Identities

Having friends, getting wrapped up in his friends, is one of the main ways your teenager finds out who he is. Friends provide a kind of workshop for your kid to putter around in, experimenting. In the end, friends help him invent himself. There's no other way he can work so hard and get so much information about who he is and who he doesn't want to be. Let's look at how this works.

In spite of the images presented on television, the world of teenagers isn't monolithic. Far from it. Every high school and college has dozens of cliques, groups, and gangs. There are usually some broad categories—the "cool kids," the "nerds," the "punks," the "jocks," the "radicals," the "wheels." The names change from school to school and from generation to generation, but the categories usually remain the same. There are also more specialized categories, from the kids who play

Dungeons and Dragons or go skiing every weekend to the kids who help the homeless or hang out at the Chinese cultural center. Each one of these groups provides an opportunity for your teenager to try out an identity and see how it feels.

The gang has an identity before your teenager joins it. So when your teen joins a group of, say, bikers (God forbid, you probably say), he's both claiming an identity and at the same time trying on a prefabricated identity. The gang keeps telling him he's terrific for being just the way they are. But no matter how much he seems to be involved with the group, your teenager's also asking himself, more or less consciously, "Am I really comfortable here? Is this really who I am? Is this group meeting my needs? Is this something I want to stick with? Is there something better out there?"

Your teenager is perfectly capable of answering these questions for himself. But the gang makes doing so harder by supporting the ideas of not asking questions and just going along with the group. This is why your relationship with your teenager is so important. He needs support. If you don't have a good relationship with your teenager, then you make it much more difficult for him to question what the group is doing; without your support, the group's support will be that much more important to him, and he won't want to risk losing it by questioning the group. And the more you push your kid to leave the group, the more he turns to it for support.

This means that you have a very difficult task when your teenager hooks up with what you consider the "wrong crowd." You're absolutely right in believing that bad friends can be a bad influence. But that's not the issue; *the issue is what you can do about it*. If you try to battle for control, it will only mean that your teenager will find the gang that much more supportive. You fight, and they win. Not a good strategy.

On the other hand, you can work at having the best possible relationship with your teenager; you can work hard with him to get your needs met. No, you won't make him turn on a dime; you could never do that anyway. But you'll make sure that he's getting his need for support and acceptance met with you. That will leave him free to figure out his identity through the gang and not need the gang for anything else.

The best gift you can give your teenager is confidence that she is a strong, healthy, normal kid who's doing just what she should be doing. So the next time your kid tells you about a new direction she's taking, just say, "I'm sure you'll be someone you [note the "you" instead of "I'll"] like and feel proud of."

Helping around the House

You can't have a good relationship with someone you resent. And you can only resent someone who doesn't clean up after himself or do his fair share. So if you're going to strengthen your relationship with your teenager, you have to get rid of the feeling that your kid treats you like her housekeeper. That's why we strongly believe that kids have to do their jobs in the house without battles.

The solution is very simple, really. Your kid's leaving home and becoming an adult. He's on his way to being in charge of himself. Well, if he had a roommate instead of a parent, he'd share the household chores with that roommate. If he really were in charge of himself, he'd have to be in charge of cleaning up after himself. So getting ready to leave home and become an adult doesn't get him off the hook when it comes to helping out around the house. On the contrary, it requires not only that he do chores but that he take responsibility for doing these chores.

Getting your kid to do his chores is really just a special case of getting your needs met. So all you need to do when he's not doing his fair share around the house is to use your good relationship with him to gain leverage. Ultimately, if telling him how you feel and listening to his needs isn't enough, you can use the magic question—"What do you need to give me what I need?"—as the basis for making an agreement.

But household chores are simultaneously so all-pervasive, so intimate, and so petty that special problems may arise, making it harder for you to get your needs met. Here are some suggestions.

No Nagging

By nagging we mean repeatedly asking him if he's done a chore or repeatedly urging him to do it. Every time you repeat yourself without getting what you want, you lose influence and give a signal that you're willing to put up with this behavior. After all, he's not a baby but a near-adult with whom you have a relationship. If he doesn't do what he's agreed to the first time you ask him, then you have a problem that you have to take care of, and repeating yourself isn't the solution.

Here's something that will work when you find yourself starting to nag.

Get His Attention

This means you have to sit him down and let him know that, for instance, it's unacceptable for him to walk out of the house without doing the dishes. Let him know how you feel. If you're very angry, let him see how angry you are. Dirty dishes may be petty, but your having to do his dishes when you're tired or even when you're not is really unfair. Don't use feelings as a weapon in the battle for control; share them as you would with a friend to keep your relationship healthy.

When we say you should get his attention by "sitting him down," that could be interpreted as trying to control him. But of course we don't mean that, and you can get his attention without being controlling. Here's how. Instead of saying, "You have to sit down now and listen to me," it's far better to say something like, "I need to talk to you. *When would be a good time soon for us to talk?*" This way you basically make an appointment to talk to your teenager. This shows your respect, shows you take your own needs seriously enough to make an appointment to deal with them, and makes it likely that when your teenager does sit down with you you'll have his attention. It won't be a time when he has to run off somewhere.

Don't Waste Your Influence Trying to Get Your Kid to Do Things around the House That Are Really None of Your Business

The classic example of this is the parent fighting to try to get her teenager to clean up his room. Now get ready for what may be a revolutionary thought: Why do you need his room to be clean? Why is it *your* problem if *his* room is a mess? It's not, is it? As long as his door's closed, what difference does it make to you? Why should you ever have to go in there?

It's just not productive to turn your teenager's room into a battleground. So make a distinction between his business and the family's business. His room, for example, is his business. The living room is the family's business. His laundry is his business. The state of the bathroom is the family's business.

Remember, adolescence is a time of growing separation between domains that are his and domains that are yours. You might as well let him have his domain now, while he's fighting for his autonomy. If he doesn't want to keep his room clean, or he can't organize himself to do his own laundry, what difference does that make to you? Taking care of yourself is something adults have to figure out how to do, so let him figure it out for himself.

The key to getting your teenager to help around the house is to make sure you get your needs met by using the relationship approach. Then the only things you'll struggle over will be legitimate family issues. But you'll have eliminated what, in many families, causes the majority of fights over chores. Really all we're saying here is what we said in the chapter on getting your needs met: the first step is to separate what you need from what you think your teenager should need.

What's the worst thing that will happen if you follow the relationship approach and don't bug your kid about things that really aren't your business? You'll have a kid with a messy room and wrinkled pants who washes the family dishes and has a great relationship with you. It's a pretty good deal. You should take it.

School

"Have you done your homework yet?"

"I want to talk to you about your grades."

These two sentences ignite thousands of fights each day across the country between parents and teenagers. In fact, few things cause more day-to-day irritation in the parent-teen relationship than a teenager's less-than-ideal performance in school. If you're a high achiever yourself, then you probably want your kid to do at least as well as you did. If you're not such a high achiever, you very likely want your kid to do a lot better than you did.

But, alas . . . normal, imperfect teenagers often fail to co-operate with their parents' expectations. It's a safe bet that you feel your teenager is not studying as hard or doing as well in school as you'd like.

What do parents give as reasons for their teenager's poor performance? Here are some: "He just doesn't apply himself." "She doesn't seem to be motivated." "He has terrible study habits." "She wastes time." "He's stupid." "She's lazy." But while any of these things might be true about your kid, they're most likely not the real reason why she's not doing well in school.

Parents need to dig deeper. OK, she seems lazy and care-less, but why? You'll be able to avoid the frustrating fights you've been getting into and be able to give her the kind of help and support she needs only when you go beyond labels and understand the real reasons for teenagers' poor performance in school.

Many Teenagers Don't Do Well in School Because of Their Immaturity

We don't mean this in the sense that there's something wrong with your teenager; rather, what we mean is that kids mature at their own rate but school rewards the few who mature earliest. If your teenager is one of the great majority of kids who don't mature early, he'll fail to shine. To a large extent, performance in school measures not intelligence or motivation but maturity.

For example, part of maturity is patience. This includes the ability to put in long hours reading dry books, plus the ability to keep studying even when you're frustrated by difficult material. So the less-than-exceptionally mature kid is likely to drop things he finds boring and to give up when he's frustrated.

Is this a problem? Only if the parent is immature enough to be impatient himself! In fact, immaturity isn't really a problem at all, because, of all the things that could possibly be wrong with your kid, immaturity is almost guaranteed to get better all by itself. *All kids mature by themselves and at their own rates.* Immaturity is a self-correcting problem.

If you don't cripple your kid by trying to be too helpful, he'll become as mature as he can as fast as he can on his own without any help. Maybe it'll happen when he's twenty-four instead of when he's fifteen, and maybe not until he's thirty-three, but at some point his inability to get organized and to tolerate boredom and frustration will diminish to the point where your now-adult offspring is able to handle easily things he couldn't handle at all before. Many veterans who go to college after serving in the armed forces, for example, are surprised at what good students they became once they'd had a little time to grow up.

What you find so upsetting about your teenager not doing well in school may be something time will take care of—while you're taking care of your relationship with your teenager. If you allow maturity to work on its own, then you won't push your kid to do better in school and he won't end up hating both school and you.

Many Teenagers Don't Do Well in School Because They Haven't Found What They're Good at Yet

Did you know that many people who are great at computer programming are terrible when it comes to math? That many brilliant business people were poor students in school? That, at least according to one study, some of the best doctors are the people who did the worst in medical school? And, most important of all, you should know that, according to Yale psychologist Robert Sternberg, *intelligence isn't being smart at everything but is the ability to know what you're good at and what you're not good at and the ability to focus on your strengths and compensate for your weaknesses.*

This is important for you in understanding your teenager and why he may not be doing so well in school right now. School measures a very narrow range of abilities. To take just a few examples, chefs, artists, salespeople, politicians, animal trainers, entrepreneurs, and cabinetmakers are all people whose talents are unlikely to show up on their report cards. Even among future academic successes, there are people whose learning styles make it difficult for them to do well in school. For example, there are some Nobel Prize–winning physicists who could not learn physics from either textbooks or lectures. They learned it from talking physics among themselves.

It can be very difficult to work hard at something you're not very good at. This is why it doesn't make as much sense as it might seem for you to say to your kid, "Well, you could at least try." *It's hard to "try" when what you're trying doesn't feel very rewarding.* Parents need to understand this the next time they feel tempted to push their kids. But the good news is that your seemingly lazy, scatterbrained kid will most likely be a very different person five or ten years from now. By that time he'll have found something he is good at and you'll notice a miraculous transformation of your teenager into a dedicated, focused, clearheaded adult.

But you can get in the way of this transformation if you're not careful. In the mistaken belief that school is life, or a predictor for life, many parents get very angry at their kids for doing poorly in school. Even when these parents try to be "encouraging," the message that gets communicated is, "What's wrong with you?" The next thing you know, their teenager has begun to think there *is* something wrong with him, that he's defective, that he's a failure.

This is one of the reasons that it's so important to have a good relationship with your teenager. The closer you are to your kid and the better you get along with him, the easier it is for you to see him as a unique person rather than as a reflection of yourself or as a standard-issue, mass-produced teenager. No, he's an individual, and somewhere out there in the world is a much better fit for him than the limited-size, off-the-rack stuff that school hands out.

In other words, you're better off helping your kid find himself than telling him how lost he is.

Many Teenagers Don't Do Well in School Because of the Necessary Scarcity of High Performers

Here's a quiz item for parents. How many kids can be in the top 10 percent of their high school or college classes at one time? The answer is . . . 10 percent! And not one kid more. It's just simple logic, but if more parents understood this there'd be a lot fewer harassed kids and discouraged parents.

Think about what this means. In the real world only 10 percent of kids can be in the top 10 percent of their class. But if the world of parents' expectations were the real world, 90 percent of kids would be in the top 10 percent. And think of what a tough time there would be trying to fit them all in!

There's a serious point here. Deliberately or not, schools organize themselves around the statistical norms of academic ability. The average kid, in the long run, will only do averagely well, by definition. It's logical that *your* kid is more likely to be average than anything else because it's more likely that *any* kid will be average than anything else. You probably don't want to think of your kid as average, but it's mathematically impossible for all the parents who want their kids to be above average to have above-average kids. It just can't happen! They won't fit there either.

What this means for you is that when the shouting is over— and even while you're still shouting—your kid's substellar performance probably isn't a sign that he's not working up to his potential. It's much more likely that it's a sign of what his potential is, at least in the limited domain of school. It's the bittersweet news that was probably going to reach you someday and is finally reaching you now: your kid is one of the 99.999 percent of people who are destined for goodness, not greatness.

Now you may be shaking your head at this point because you're sure that, while not a genius, he could do better if he just tried harder. But as we've said, as he becomes more mature and gets closer and closer to what he's really good at, he will try harder. It's very difficult to separate effort from talent. People tend to work hard at things that are rewarding. And those things are rewarding because they come relatively easily. Paradoxically, then, people tend to work hard at things that are easy for them. This is reality, not the myth of your kid pushing the boulder of excellence all the way to the top of the mountain of success in triumph.

Regression to the Mean

You did well in school, but your kid isn't doing so well. Why? It must be because he's not applying himself, right?

But that is very possibly *not* the reason. While bright people often have bright kids, exceptionally bright people are, after all, exceptional. Unusual. Out of the ordinary. In other words, a statistical anomaly. The very fact of their amazing excellence points to the likelihood that that excellence won't be repeated in the next generation, at least not to the same degree. Another way of looking at it is to say that if the odds are one in 10,000 that you would be a superstar, the odds are one in 100,000,000 that your kid would be a superstar too. Some odds.*

---

*The probability of two independent events both happening is the product of their individual probabilities. So if the probability of you *or* your kid being a

And in his attempt to become his own person, your teenager will probably decide he doesn't want to compete head to head with you; instead, he leaves your field to you and goes off to find his own field. You may be the brilliant surgeon who graduated first in your class in medical school; your kid will try his hand at writing catchy TV commercials. And he doesn't need good grades for that.

However much you've achieved, your job as a parent is not to push your kid to excellence. People become excellent all by themselves. If your ability to accept your kid depends on his being excellent, then you have to be prepared for the likelihood that your expectations will damage your relationship with your teenager while doing nothing to enhance his performance. For example, Phil, a brilliant scientist, had been giving his teenage son Ben a very hard time. Finally, after working with a family therapist, Phil went off for a fishing weekend by himself and spent two whole days trying to decide if it would be OK with him if his son were really as mediocre as he seemed. What it came down to was whether he'd say to his son either, "You're not good enough the way you are," or "You're OK the way you are." It really felt as if it had to be one or the other.

In the end Phil realized he had to say, "You're OK the way you are," or lose his son. In other words, he could lose his dream of having a brilliant son or he could lose Ben. And it became clear that the dream, while painful to give up, was far less important than the real young man he loved.

What You Can Do about Your Teenager's Performance in School

High parental expectations result in low parental performance. If you accept the fact that your kid will mature, that he will find what he's good at, and that he will one day achieve his own personal level of excellence, then you can let go of the battle for control over his study habits and stop

---

superstar is one in 10,000, the probability of *both* you *and* your kid being superstars is $1/10,000$ times $1/10,000$, and that equals $1/100,000,000$.

doing the things that have been hurting your relationship with him. At that point he'll be able to stop the hiding, defending, and promising that you've pushed him into. You'll be able to talk to a teenager who offers insights instead of excuses.

If you push your kid and ask him if he's done his homework, he's likely to try to get you off his back by lying and telling you he has. On the other hand, if you don't push your kid, he's likely to tell you if he's been having a problem. You'll become more like a wise, older friend, and the more you do, the more you'll be able to be genuinely helpful to your kid.

Suppose you're worried about the effort your teenager's putting out in school. Perhaps he comes home one day with a terrible report card after a semester during which you're sure he's done little studying. It's useful to ask simply, "Is this your best work?" If he says no, ask him if he wants to do better. If he says no to this, ask why. If he says he does want to do better, ask what you can do to help him or if there's anyone else—a tutor, a relative, or a friend—whose help he'd like.

Another way you can be helpful is to ask, "Do you know why you're having difficulty?" The better your relationship with your teenager, the easier it will be for him to talk to you about this. If he doesn't know, he might be willing to brainstorm possibilities with you. If he does know, you can ask him if there's some way you can help with the difficulty.

As you talk about what's going on with your teenager, it's important to remember how crucial it is to him to achieve his own identity. "Helping your kid do better in school" can all too quickly turn into forcing your agenda on him. Often when a teenager seems to be resisting help he's really resisting efforts to prevent him from being in charge of achieving his own identity. So all talk about helping him do better must be in the context of helping him achieve *his* goals. It's terrific, for example, to learn math, but pushing a kid to do better in math can backfire if he wants to be an artist. If his goals seem really stupid and harmful to you, then all you can do is make sure your relationship is good enough so that he'll listen when you give him information about what's wrong with his goals.*

What if you see him doing that dread thing—not studying? If you have a good relationship with him, you could simply ask, "Are you doing what you need to be doing for yourself?" And you can always ask, "Is there any way I can be helpful with your studying?"

Finally, you can always use the permission technique. If your kid's having problems and *if he wants help*, you can ask for his permission to get actively involved, and you can decide together specifically how you'll get involved. There's nothing wrong with your dragging your kid to his desk every evening at seven, for example, *but only if he's asked you to do that*. You're infinitely more powerful with his permission than without it. But you won't get that permission unless things are going well between you, and that means getting closer and stopping the pushing and criticizing.

Money

Your teenager needs money for new clothes; you say no; your kid persists; you feel torn between being firm and giving in; your kid keeps coming at you—and this goes on until both of you are miserable and exhausted. This is the world of parents, teens, and money.

Well, now you can say good-bye to all that.

Here it is, finally, an end to struggling with your teenager over money. Here's a solution where you can balance what you feel you can afford with what he needs without fighting over it. This solution comes right out of having a good relationship with your teenager.

You make a budget together.

*If your teenager has unrealistic or self-destructive goals, much better than arguing with him is helping him find real people who are doing what he is thinking of doing. A half an hour's conversation with a real artist (if that's what he wants to be) can put your teenager's feet on the ground faster than anything else, whereas screaming fights with you will just put his head higher up in the clouds.

Step one. Try to come up with an annual budget for your teenager by thinking of all the possible expenses he has. The final amount you come up with is based on your own best judgment, and it should include necessities as well as extras. Include everything your teenager needs money for, like toiletries, transportation, and school supplies, as well as more discretionary items like clothes and entertainment. Don't forget to include one-time expenses like a new winter coat or the junior prom.

Try to arrive at some figure that takes into account how much money your kid needs, how much he'd like, how much you can afford, and how much you've given him in the past. Some parents exclude from the budget things like school supplies (since they want their kid to feel he can have as much as he needs) and special items (like the cost of plane tickets to visit relatives). Keep in mind that this is a provisional figure and that in step three you'll negotiate the final amount with your teenager.

Step two. Explain to your teenager that you've come up with a way to end the almost daily battles over money. Tell him you're going to give him an annual budget that will cover absolutely all of his needs to the extent that you can afford it.

Tell him the dollar amount you're prepared to give him for the year. Depending on his age, preference, and maturity, and on whether it's possible for you, offer to give him the money all at once or quarterly or monthly or weekly or whatever. You can give him the money either by handing it to him or, to reduce the temptation to spend it all at once, by creating an account where he asks you for *his* money and you subtract it from the amount he has left in his budget. Make it clear that when he spends his money it's gone and there will be no more until the next budget comes into effect.

It's possible that your kid won't like the idea of a budget. A teenager can be very hesitant. He may not understand the concept at first. He may even think that this is an attempt to control him.

Make it absolutely clear that the point of the budget is liberation, not control. You could say something like

Look, I added up everything I gave you last year and it came to about X dollars. Since you're older, I'm prepared to give you a little more this year. The point of this is to give you control of your money, not for me to be in control and not for me to cut back on your money. If you have money in your budget and you ask me for it, you'll get it, with no questions asked. You won't have to beg for your money anymore. I'm not going to have to fight with you when you ask for money anymore. I'm not even going to ask you how you're going to spend it.

In other words, talk to your kid until he gets the idea that you're giving him a budget to make things better for both of you.

Step three. Make sure you negotiate the final amount of the budget. This is critical. If you don't negotiate the amount, then after he's had some time to think about it, he'll almost certainly say it's not enough. And if you have to keep renegotiating the budget in the middle of the year, you're back to where you were before you began. Work out an agreement on the final amount before the budget goes into effect. If he wants to, let your kid prepare his own detailed budget. If he can make a good case for getting more and if you can afford it, then be flexible. If you absolutely can't afford more, then explain why.

Two things have to happen in this third step. There has to be some kind of mutual acceptance and understanding of the final amount. And it must be clear that once the amount has been agreed upon, *it's final.* No more negotiation. No extra money. Nothing but what you've agreed upon.

But there's one thing you have to allow for, as we said in our discussion about agreements. Both of you are learning how to do this the first time through. During that first year of the budget, your kid might spend his money too fast. Or you might find you've miscalculated and not allotted him enough money. You'll have to decide what you'll do about giving advances, particularly since your kid will probably spend too much too soon. Getting in the habit of giving advances destroys the idea of a budget, but an occasional advance may be necessary the first year.

The beauty of the annual budget is that once you work out the kinks, once you've had that one struggle to arrive at an agreed amount, there is no more fighting over money for an entire year. You have 364 days of peace until it's time to give him his budget for the following year. The other beautiful thing about this system is that in determining the amount of the budget and the payment schedule, everyone's needs get taken into account. And the third beautiful part of it is that this will force your teenager to think about how he spends his money.

Moods and Attitudes

Your kid walks in the house. "Hi! How was school?" you ask, in a bright, friendly voice.

Silence. You try again, "Did you have a good day?"

"Why can't you leave me alone?" your teenager says in a mean, furious way.

Or perhaps you call up your kid at college, and she just has nothing to say, as if she just can't wait for you to get off the phone. Or your fourteen-year-old not only acts gloomy but depresses the hell out of you by telling you everything that's wrong with you, from your hair to your breath to your clothes to your entire way of being.

This kind of behavior is a joke when you see it on television, but it's certainly no joke when you're living through it. Besides making you angry, it makes you wonder whether there's something seriously wrong with your teenager. Especially if everything you do to snap him out of it seems to make him only more sullen.

The good news is that if you're patient, you'll be able to bring this obnoxious behavior down to its absolute minimum. Here's how.

Understand that for most kids most of the time, moody, sullen, obnoxious behavior is a sign of neither mental illness nor deeply ingrained rudeness. Instead, for one thing, it's a normal, common feature of adolescence. Studies show clearly that normal teenagers have lower lows and higher highs than adults, and teenagers often have no idea where these feelings come from. One thing that is known is that bugging teenagers about their moods makes things worse.

Another fact about adolescent moods and attitudes is that they sometimes serve as the best way your teenager knows to perform the complicated task of balancing his need to leave home with his need to remain at home. A bad mood can be your teenager's way of drawing a line between the things he needs from you and the things he doesn't. It's his way of saying, "I need you for a lot of things, but I don't need you for the kind of dumb parent-child chatter you try to engage me in. 'How was school today, dear?'! What do you think I am? Eight years old?" No one is saying that you're intending any of this, but that's how it feels to your teenager. You just need to understand that once the process of leaving home has started, some of it's going to have to take place in the home and in the family, and some of it won't feel very good to you.

To make things easier, you can, for instance, sometimes ignore your teenager when he comes into the house. You can drop constant efforts to include him in the conversation at dinner. When he acts moody and cold, you can simply and wordlessly back off and leave him alone. But it's important to do this in a matter-of-fact way, as if you were simply being polite, rather than in an angry, sullen way of your own.

In fact, one of the best guides to dealing with a teenager is to use politeness as a key. Treat your kid like a beloved houseguest who is going through a tough time and needs a great deal of privacy.

In spite of your kid's "bad attitude," you can still ask him about your relationship. You can ask him if he wants more distance. You can ask what his actions mean to him. You can ask what he wants you to do. And you can tell him how you feel about the way he's acting.

You might wonder how we can say both "back off" and "ask questions." But you really can do both at the same time. You can refrain from asking your teenager most of the questions you might ask him most of the time. That will give him the feeling of being left alone. And you can also occasionally say, if only once in a day or once in a week, "Do you feel things are OK between us?" or, "Is there anything you're needing from me that I'm not doing?" If you just ask once and then drop it if your teenager isn't responsive, you'll convey both your caring and your intention to leave him alone.

It's sad enough to see your kid growing up and getting ready to move away, so it's doubly scary to do what feels to many parents like contributing to an already-painful distance by allowing your kid his space and silence. But if you think about it for a moment, it's not hard to guess what will happen if you allow your kid to build up a bit of privacy around him.

He will come to you.

It always happens. Parents who give their kids space to have their moods and to keep the distance they feel necessary find that once their teenagers feel secure in their bubble of privacy they are quite willing to leave it. The same teenager who wouldn't give you the time of day will seek you out in one way or another when he feels you won't violate his space. He might seek you out to ask you about a very important personal issue, or it might just be to ask you a simple question about his homework. And it might take a lot longer than you'd like. But it *will* happen.

It's crucial that you reward your moody teenager for even the slightest gesture toward reaching out of his sullen state. It doesn't have to be a big reward—just a simple "I'm glad you asked me," followed by a brief and non-resentment-laden answer to his question. For most teenagers, that will be reward enough, because it doesn't take much for them to feel that their foray outside of their privacy bubble went well and might be worth doing again.

You may feel there's a contradiction here: we've said over and over that battling for control leads to silence and distance. Now we seem to be saying that silence and distance are good. Which is it?

The answer is that there is all the difference in the world between a teenager's natural need for privacy and his feeling he can't talk to his parents. When you respect your teenager's moods, you respect his privacy and support him in his journey toward leaving home. In the normal course of affairs, he'll move in and out between talking to you and keeping things private, between getting close and moving away.* Battling for control, on the other hand, keeps your teenager stuck in his distance, and then the gap between you is wider. Even the best parent-teen relationships have times when the teenager needs distance. The difference is that battling for control makes it impossible for him to bridge that distance.

What many parents say at this point is, "Maybe this is all well and good for my teenager, but you seem to be asking me to roll out the carpet for his every mood and whim. Do you really expect me to tolerate rudeness, insolence, and disrespect? What about my needs?"

Your needs are no less important than your teenager's. For the relationship approach to work, both persons' needs must be met. But before you can get your needs met, you have to separate what you need from what you think your teenager needs. More often than not, parents battle for control because they think they're helping their kid. When he acts moody they think something is wrong with him or that he's being spoiled. They want to fight for control in an effort to save him from himself.

It's much easier if you focus on your own needs. You have every right to be treated with respect, just as your kid has a right to privacy. Once you understand that the average teenager, rude and sullen like other teenagers, generally grows up to be a normal adult no more rude or sullen than other adults, you can let go of your concerns about saving him from himself.

---

*This is why you shouldn't think it's a black mark against your relationship with your teenager if he occasionally keeps something from you.

And once you understand that your kid's attitude is part of his doing his job of leaving home, you'll feel differently about some of the ways he behaves. What before might have felt like a slap in the face will now clearly seem like your teenager's attempt to maintain his privacy. It's not personal and it's not directed at you. So at least some of the behavior you found so difficult will now feel tolerable, like something you can ignore.

But some of it won't. Sometimes, even though you understand why your teenager is acting the way he is, his behavior will still hurt or make you angry. Then how do you respond?

First of all, when your kid acts in a way that hurts or upsets you, let him know just how you feel immediately, just the way you'd say "ouch" if someone stepped on your toes. For example:

- "All I did was say 'How was school?' You didn't have to jump down my throat as if I'd attacked you. It's not fair."
- "If you don't want to talk, that's fine. But there's no need to act so mean when I talk to you. It really hurts me when you act so mean."
- "For God's sake, you were asking me to help you. Why did you have to ask in such a miserable, unpleasant way? That doesn't make me want to help you."

OK, good, you let your kid know how you felt and what impact his behavior had. People in a relationship need that kind of feedback. But then, for the moment anyway, you should cool it. Don't harp on it, because by his very behavior your kid's letting you know that this is a time when he needs to have the barrier up.

But you're not finished. You didn't avoid letting him know exactly how you felt in the moment, and you shouldn't let things drop. Later, when you sense that your teenager might be a little bit more open to talking and listening, you can go beyond saying how you feel. Ask directly for what you want. You could say something like

Look, I understand you're not always in the mood to talk. That's fine. But I'm not a genius. I don't always know when that is. So if I ask you how school was or how your date was or something and you don't feel like talking about it, don't jump down my throat. I'm not putting you on the rack or anything. I'm just asking a question. All you have to do is say, "I really don't feel like talking about it now. Can we talk about it later?" And I'll say fine. But it's not acceptable to me that you respond to me as if I'm a horrible person. If you've got some problem with me, talk to me about it.

The exact words don't matter. What does matter is that you're taking your needs seriously enough to follow up on them, and at the same time, you're recognizing that your teenager has needs too.

It's possible that your teenager will have a problem with giving you what you want, perhaps because teenagers are such advocates of authenticity. He might say something like "Why should I have to be nice when I don't feel like it? What do you care how I act? Just don't pay any attention to it."

But you want more. That's what the magic question is for. "Well, I do pay attention. What I'm asking you is what do you need to respond politely when I ask you how school was or something? I'm not asking you to tell me how school was. I'm just asking you what you need to respond politely in letting me know you don't want to talk about it."

Maybe you'll have to go back and forth with this a few times. Teenagers often say they don't know what they need; in that case, you can offer suggestions. Sometimes a kid will say, "Look, it doesn't matter what I need, it won't make a difference anyway, you'll just forget to do it." You can offer to let him remind you. Or maybe your teenager will say that what he needs is something you just can't give, like a promise that you'll never ask about anything. Then you can make some kind of counteroffer.

There's one more thing you can do. You can remember to talk about your relationship with your teenager. You can say something like "I know you need your privacy and I know that you're sometimes in a pissy mood, but I want us to have a good relationship. I don't want our relationship chewed up by bad feelings. Let's talk when you're feeling better."

The point is that as long as there are two people taking not only their own needs but each other's needs seriously, then there are no limits to what you can accomplish. It won't happen overnight, but it will happen.

Parents with and without Partners

17

It's tough bringing up a teenager, no question about it. But some things make it tougher.

Like being a single parent. How, for example, do you cope with a teenager when you're exhausted and don't have a partner for backup and support?

There are also ways in which *having* a partner can make it tougher. Being part of a parenting team is great in theory, but in practice many parents find that their current or ex-spouses undermine and complicate the job of bringing up a teenager.

Whether you have a partner or not, this chapter will show you how to cope with some of the special problems that your situation entails.

Single Parents

Ruth doesn't talk to her mother at all anymore. Her teen years were such a nightmare of fighting and anger that not only doesn't Ruth believe that reconciliation is possible, she doesn't even want it.

Now that she has kids of her own, Ruth realizes how tough it must have been for her mother to bring up a daughter all by herself. But she can't find it in her heart to forgive her mother for the screaming and name calling, the absurd rules and endless punishments that filled her home life. Perhaps, most of all, she can't forgive her mother because, "You know, I was really a good kid, but she always made me feel like such a bad kid. What did I ever do that was so terrible?"

Today, Ruth's mother, Lydia, is a small, sad old woman who just can't understand how things could have gone so wrong when her intentions were so good. "What could I do? I was all alone. I had to be both father and mother for Ruth. I had to provide some discipline or she'd just have run wild."

There may have been an earlier time when Lydia was congratulating herself with the grim satisfaction so common to people who battle for control. After all, most of the wildness that Lydia tried to control during Ruth's teen years took place in the house. It was afterwards, when Ruth "grew up," that Lydia's illusion of success began to unravel.

Once she finally left home and got beyond the grasp of her mother's control, Ruth did in fact run wild. She bounced from relationship to relationship, generally with men who treated her poorly, the way her mother had treated her. She had children in one relatively stable relationship, but the structure of that life felt so much like control that Ruth had to get out, and so she left her husband.

The bad news is that this story is all too common. The good news is that it doesn't have to be.

It's true that many single parents feel isolated and vulnerable. They feel everyday life is difficult enough; they must, at least, try to get control over their kids. It's as if their message were, "Look, things are tough, so the only way we are going to get through this is if you do what I say, when I say it, the way I want it done."

This is certainly understandable, but even the most isolated and vulnerable single parent has a much better alternative. If you're a single parent you really don't have any *less* control than two parents, even if one of them is a full-time parent. With teenagers, particularly as they get older, control is an illusion; any victories you think you win are either temporary or false.

Some research indicates that most single parents are at least as successful as parents with partners, if not more so. And as a single parent you have a secret weapon. Your teenager can understand how tough things are for you. He can sympathize with your difficulties. All you have to do is avoid eroding that sympathy with endless battles for control.

And you have more going for you than just your kid's sympathy. Many single parents find they tell their kids things about themselves and their daily lives that they would tell their partners if they were in a relationship. This helps foster an atmosphere of closeness and communication. It makes it easier for your kid to share with you if you're sharing with your kid. Free and full communication is one of the most important determinants of successful single parenting.

What we're saying, then, is that as a single parent you have two choices. Feeling that control is going to be particularly hard to get, you can fight all the harder for it. Or, you can let go of the illusion that you can have control and build on a potential strength—the special intimacy that arises between a single parent and her teenager.

Parents with Partners

First of all, you should understand that we're not only talking about married (or living-together) parents here. We're also talking about divorced parents who, through joint custody or visitation or some other arrangement, share the parenting even though they're no longer married. And we're also talking about parents who share the parenting with a person who is now their teenager's stepparent.

How can we lump all these situations together? Because the common problem is coordination, the difficulty two people have getting their joint parenting act together. Any two parents are very different people, and often even subtle differences can be enormously magnified by the pressures and confusions of bringing up a teenager.

Of course the lingering bitterness of divorce can infect parents' ability to agree about what to do with their kid. On the other hand, even without that special bitterness to contend with, parents can find that day-to-day life with a teenager brings out resentments all by itself. So in this section we'd like to emphasize the common difficulties faced by all parents with partners.

It's all based on disagreement. It really doesn't matter very much in the end whether this disagreement comes from mutual hatred, philosophical differences, or having been brought up differently as kids. Whatever the case, the problem lies in a common misunderstanding: many parents think it's important to figure out which one of them is right. "You'll spoil the kid," one says. "No, I think you're being too rigid," the other answers. Or one says, "You've got to set limits," and the other says, "You'll just antagonize her."

And back and forth the parents go, trying to convince the other that he or she is right. Of course they both have a secret weapon: when they're alone with their kid they do whatever they want. And of course the secret weapons end up cancelling each other out. By the time the strict and the lenient parent get through dealing separately with their kid, the strictness of one plus the leniency of the other add up to no clear impact of either parent on the kid.

What does have an impact is the disagreement itself. When two parents are busy undermining each other, even very young kids quickly learn to play politics. They learn to manipulate the situation to their own advantage.

Now here's a way for all co-parents, living together or not, to get their act together.

First of all, understand that your success or effectiveness probably has very little to do with the kinds of things you think are so important to fight over. The research is clear that strict parents and lenient parents *both* turn out terrific kids. As bad as you think it would be for your teenager to be brought up completely under the hated teen-rearing philosophy of your co-parent, it's generally much worse for your kid to be whipsawed back and forth between you. Most of the time, if you really care about your kid, you'd actually do better to go along with the other parent, even though you're sure he's wrong, than to have endless unresolved fights with the other parent over what you think is right.

But it's unrealistic to think that most parents are going to do this. And anyway, you have a much better alternative. If the way you parent is based on strengthening your relationship with your teenager instead of battling for control, then a lot of the issues you and your co-parent fight over drop out. What to control and how much to control stop being issues. Instead, you can focus on getting your needs met—and it doesn't matter that much if you have different needs. Your teenager can meet your needs and your co-parent's needs whether they are the same or different.

That will still leave many areas for you to disagree about. But we can offer something that works to dissolve those disagreements. You and your co-parent talk and make a list of your disagreements. It doesn't matter how long the list is or how far apart you are on each item. Then divide the items between you. Decide who's going to be in charge of what. You can do it by preference, tossing a coin, who's good at what, who tends to be in what place, who has the time, or anything else you both think is fair.

The important thing is it doesn't matter who gets to be in charge of which item. What does matter is that the authority be clear between you. You want to be able to get to the place where you can say things to your teenager like, "Your father's in charge of school stuff, and if he says you can't go out on a school night then that's it." Or, "Your mother gives you your allowance. Money is her department when it comes to you. You ask her if it's OK to get an advance on your budget and whatever she says goes."

What you gain from this is enormous. You have much more influence with your teenager because you can't be divided. At the same time you have half the work because you only have to be responsible for half the decisions. And, you remove a huge source of conflict from your relationship with your co-partner.

Most of all, you know you're doing the very best thing for your teenager.

What Do You Do When Your Kid's All Grown Up?

18

If you've used the relationship approach throughout your kid's adolescence, you'll find that when your kid finally becomes a full-fledged adult and leaves home the two of you can spend the rest of your lives in a warm close relationship unburdened by bruises and bad memories. And you'll find you have the skills to maintain that relationship as long as you're both alive.

But if your kid's now an adult and you find yourself having to play catch-up, here's some help. Let's look at the world of parent–*adult* child relationships. It will help you see some of the traps you can fall into and some of the ways out of these traps.

Problem Parents

Here are the main roles *problem* parents of adult children play.

- *The Criticizer.* "My mother's coming for a week," your friend says, and groans. Why the groan? Why so many groans from adult sons and daughters at the thought of contact with their parents? It's a good bet that it's The

Criticizer who's causing these groans. These parents must have liked battling for control so much when their kids were teenagers that they wanted never to stop. The endless unpleasantness doesn't seem to deter them, so we can only assume that they reward themselves, mentally, by telling themselves, like Don Quixote, how just and noble their cause is, regardless of the outcome.

- *The Guilt Producer.* Another groan maker, this kind of problem parent is probably a Criticizer in sheep's clothing. "You're too busy to call your mother?" she says, as if by this nagging, complaining, and guilt-making she is thereby making herself so unbelievably interesting, attractive, and pleasant to be with that no one in his right mind would ever not want to call her. When we talk to these parents we often find they're afraid that without these indirect attempts at control they would have no hold on their adult children at all.

- *The Needy Victim.* A devious plotter, this one. "Let's see [he might say if he would ever put this into words], I can't seem to control my kids by acting like a parent. Maybe I can control them by acting like I *need* a parent, like I need them to take care of me." More groans from the kids. And impatience and pity. Like the other two types, this problem parent can't find a way to relate to his adult children as an adult friend.

- *The Unavailable Parent.* If he can't win he won't play. His teenager committed some terrible crime now or in the past, some crime of not being controllable in some crucial way, and now the kid must pay. So the parent is silent and withdraws. "My father won't talk to me," his kid says. Maybe this type of problem parent really doesn't care. Does this role make sense if he does?

- *The Parent Who Is Stuck in the Past.* For this parent, his adult child has simply never grown up. Whatever his adult son's or daughter's triumphs, however weighty his kid's responsibilities, this parent will want to know if his kid is getting enough to eat and has remembered to wear his galoshes. While cute on television, real-life parents who play this role almost murderously cut their kid down to size. This parent all too often annihilates whatever his kid accomplishes as an adult.

How Not to Be a Problem Parent to Your Adult Child

OK, that's what you should *not* to do. But what kinds of roles can and should you play with your adult child? Actually, this question is important for *all* parents of teenagers, regardless of what stage your teenager is in, because the answer to it will tell you what kinds of roles you can and should be starting to play *right now* with your teenager.

- Instead of being The Criticizer, be *The Advisor*. Here's the critical point about advisors: they accept the decision of the person they're advising. Presidential advisors, for instance, wait to be asked for their advice before giving it. And that's what you should do. An advisor to a CEO, say a board member, might volunteer his advice, but once the boss decides, the advisor supports the boss's decision—even if it goes against his advice. And that's what you should do.

    The critical components, then, of the parental advisor are waiting to be asked and accepting your kid's decision. These components mark out the beginning and end of your involvement: it begins when you're asked for advice and it ends when your kid makes his decision. What about in between?

    That depends on your relationship. The better it is and the more respect and openness between you, the more you can get into a freewheeling discussion and even argument with your kid. There's nothing wrong with conflict and controversy in a relationship. What good parent-teen and parent–adult child relationships have going for them is the parent's sensitivity to the kid's independence, to the boundaries the kid has set up for himself. As long as you respect his independence and his boundaries, you'll find that you can play a gratifying role in your kid's life.

- Instead of being The Guilt Producer, be *The Direct Parent*. Maybe there's nothing you can do about it. Maybe a whiner is a whiner and that's it. But we hope not. Maybe the whining, guilt-producing parent is really someone who just feels helpless. Feeling helpless is a bad habit to get into in your relationship with your teenager, both for now and in the future, if for no other reason than the fact that it leads to becoming a Guilt Producer. The way to get out of this habit is to look at parents who manage *not* to feel helpless. What do they have going for them, in addition to getting along with their kid?

One reason they don't feel helpless is they don't try to control the uncontrollable. They draw the line between what they *can* get and what they can't get. This makes a huge difference.

Take, for example, the classic case of the mother who complains because her kid doesn't call more often. Parents who get themselves into this situation are almost always parents who think their kid *should want* to call them. That's why they say things like, "I guess I'm not important to you anymore," or, "What's the matter, don't you have any time for your mother?" or, "Don't you love your mother?" Whether he says it or not, the kid will be driven to feel, "Why can't you leave me alone?"

What successful parents understand is that since they've been demoted from parent to person they're not at the center of their kid's life anymore. And even though spontaneous feelings of love and gratitude *should* constantly be bubbling to the surface, they *don't*. If you're not trying to control the uncontrollable, then you're letting whatever is going to happen happen.

Now that may not be enough, and, fortunately, it doesn't have to be enough. The other thing successful parents have going for them, once they focus on what they can get instead of focusing on being upset about not getting what they think they should be getting, is that they ask directly for what they want.

So while you can't get a kid who *wants* to call you all the time, you can get a kid who *does* call you regularly. Instead of asking him to be filled with desire to talk to you, you can ask him to call at stated intervals. It could be an agreed upon time (say every Sunday evening) or it could be with an agreed upon frequency (say every week). It could even be simply the agreement that whoever calls one time is owed a call by the other next time.

The point is you can stop feeling helpless by having a real give-and-take with your kid over what you can get. Somewhere not too far from what you ask directly for is what your kid can give you. If you don't ask directly you won't get even that. If you try emotional arm twisting you'll get still less, plus you'll get a resentful kid who is always pulling away from you.

- Instead of being The Needy Victim, be *The Adult Friend*. If The Guilt Producer is caused by a parent feeling helpless, it's fear that turns a parent into a Needy Victim. Fear of what? Fear of being abandoned, fear of the kid having no reason to stay connected to the parent. Often these parents have victimized themselves, in the sense that the years they spent battling for control over their teenager so eroded the parent-teen relationship that suddenly, when the kid physically left the house, there was no more bond between them. So the only way these parents can think of to re-create a bond is to arouse the kid's sense of pity and obligation.

  There's hope, but only if you're willing to be patient. If you have a good relationship with your adult child, then you already are his adult friend. But if the relationship has been damaged, then it's going to take time to build it up. Impatience will only translate into some kind of move to gain control, even if it's only the indirect control attempts of The Needy Victim, and this will just hurt the relationship even more.

  How, then, with patience, do you become your adult child's adult friend?

  All you can do is what you already do to become anyone's friend. You do the kinds of things that would be much too obvious to mention except that with their kids people forget the obvious. So to become friends with your adult kid you do obvious things like being nice to them, getting to know them, finding things in common, spending time with them, being someone *they* would want to spend time with, and at the same time avoiding pushing yourself on them.

What you have going for you is the fact that the two of you have a real connection. What you have going against you is the fact that there may be a history of anger and hurt. It's critical, starting now, not to add any more anger and hurt, even if your own anger and hurt come from the fact that you're not as close to your kid as you'd like.

One thing you can do, though, if you have nothing else in common, is to heal the past. For this to be successful, two things are key.

One, you have to make sure your kid gets at least as much time, if not more, talking about his anger and hurts as you do talking about yours.

Two, you have to absolutely refuse to let yourself get drawn into being defensive or judgmental. This means that when your kid mentions some "horrible crime" you committed against him, whether it was the time you whacked him or the time you failed to praise him for getting an A, or whether it was his perception of a long-standing pattern on your part of being critical, you have to just accept what he says without denying it, trying to justify it, or blaming him for it. All you need to say is, "Yeah, that must have been tough for you." You'll know that you're beginning to have a better relationship with your kid when he can begin to listen to your telling him, nondefensively, what was going on for you when you committed your "horrible crime."

- Instead of being The Unavailable Parent, be *The Available Parent*. Here's a story. Robert had worked hard to become a very successful civil engineer. More than anything else he respected brains, hard work, and getting the job done. His son Chuck, starting in high school, became more and more of a flake in his father's eyes. Chuck let his hair grow long, played in a rock band, and drove around on a motorcycle. Chuck was good in math like his father, but, unlike his father, he gravitated toward pure mathematics, which Robert thought totally useless.

Finally Robert couldn't take it anymore. Everything Chuck was doing seemed like an assault on his father's values, and so finally Robert just wrote him off. He refused to have anything to do with Chuck.

Now some of the Roberts of this world can't and won't change. But some can be reached, once they realize they're trapped. They are acting as though some standard of theirs is more important than their kid, but they don't really mean it. Pride and blindness have pushed them to hold on to a position they'd love to abandon. All they need to do is ask themselves a simple question: "Are the standards I'm holding on to more important to me than my kid?"

Some parents say yes, my standards are more important. But some—enough—say no, I've been making a mistake; as hard as it is for me to take, my kid is really more important to me than my standards.

This situation frequently comes up when gay young adults come out to their parents. Many parents are so upset they refuse to have anything to do with their kids. But some of these parents who cut themselves off have been brought around when their kids have sent them a note saying, "I know you're very upset by this and that it's something you feel you can never accept. But I am your child and I love you. Is your hatred of my being gay [or whatever it is the parent is objecting to] really more important to you than your love for me?"

One woman sent this note—just these three sentences—to her mother every year on Mother's Day for seven years. Finally, in the seventh year, her mother called her and said, "I'm sorry, I've made a mistake."

This daughter had made it possible for her mother to find a way out of her unavailability.

- Instead of being The Parent Who Is Stuck in the Past, be *The Parent Who Accepts His Kid as an Adult*. Some of the problems we've just mentioned are very dramatic. The problem of the parent who is stuck in the past is much less dramatic. It can even be comical at times. But it is so widespread and insidious that it creates at least as much trouble as the other problems combined.

Bringing up a child is a very strange kind of activity. With most of the other things people do, the better they get at doing them the more responsibilities and rewards they get. A good secretary becomes an office manager or an executive assistant. A nurse takes on more important, more difficult, and more responsible jobs. A lawyer will find the bigger and more interesting cases coming her way. Even a family doctor who does essentially the same work throughout her career will find that she's built an edifice of respect and accomplishment.

But it's the opposite with a parent. Parents start out with the greatest responsibilities at the beginning. Then even the best of parents, like hopeless bunglers, are repeatedly told they are not needed for this and not needed for that, that everything they do is wrong, that they're just in the way, until eventually all they're needed for is money, and then nothing.

If you have a good relationship with your kid it can make this bearable. In fact, the relationship can take the place of the job you are losing. But many parents are only aware of the loss. All they can do is to compare the good old days when things were the way they should be with the terrible upside-down present when they feel they must demand the right to play their old role.

But the old role is over, and if you need it to have a sense of self and self-worth then not only are you in trouble, so is your relationship with your kid. How can you accept your kid as an adult if that forces you to acknowledge that you're unemployed in mind, body, and soul?

The answer for your relationship with yourself, as with your relationship with your teenager, is to take care of it as early as possible. If you can acknowledge the very temporary nature of your parental employment when you hold your baby in your arms, then that's best. Whenever you do it, sooner is better. And now is better than never.

The point here is that parents who are most successful at acknowledging their grown-up kid as an adult are the ones who are least invested in an image of themselves as parents.

In a sense, bringing up a teenager successfully is the mirror image of bringing up a baby successfully. Babies soak up their parents' time. Teenagers give time back to you. The more you use that time for yourself, the better off you and your teenager will be. The trick with a baby is learning how to get involved in the right way. The trick with a teenager is learning how to get *un*involved in the right way.

Appendix:
What to Do If You Think There Might Be Something *Seriously* Wrong with Your Teenager

Throughout this book we've tried to provide you with reassurance that in spite of the weird and obnoxious things your teenager does sometimes, the odds are overwhelming that your kid is normal and that he'll turn out fine. We've tried to provide this reassurance, first, because it's true: most of the things kids do as adolescents are not only normal but are actually nature's way of helping him do his job of getting ready to leave home. And, second, this reassurance is important because worry about behavior that is an inevitable part of adolescence drives parents into harmful battles for control.

But occasionally there's good reason for parental concern: not often, but once in a while, there really is something seriously wrong with a teenager. What do you do then?

Think of it like this. If you have a cold, you can be your own doctor no matter how miserable you feel. But if you have pneumonia, you have to consult an expert. And it's the same with teenagers. First you have to figure out how serious the problem is and then you have to figure out what to do about it.

How to Tell When Something's Seriously Wrong

The criteria for something being seriously wrong are *not* whether you like what your teenager does or whether he behaves the way you behave or whether he makes you worry that he won't be a success or whether you think your teenager is making stupid choices. The criterion isn't even whether he's like most kids his age.

Instead, our position is that the criterion has to have something to do with damage.

It's generally neither useful nor appropriate to assume something is seriously wrong unless what your teenager is doing will seriously damage him now or will have a good probability of leading to serious damage in the future.

Clearly, just where to draw the line is something parents will have to decide for themselves. Here are some illustrations that might clarify the distinction between a normal and a serious problem:

- It's a serious problem when a teenager refuses to go to school for three weeks, not when he plays hookey occasionally or when his grades are disappointing and you're sure they could be better.
- It's a serious problem when a teenager is drug-dependent and his life revolves around drugs, not when he experiments once.
- It's a serious problem when a teenager diets so strictly that she's significantly below her optimum body weight, not when all she does is keep going from one diet to another and constantly talk about how fat she is (while her body weight stays within the normal range).
- It's a serious problem when a teenager is involved in major and repeated thefts, not when she shoplifts a pair of earrings.

Lots of teenagers, for example, have bad grades, experiment with drugs, and commit a couple of acts of minor shoplifting. These kids certainly need to be dealt with, but they're

not involved in anything so serious that you should think
they're doomed.

What can make assessing their teenager frightening and
confusing for parents is the "slippery slope" theory of teen
problems. This theory says a couple of C's on a report card
aren't that bad in themselves, but if they're not attacked vig-
orously your teenager will slide into total academic failure.
No, a couple of joints won't kill your teenager, but, the "slippery slope" theory says, aren't those joints evidence that your
kid is already sliding toward serious drug addiction? In other
words, lots of things are dangerous not because of what they
are but because of what they can lead to.

But the "slippery slope" theory is wrong. It's a fallacy to
say that because many drug addicts start out with marijuana,
experimenting with marijuana necessarily leads to drug addiction. This makes no more sense than saying that since so
many rich people started out poor, poverty necessarily leads
to becoming rich. Most poor people aren't even in danger of
becoming rich.

What's more, the people who are most in danger of falling
down the slippery slope are the parents themselves. After all,
once you start down the slippery slope of thinking about what
your teenager's behavior *can* lead to, you can think any im-
perfection will lead to a terrible problem. No wonder parents
so easily fall into battling for control.

So how can you tell when something's really wrong with
your teenager if you're not sure?

One thing you can do if you're afraid that your kid's problem is serious is to use the fact that you get along and care
for each other to ask directly for the reassurance you need.
Talk to your teenager about your fears that, for example, his
occasional use of pot will lead to serious drug addiction. Work
out ways to keep the lines of communication open so that you
can maintain your influence with your teenager.

Steve, who knew his son Mark did a lot of drinking in
college, confronted him with his fears that Mark was becoming an alcoholic. Mark used the standard "everyone does it"
explanation, and Steve pulled out the traditional "slippery
slope" theory. (In fact, many parent-teen arguments consist

of a contest between "everyone does it" explanations and "slippery slope" theories.)

But since Steve was not interested in a battle for control, they were able to move beyond a pointless argument. At one point Mark said, "Look, I know that alcoholism is a disease of denial, so I know it doesn't mean that much to you when I say I don't have a problem. But I'll tell you what. If I'm still drinking like this after I finish college, then I'll know I have a problem and I promise I'll deal with it."

"Will you put that in writing?" Steve asked.

Mark agreed. As it turned out, well before Mark became a college senior his partying tapered off and so did his drinking.

There are two ways parents can make a mistake: overreacting to something they should ignore and underreacting to something they should deal with. We've warned against overreaction throughout this book because it's the most common way parents of normal teenagers respond. The only time you should worry about *under*reacting is when you're afraid your kid is likely to do himself harm.*

What to Do When You Think Something's Seriously Wrong

The first thing to do is to work even harder at strengthening your relationship with your teenager. We're not saying this will be easy. In fact, it will be harder because you're scared and angry and because you're sure your kid is out of control. But it's more important now than ever because, after all, if your teenager has a serious problem, free and full communication back and forth is important, your ability to influence her is all the more critical, and whatever caring there is between you is all the more precious and powerful.

If your teenager really does have a serious problem, then

---

*But how can you tell whether you're ignoring a serious problem or getting too upset over a problem that isn't serious? There's an excellent book that can help you—Douglas H. Powell's *Teenagers: When to Worry and What to Do* (New York: Doubleday, 1987).

the extra that's needed isn't control but competent, professional help. Many parents put off getting help because they feel that seeing a professional is a sign of their own failure and incompetence. It's understandable they'd feel that way, but it's a mistake. Good professionals today are not interested in blaming parents or looking down on them or criticizing them. The point isn't blame at all, but change. No one's saying you're part of the problem, only that you have to be part of the solution.

The most important decision you have to make, once you've decided to get help, is what *kind* of help to get. This is where it's possible to make a serious mistake. Too often, when a kid has serious problems, parents ship him off to his own therapist, putting the whole burden for change on their teenager and not getting involved themselves. But your teenager is part of your family, and if he's going to change, other members of the family will have to change too.

So the best kind of help generally comes from a *family therapist*. We believe it's at the family level that the best and most effective solutions can be implemented, because when all the family members are involved change happens most quickly and lasts longest. It's certainly possible that at some point a family therapist would recommend individual therapy for your teenager, and that would be fine. But by starting with family therapy you'll know you're doing your full share in helping your kid. If there are a number of family therapists in your area, select a family therapist experienced in dealing with teenagers and their families.

One feature of any good solution is that it keeps your teenager on his normal life track as much as possible. This means staying in school, staying connected to friends, and staying involved in his activities. All of these are generally very powerful in grounding a teenager in the normal world and in preserving his roots there. Any intervention that uproots him runs the risk of cutting him off from sources of strength and from the feeling that he's basically OK. If there's a serious problem, it's important not to deny it, and to deal with it. At the very same time, it's important to preserve your teenager's sense that he's basically OK.

That's one reason you should watch out for a cure that's worse than the disease. A mini-industry has risen up to deal with teenagers whose parents are failing with the control approach but who keep on trying to use it: many private psychiatric facilities advertise aggressively and are eager to use your health insurance coverage to hospitalize your teenager. Such institutions are willing to agree with the parents' view that lack of control is the problem.

But most often, use of these facilities results in making the teenager feel that there is something permanently and essentially wrong with him. Both parents and teenagers get labeled as defective, and then spend the rest of their lives living up to those labels. It is more likely that, instead of helping, hospitalization results in increasing the probability that your teenager will need further hospitalization in the future. So treat hospitalization the way you would an experimental drug with very serious side effects: something to be avoided at all costs and to be used only when all else has failed.

So if you think your teenager has serious problems, the best professional solution is one that treats the family, does no labeling, avoids hospitalization, and as much as possible keeps the teenager on his normal life track.

Additional Readings

Coleman, John C., and Leo Hendry. *The Nature of Adolescence*. New York: Routledge, 1990.

    This scholarly but readable book surveys all the best and most recent research on what adolescence really is and what happens to kids as they go through it.

Csikszentmihaly, Mihaly, and Reed Larson. *Being Adolescent: Conflict and Growth in the Teen Years*. New York: Basic Books, 1984.

    This is a wonderful book about what it's like to be a teenager. It's based on a study of how teenagers actually spend their time and how they feel about what they're doing.

Faber, Adele, and Elaine Mazlish. *Liberated Parents, Liberated Children*. New York: Avon, 1976.

    While this is a book about parenting children, its excellent, practical advice is useful for dealing with some of the most difficult situations that come up.

Fisher, Roger, and William Ury. *Getting to Yes: Negotiating Agreements Without Giving In*. New York: Penguin Books, 1983.

    Since control can't work, you *have* to negotiate with your teenager. This short, entertaining book will teach you what you need to know to not only be an effective negotiator but a fair one as well.

Napier, Augustus, and Carl Whitaker. *The Family Crucible*. New York: Bantam, 1984.

This almost-novelistic book is both about families and about family therapy. It will help you understand a lot of what's going on inside of your family.

Powell, Douglas. *Teenagers: When to Worry and What to Do*. New York: Doubleday, 1987.

This is a terrific book to turn to when you're afraid your teenager might be seriously disturbed. It gives specific guidelines for how to know when things are bad enough to seek help.

Satir, Virginia. *The New Peoplemaking*. Mountain View, CA: Science and Behavior, 1988.

This book by a family-therapy pioneer describes how families work and the impact of families on their members. It will give you both insights and ideas for how to make things better in your family.

INDEX